Expert Praise for
Follow That Customer!

To me Event Driven Marketing (EDM) is the ultimate marketing machine. Target the right message on exactly the right moment at the one customer fitting that message. For sales, services, information or win-back . . . Hey, I love EDM!

>A.J. Nyhuis
>Program and Change Manager
>ING Bank

van Boel, Sander and Weber provide the next step in the evolution of direct marketing. Event-driven Marketing takes the critical elements of consumer's behaviors and helps turn them into actionable programs. Wonderfully readable, yet concise and focused. Great information for direct marketers wanting to move to the next level.

>Don E. Schultz
>President, Agora
>Emeritus, The Medill School, Northwestern University

The authors have discovered the central flaw in most direct marketing: That it is based on past behavior. Event-driven marketing is about future behavior—the kind triggered by events. And we're not just talking about birthdays. This compelling new book is filled with both B2C and B2B case histories. You'll learn how well-timed event marketing can move customers into the sales funnel. You'll learn how to leverage EDM through mobile devices. And you'll find out about the changes you need to make to exploit this marketing phenomenon.

>Ray Schultz
>Former editor of *DM News* and *Direct*
>President, TellAllmarketing

EDM takes direct marketing beyond the world of traditional campaigning and into the more complex—and more effective—world of managing ongoing customer relationships, in a way that is both welcomed by customers and more profitable for marketers. I particularly appreciate the authors' inclusion of several useful methods for measuring the ROI on multi-touch programs—a vexing challenge in much of B-to-B marketing. Also, their introduction of the notion of scoring and scorecards to predict the likelihood of an event, to identify target audiences appropriate for EDM treatment, will be a boon to marketers everywhere.

Ruth P. Stevens
President, eMarketing Strategy
Adjunct professor, Columbia University School of Business

Follow That Customer! Is an excellent contribution to the literature on marketing and not to be missed! It puts the customer centre stage, which is exactly where he/she should be in any marketing strategy."

Alastair Tempest
Director General
FEDMA

CRM (customer-focused entrepreneurship) is about balancing the value of the customer and the value for the customer. Even Driven Marketing is about the right timing of customer contact and therefore bridges traditional marketing and CRM. This book is a unique travel guide to follow your customer's journeys.

Wil Wurtz
Director
CRM Association, Netherlands

Alan Weber is a master database strategist and this book adds another chapter to his rich teaching and writing history. This book demonstrates that event-driven marketing influenced by life-stage changes is at the center of the next generation of marketing.

Jack Schmid
President
J. Schmid & Assoc. Inc.

Follow That Customer!

Follow That Customer!

The Event-Driven Marketing Handbook

Egbert Jan van Bel
Ed Sander
Alan Weber

150 N. Michigan Ave. • Suite 2800
Chicago, Illinois 60601

© 2011 Egbert Jan van Bel, Ed Sander, and Alan Weber

Editor: Richard Hagle
Cover and interior design by Sans Serif, Inc., Saline, MI

Published by:
Racom Books/Racom Communications
150 N. Michigan Ave.
Suite 2800
Chicago, IL 60601
312-494-0100 / 800-247-6553
www.racombooks.com

All rights reserved. Printed in the United States of America. Except as permitted under the United States Copyright Act of 1976, no part of this publication may be reproduced or distributed in any form or by any means, or stored in a database or retrieval system, without the prior written permission of the publisher.

ISBN: 978-1-933199-26-9

Contents

Acknowledgments	ix
Preface	xiii
Introduction	xv

CHAPTER 1: A New Day Marketing — 1

The Roots of Event-Driven Marketing	2
EDM and Direct Marketing: Important Distinctions	4
EDM Prospecting	7
Other EDM-related Concepts	8
Segmentation: Old and New	10
Taking the Event-Driven Approach	10

Case 1 Birthday Clubs — 14

CHAPTER 2: Customer-Related Terminology and Marketing Myopia — 22

Market Segmentation: From Old Economy to New?	24
Put Down That Scatter Gun	25
Viewing from the Customer's Point of View	26
"Stuff" and Self-Image	28
Sales Funnel	30
Regulars, Buyers, and Tryers	33

CHAPTER 3: THE EDM QUADRANT — 34

From Internal Planning to Customer-Oriented Supply	34
Event-Driven Marketing: Choosing the Right Moment	35
Key Roles in the Marketing Process	39
The EDM Quadrant	40
Time versus Predictability	43
EDM in Mobile Telephony	44
Events in Mobile Telephony	45

Chapter 4: Process Management and the Implementation of Event-Driven Marketing — 47

    The Customer Comes First — 47
    Marketing and IT Merge — 49
    The FBC Formula: Faster, Better, Cheaper — 50
    Keep IT Simple . . . — 54
    The Customer: In the Driver's Seat — 55
    Campaign Management and the Event-Driven Marketing Cycle — 56
    EDM Execution — 62
    The Impact of EDM Execution — 63

Case 2: Folksam's Moving Birds — 66

Case 3: Product-Phase Event-Driven Contact Strategies — 73

Chapter 5: Loyalty Versus Retention — 83

    The Goal of Marketing — 83
    The Focus of Marketing — 83
    Loyal People Don't Exist, So Neither Do Loyal Customers — 84
    Loyalty and Switching Costs — 86
    What Is Churn, and What Is Its Significance? — 87
    Loyalty Versus Retention — 88
    Don't Give the Customer a Reason to Leave — 90
    Loyalty and Branding — 91
    Organizing a Customer Retention Strategy — 92
    Survival of the Fittest — 92

Chapter 6: Customer Value and Profitability — 93

    The Elements of Customer Value: Acquisition, Development, and Retention — 95
    Five Methods for Calculating Profitability — 98
    Technical Terms — 100
    Method 1: Understanding Break-Even — 101
    Method 2: Understanding Profitability by Campaign — 102
    Method 3: Understanding Profitability of Multistep Campaigns — 106
    Method 4: Understanding Lifetime Value — 109
    Discussion — 112
    Method 5: Understanding Payback Period — 115

Case 4: EDM in Fast-Moving Consumer Goods and Baby Care — 119

Case 5: Event-Driven Marketing for Premium Pet Food — 134

Chapter 7: CRM, Databases, and Marketing Information — 144

Data Warehouses — 146
Logic, Matching, and Understanding — 146
Harmonizing Supply and Demand — 147
Information Versus Data — 149
Useless Information — 150
Database Marketing and Data Mining — 151
Analyzing Data — 152
Analysis: From Theory to Practice — 153
Database Analysis Techniques — 154
Formulating Analytical Objectives — 157

Case 6: Developing an Event-Driven Marketing Program — 160

Chapter 8: EDM and Legislation in the European Union — 172

Introduction: Local Regulations — 172
Universal Principles: Transparency and Confidence — 173
European Directive Unification — 174
EDM and Awareness — 175
Legal Information Requirements under the Data Protection Directive — 176
Absolute Right to Object — 177
Transborder Flow of Personal Data within the European Union — 178
Establishment of the Controller
Transfer of Personal Data to Countries Outside the European Union — 180
Legal Information Requirements under the E-communications & Privacy Directive — 181
Use of Electronic Messages for Commercial Communication — 181
Channel Management: A Legal Necessity — 182
Channel Management Matrix — 183
Legal Information Requirements under the Distance Selling Directive — 186
EDM-related Directive: the Unfair Commercial Practices Directive — 188
Development: Event-Forbidden Marketing — 189
Transborder Event-Driven Marketing: Good Taste and Decency — 190
Conclusion — 190
Forthcoming Event: Revisions and Discussions — 191
The History of Legislation for Direct Marketing — 193

CHAPTER 9: EDM and Legislation in the United States   194

    Introduction   194
    US and European Law Briefly Compared   195
    Industry and Media-Specific Legislation   197
    Consumer Credit Information   197
    Information Notices by Financial Institutions   197
    Protected Health Information   198
    Media Channels   199
    Telephone, Mobile, SMS, Fax   199
    Email   200
    Direct Mail   201
    Enforcement and Conclusion   202

Appendix 1   Tips and Checklists   203
Appendix 2   ROI Case Studies   209
Appendix 3   Lists of Exhibits   215

Index   218

About the Authors   227

Acknowledgments

Many thanks ...

... to all who inspired us, thought with us, supported us: Jessica Jonasse (Service Check), Tjessica Stegenga & Tim de Boer (Pleon Europe); Nathalie Scholman, Anke Kusters; Hans Molenaar (Beeckestijn Business School); Ugo & Anna Galiussi (grazie per la settimana nella vostra casa in montagne!); Willem Smit (Erasmus University); Rob van Vroenhoven (Wij Special Media); Annemarie Schonewille (Aprimo); Frans Reichardt (Holy Cow! Direct Communications); Miranda Karreman (web designer of www.eventdrivenmarketing.net); Tanya Polyakova (De Lage Landen); Judd Goldfeder (The Customer Connection); Louis, Billy & Gringo and last but not least Rich Hagle (Racom Communications) for his limitless patience.

... and to all who contributed to this book: Arthur Middleton Hughes (Database Marketing Institute); Charles A. Prescott (Prescott Report); Alexander Singewald (Singewald Consultants Group BV); Dick Vanderzaken & Ronald Morcus (2Organize) and Ruud Verduin (Verduin Marketing Consultants).

Contributors
Arthur Middleton Hughes

Arthur Middleton Hughes is a recognized expert in email, database and telecom marketing strategy. Arthur serves e-Dialog (www.e-dialog.com) as their Senior Strategist. In this role he advises e-Dialog staff and e-Dialog clients on profitable strategies for using electronic communications in their marketing programs.

A graduate of Princeton University with a Masters in Public Affairs, Arthur taught economics at the University of Maryland for 32 years. When it comes to database marketing, he wrote the book! He is the author of *The Complete Database Marketer*, 2nd Ed. (McGraw-Hill, 1996), *Strategic Database Marketing*, 3rd Ed. (McGraw-Hill, 2006) and *The Customer Loyalty Solution* (McGraw-Hill, 2003). His book, *Customer Churn Reduction and Retention for Telecoms* was published by RACOM in 2007, and in 2009 he co-authored with Arthur Sweetser *Successful E-Mail Marketing Strategies: from Hunting to Farming* (Racom 2009).

Arthur is the founder of The Database Marketing Institute, Ltd. Through the Institute, he gave 28 two-day seminars on database marketing from 1993 to 2000 with Dr. Paul Wang of Northwestern University. Graduates of the Institute's training include 1,200 senior marketers from major US corporations. The Institute's websites are www.dbmarketing.com and www.telecom-marketing.com.

Arthur's articles appear regularly in leading industry publications. His consulting assignments and lectures on marketing and economics have taken place in the US, Canada, Europe, Latin America and Asia. He has been a key speaker in

marketing conferences in the US, Canada, U.K., Japan, Taiwan, Australia, New Zealand, Brazil, Venezuela, Columbia, Malaysia, Thailand and Portugal.
arthur.hughes@kbm1.com
http://www.dbmarketing.com/

Charles A. Prescott

Charles A. Prescott has spent his career in international corporate, securities, finance, and new country development law and projects. During his career he has worked in law firms in Tokyo and New York and has been in-house corporate counsel with privately owned Continental Grain Company and publicly listed The Reader's Digest Association, Inc. Most recently he was Vice President, Global Development, at the Direct Marketing Association, Inc., of the United States. The DMA is the largest trade association for businesses interested in interactive and database marketing,

Most recently he represented the direct marketing industry in numerous US government and international bodies, including the US Department of Commerce, the State Department, the International Chamber of Commerce, and the Universal Postal Union. He also served on the Board of Directors of FEDMA (Federation of European Direct and Interactive Marketing). Currently he represents the Global Envelope Alliance at the Universal Postal Union where he also serves as Chairman of the Consultative Committee, which consists of private sector associations and organizations with interest in the international postal network, including competitors, customers of, and suppliers to post offices worldwide. He also serves on the Industry Technical Advisory Committee to the US Department of Commerce, which advises the government on international trade agreements and issues and a similar committee which advises the State Department on postal matters.

He earned his J.D. (cum laude) in 1974 from Harvard Law School, after earning an A.B. in 1969 from Hamilton College. He has been admitted to practice in California and New York and is a member of the American Bar Association and the New York State Bar Association.

He is a frequent speaker around the world on direct and interactive marketing developments and privacy and data protection and has authored numerous works to assist data processors to understand and comply with laws and best practices world-wide. His work at the UPU has resulted in engagement in numerous postal issues impacting international mailers.
chaspres@optonline.net
www.prescottreport.com

Alexander Singewald

Alexander J.J.T. Singewald LLM is a legal consultant of Singewald Consultants Group BV, based in Aalsmeer, The Netherlands. Singewald Consultants Group BV advises in the field of all matters pertaining to data protection, primarily within the direct/database marketing, distance selling, and sales promotion sectors and (multi)national companies that consider the database as a part of their (primary) business process. Singewald Consultants Group works for a wide range of companies such as publishers, transport companies, power companies, financial service providers, address suppliers, fundraisers and health organizations, software developers, and advertising agencies. Singewald Consultants Group also advises on outsourcing agreements, the legal implementation of Enterprise Content Management Systems, and guides organizations if PR and PA are important aspects.

Alexander J.J.T. Singewald LLM was elected as DM man of the year in April 2004. He is treasurer of FEDMA, advisor of Stichting DM en SP Prijzen Esprix (the European equivalent of the American ECHO Awards), chairman of the Dutch Plantronics Telesales Team Trophy and speaker/tutor on the legal aspects of direct marketing.
singewald@privacy.nl
www.privacy.nl

Dick Vanderzaken & Ronald Morcus

Since 2000, Dick Vanderzaken (1965) has been business development director at the Dutch specialist in multichannel campaign management 2organize. In this role he is responsible for consultancy and project management activities. Previously, he was senior account manager with PlantijnCasparie (part of RSDB). During the last two decades Dick has developed a broad expertise and a strong vision in the field of multichannel campaign management.

Since 2000, Ronald Morcus (1960) has been managing director of 2organize. Before that he held various international management positions with Philips, Brother, and Yamaha. He holds a degree in Business Economics and did an MBA/MBI at the Rotterdam School of Management.

Since 2007 Dick Vanderzaken and Ronald Morcus are co-owners of 2organize.
dick.vanderzaken@2organize.com
ronald.morcus@2organize.com
www.2organize.com

Ruud Verduin
Adviser and consultant
Special thanks are due to Ruud Verduin, with whom Egbert Jan van Bel has advised on and implemented EDM projects. He is author of the book *Introduction to Customer Relationship Management* and co-author of the original Dutch edition. He has made a valuable contribution to the preparation of this book as a "sparring partner" for the writers, as well as generously lending his ideas to reinforce the theories and vision expounded. Ruud is widely recognized as an expert in CRM and

Customer Experience Management, with a particular expertise in customer-centric change management.

He is principal of Verduin Marketing Consultants, a consulting group that helps clients develop and implement effective relationship marketing approaches. Ruud's consulting clients have included large organizations as well as middle-market businesses in industries as diverse as distribution, financial services, high-technology, telecom, not-for-profit, agricultural, and manufacturing. Ruud's passion is helping organizations exploit their marketing potential to the full. His knowledge and experience in achieving the transition from product-oriented to customer-oriented operation make him a sought-after adviser, consultant and speaker.

His experience with the transition from product-driven to customer-driven organizations has made him a popular public speaker and commentator on customer relationship management in The Netherlands.

Ruud holds a BA in information management and received his MBA from Newport University, Utrecht. Prior to establishing his own company, Ruud held management positions at one of the big international consultancy firms as well as at several other companies. He is lecturer in various MBA programs and serves as a judge for the CRM Association.nl's CRM Award.

ruud@verduin.nl

www.verduin.nl

Preface

How do you get customers to buy your products? That has been the marketing problem for centuries. In *Follow That Customer!*, the authors have provided an extremely useful and practical answer to this question: you communicate with them based on events that are important to them.

We often hear marketers claim that they make "the right offer to the right person at the right time" as if that were an obvious method of gaining sales. Perhaps it might be, but assembling the information necessary to carry out that claim has proved to be very difficult for most marketers. In fact, today, most marketers are thinking about what they want to sell rather than about what their customers want to buy. This book should change that approach for those who read it and take its lessons to heart. It tells just how to obtain and use the information needed to send messages based on customer events.

In six very detailed and useful case studies, *Follow That Customer!* explains how several companies have succeeded in using events in their customers' lives successfully to trigger their marketing campaigns. Following the case studies, the authors explain the principles behind the case studies in useful ways that can be adopted by the thousands of corporate readers of their useful book.

For me, one of the best parts of this wonderful book is the Eleven Lessons Learned. Included in these lessons are the following:

- Think like a customer.
- Test on a small scale first.
- Keep asking questions.
- EDM is a permanent process, not a one-off promotion.
- Be different—make your EDM program special enough so that people stick with your program.

This valuable book should be on the bookshelf of the marketing staff of every significant company in America or Europe. Those following its lessons will earn millions of dollars in profit for their companies as well as making their customers happy.

Arthur Middleton Hughes
Fort Lauderdale, Florida
2010

Introduction

The Quest for Event-Driven Marketing

It's evident: The customer is the most important person for reaching your goals. A customer is a person, not a concept. It is important in your business to get a hold of your customer's moves, their interests, behavior, their needs and wishes, and how they relate to your company. One of my clients wanted to keep track of his customers' moves, their needs and desires. His vision was to put more energy in keeping clients, making them both more loyal and more profitable. "I want to *follow* my customer," he said. That was more than eight years ago. He was ready for a customer approach in his marketing and sales.

Back then I already had some experience with Event-Driven Marketing (EDM). I asked my client—an international marketing director at a large financial services provider—to have a look at this concept and see how it could fit to his ideas. In my preparations, I wanted to find out more about EDM. I was surprised to find that neither my regular "brick" bookshop nor even the "click" stores like Amazon.com could provide me with a single book dedicated to the subject.

That can't be true!

EDM wasn't invented yesterday, or even the day before. The term is at least fifteen years old! But not even googling "event-driven marketing" brought up anything worthwhile. Megabyte after megabyte of PowerPoint presentations, and lots of other publications later: still no concise definitions or explanations. No "how to's" and certainly no models, checklists, or frameworks.

Unbelievable...

After all, EDM is the logical next step from direct marketing and database marketing, from customer relationship management (CRM). EDM is a strongly customer-oriented concept, making the most of new media like the Internet, new technologies in the field of databases, and the latest campaign-management software. EDM is results-oriented because through it you try to offer the right message to the right individual customer at the right time.

In short, EDM is for today!

My own experiences with EDM in my day-to-day consultancy work have been totally positive. So why has the concept failed to catch on in a big way with modern-thinking, modern-working businesses? Perhaps because it is not easy to implement. You need considerable experience with database marketing; your personnel, customer, and IT processes must be in order; and you have to really understand your customers and all their needs and wishes. No easy task!

So EDM is not for the simple-minded.

The book you are now reading is the first dedicated, comprehensive publication on the subject of event-driven marketing. As well as describing our own experiences in this field, it contains inspiring contributions from a number of leading specialists. *Follow That Customer!* combines theoretical background and visionary thoughts with companies' real-life experiences with event-driven marketing. We discuss how EDM fits in with marketing and sales, the new marketing terminology it uses and EDM process management. We also elaborate on subjects like loyalty, ROI, analytics, databases, and legislation, thereby providing a full handbook for those who want to make EDM work for them.

The original Dutch edition of this book was an instant bestseller in its field. Within a year it had become essential business reading, with every subsequent edition—it is now in its fifth—selling fast. And not only did the readers devour it, they used it! The theories we set out have been put into practice, with many companies making a lot of money from event-driven marketing as a result.

When we started working on a new book on event-driven marketing for the US, it gave us the chance to completely revisit the material from it's European "predecessor." The first edition might have been a prize-winner (winning the Best Marketing Book Award), but as with most projects there were parts that we would have liked to have done differently in hindsight. Besides, marketing constantly evolves, making it necessary to update some chapters. This being the first international edition, we decided that it needed more international content. While we kept one of the original Dutch cases on baby care we decided, with the help of some contributors, to add cases from the US and Scandinavia. These cases illustrate how the theories from the previous chapter(s) can be put to practice. Six case studies illustrate what really happens when event-driven marketing programs are set up.

What's more, we teamed up with renowned database marketing expert Alan Weber who added his own US perspective and knowledge to most of the theoretical chapters. The end product outshines the original and, we hope, is a solid addition to marketing literature.

So who is it for?

For those who want to stand out from the crowd. Those who want to outperform their competitors and serve their customers as effectively as possible. Those seriously committed to improving their margins. Because isn't that what it is ultimately all about? So . . . *Follow that customer!*

We also had great pleasure writing this book, and that makes a real difference. I hope that you enjoy reading it just as much, because that is why we wrote it. And good luck with following your own customers!

Egbert-Jan van Bel
September 2010

A New Day in Marketing

It's a new day in Marketing. Actually it's more like "midday," and this book is about the latest hour. Marketing is undergoing an enormous revolution. The center of gravity or the center of power has been shifting from the marketer to the customer. As recently as a generation or two ago, marketers talked about choosing between "push" and "pull" strategies. Marketing was "war," with marketing executives driving their departments like Patton drove his tanks.

That day—or that part of the day—is gone. Customers have nearly limitless access to information and, thus, nearly limitless choice. And nearly limitless power. Beginning in the 1960s and 1970s, the computer and, in the 1990s, the Internet put instant access to information at consumers' fingertips. Customers no longer are product information "receptacles." No longer must they accept unproven claims of being "free," or "one of a kind" or "the lowest price," or the "highest quality." If you make such a claim, you had better be able to prove it because potential customers will be able to disprove it if it isn't true. And you will pay the price, a lost sale, customer disloyalty, and customer churn.

While these changes have been coming for quite a while, their impact has grown steadily. The most significant, bottom-line change is in customer loyalty and retention. It is increasingly difficult to get customers and more difficult than ever to hold on to them.

Why is this so important? It has long been known that it costs at least five times more to sell to a new customer than to sell to a current customer. Thus, on one hand, customers are a company's most valuable asset. The current customer list is, in the words of the old-time bank robber Willie Sutton, where the money is. On the other hand, customer churn—the opposite of customer retention—can be one of the most serious revenue-depleters a company can have. Retaining customers has become the most significant marketing challenge that executives face. Customers—not one-time buyers, but real customers—are the lifeblood of an enterprise—any enterprise—and customer churn is the vampire at the window.

This book is about using Event-Driven Marketing (EDM), which uses the latest in data-mining techniques to identify those factors (events or conditions) that signal a significant change in circumstance. The change in circumstance signals a new set of needs that increases a potential customer's likelihood to buy—in other words, significant events in the customer's life or circumstance that functions in EDM as marketing triggers. By focusing on these life-stage or event triggers, a marketer can better anticipate and appeal to a customer's needs and thereby create customer loyalty, increase customer retention, and improve profitability. EDM is the philosophy that drives this strategy.

The Roots of Event-Driven Marketing

Marketing has always been devoted to proactive selling on a mass basis. Philip Kotler's classic 4Ps definition still applies: "the right *p*romotion for the right *p*roduct in the right *p*lace through the right method of *p*hysical distribution." More recent definitions (e.g., by Christian Gronroos) have tended to emphasize the qualitative side of the seller-customer relationship—that customers (as opposed to one-time purchasers) buy because of the quality of the relationship as much as the product or service.

Whatever your specific definition, marketers have evolved to meet new challenges and capitalize on new opportunities. Direct marketing might be the best example. Modern direct marketing grew out of the ventures of such nineteenth-century mail-order entrepreneurs as Richard Warren Sears and Aaron Montgomery Ward. The term *direct marketing* didn't become standard usage until the late 1970s, at which time it became an umbrella term covering mail order and telesales.

The difference between general marketing and direct marketing? Direct marketing tracks customer buying behavior and/or characteristics and structures future sales offers based on that information. Such knowledge enables a marketer to group offers according to similar behaviors or look-alikes of their customers. Traditional marketing, on the other hand, uses attitudinal marketing research to identify how people feel and make mass appeals on that basis..

Mail order sellers a century and more ago knew how to manage a mailing list of customers. They just lacked today's powerful analytic tools. The rise of the computer and increasing sophistication in analyzing mailing lists (aka databases) enabled direct mailers/direct marketers to drill down into their lists more completely and identify buying behaviors more precisely.

A landmark article in the 1960s in the *Harvard Business Review* by Martin Baier explained how future marketers would use newly developed postal ZIP codes to segment markets. Increasingly powerful computers and increasingly sophisticated analytical models and techniques made it possible to develop databases that went beyond organizing markets only by location (geographic segmentation) to organizing them by purchase behavior (behavioral segmentation). The ability to segment markets into smaller and smaller segments led to the term *mass customization*, popularized in the 1990s by Joe Pine. And, of course, the 1990s also was the time when "one-to-one marketing" (Don Peppers and Martha Rogers) was all the rage. And then there was customer relationship management (CRM).

EDM is a logical extension of direct marketing and these other marketing developments. Here are some basic working definitions:

Direct Marketing (DM) is a method of marketing and selling at a distance (without an intermediary) based on making offers that appeal to the needs and wants of prospects as identified by their past buying behavior and then creating and maintaining valuable, lasting relationships with prospects and customers. Direct marketing is increasingly being done by the focused use of direct and interactive electronic media and less by direct mail. In other words, direct marketing is no longer tied to any one media, but instead viewed as a marketing discipline.

Event-Driven Marketing (EDM) expands the relationship with customers by monitoring them (and their personal or commercial situation) on a constant basis and responding immediately to relevant changes in their circumstances. This includes monitoring both their transactional behavior with you (as is done in direct marketing) as well as their life or business circumstances beyond your immediate transactional relationship.

Without a doubt, you have noticed that there is a subtle difference between the two descriptions above. Whereas we still refer to both the "prospect" and the "customer" when it comes to direct marketing—meaning, in fact, your entire target group or market segment—in event-driven marketing we are talking mainly about "your customers." It is actual customers who are at the heart of EDM.

Lifecycle stage becomes a major driver in customer relationships with EDM, whereas in direct marketing it may be little more than a tool to identify prospects if it is used at all. Understanding a customer's behavior and lifecycle stage give real insights into a customer's change in desired benefits they seek and their perceptions of their needs.

In light of the preceding, we have developed the following definition:

Event-driven marketing (EDM): a discipline within marketing, where commercial and communication activities are based upon relevant and identified changes in a customer's individual needs.

Terms like *marketing, direct marketing,* and *customer relationship management* are used by a lot of people, all of whom interpret them in their own way. But the above definition of event-driven marketing clearly delineates its scope: as the marketing discipline concerned with circumstances affecting your *customer.*

There are many different kinds of events. Some are obvious, like marriage, the birth of a child, moving house, or acquiring a pet. For all of these events, a need for new products or services arises from one moment to the next. But the expiration of a supply contract, the depletion of a stock, or a failed attempt to use a bank card are also events that can be exploited. These, too, are "relevant and identified changes in a customer's individual needs."

An example of an event in EDM?

You are a marketer at a bank. Through the database you are notified that a customer has failed to complete three card transactions during the past month because he has reached his overdraft limit. What can you do? Why not help the customer by offering him a flexible loan?

In this example, EDM seems straightforward, but good event-driven marketing means having your communications and database marketing in very good order. Speed of response and triggering the right action at the right moment are the essence of EDM.

Event-Driven Marketing is in part a response to the overtargeting of direct marketing. Direct marketing focuses primarily on RFM (recency, frequency, monetary value) and profile characteristics and less so on market share, market penetration, or share of customer. Narrowly focusing on a relationship based on past transactions often ignores changes in customer needs. For example, college seniors may appear to be excellent customers for a seller of textbooks. They have several years of buying history, buy every year, and spend a substantial amount. However, once they graduate, they will no longer need textbooks. What appeared to be "best customers" will simply become "lost customers."

Event-Driven Marketing avoids the marketing "spiral of death" that comes from overtargeting a core group of buyers while ignoring changes in needs due to circumstance. In our textbook example, new college freshman with no purchase history are seen as excellent prospects and recently graduated seniors are no longer seen as best customers by the marketer.

Granted, past behavior is generally the best indicator of future behavior. In the shorter term, buyer behavior for items such as textbooks, diapers, or retirement investments can be explained well with direct marketing techniques alone. But, as is the case with our textbook example, certain abrupt changes in buyer behavior simply cannot be explained by past behavior alone. Event-Driven Marketing provides additional insights and opportunities that help marketers find customers and serve their changing needs.

EDM and Direct Marketing: Important Distinctions

EDM is very closely related to disciplines like direct marketing, yet there are also significant differences.

DM and EDM differ in how they go about generating new leads (and, hopefully, customers) as well as cross-selling and upselling to existing ones. The best

Exhibit 1.1. Differences between Direct Marketing and Event-Driven Marketing

	Direct marketing	Event-Driven marketing
Nature	Targets customers with what we have been selling based on what they have bought. Does not specifically rely upon customer needs or circumstance. This is mass media advertising. DM targets segments.	Targets customers based on their needs due to changing circumstance. Does not specifically rely upon past purchase behavior.
Background to customer contact	Need(s) distilled from target-group buying behaviors and characteristics and objective, for the most part.	Need distilled from individual customer characteristics, statistical and other forecasts and subjective customer needs—"microsegmentation."
Reason for customer contact	Customer forms part of campaign target group, which has been identified as having a propensity to buy under certain circumstances based on prior purchase behavior.	Customer needs derived from individual customer data including circumstance and behavior.
Timing	According to marketing and/or sales plan; passive agenda, which is derived from determination/indication of customer propensity to buy, based on past behavior. Often possible to fit into a promotional calendar.	When the customer needs the product: which depends upon when an event takes place. Not easily fit into a promotional calendar.
Effectiveness	Comes from the match between campaign proposition and past buying behavior.	Comes from correct timing of the response to changing needs.
Efficiency	Economies of scale from campaign volume.	Efficiency based on precision of individual targeting based on timing and need.
Driving force/source (data)	Driving force is prior buying behavior which predicts future buying behavior. Key source is transactions summarized into RFM.	Driving force is customer needs based on circumstance. Key sources are buying behavior and characteristics that relate to circumstances and needs.
Marketing	Suitable for targeting customers for greatest response or highest average order.	Suitable for targeting prospects or leads with no prior buying history based on changes in needs. Suitable for maintaining and upgrading customer relationships by targeting new or different offers based on changes in needs.

Exhibit 1.2. DM and EDM Processes

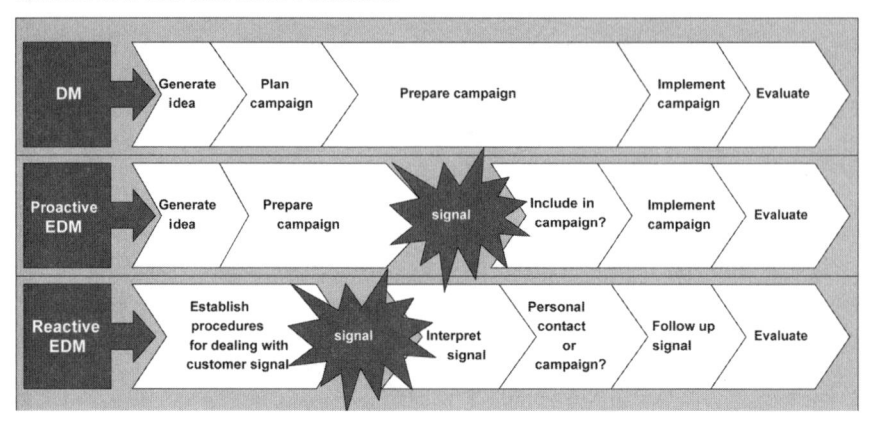

DM	Generate idea → Plan campaign → Prepare campaign → Implement campaign → Evaluate
Proactive EDM	Generate idea → Prepare campaign → signal → Include in campaign? → Implement campaign → Evaluate
Reactive EDM	Establish procedures for dealing with customer signal → signal → Interpret signal → Personal contact or campaign? → Follow up signal → Evaluate

way to find a good prospect list in DM is to find a response list of people who have bought the same or a similar item. The best way to find a good prospect list in EDM is to find a list of people that had or will have a change in circumstance that signals a change in needs.

For example, if we were to offer wedding receptions, a list of people who were just married would not contain likely buyers. An EDM approach would be to send offers to the recently engaged as opposed to the recently married.

EDM does not replace DM. It builds on it. They share many elements but EDM is an additional set of disciplines that helps marketers find opportunities or explain behaviors that cannot be found or explained by DM principles alone. DM can explain future behavior most of the time by using past behavior. When it cannot, EDM can explain why behavior changed or will change due to a change in circumstance. EDM allows for greater targeting precision by adding need-based qualifiers to behavior-based qualifiers.

Because EDM is so tightly focused on individual customers and offers are more precisely targeted than traditional DM or database marketing can be, it tends to generate higher response rates. Since the beginning of time, Marketing has tried to reproduce the individual, face-to-face sale on a mass scale. Direct Marketing and Database Marketing have improved on the level of individuality or customization of offer appeals. EDM represents the final evolution of Marketing to develop truly personal, customized offers. It is the final step in bringing mass and personal selling together.

EDM is much like the two ears and one mouth approach to marketing. The "DM" ear, listens to what customers and prospects are doing. The "EDM" ear listens to what customers and prospects need. Then the mouth delivers the message. Or as a carpenter might say, "measure twice, cut once."

Organizing an EDM campaign requires a different way of thinking and a different approach from a standard DM campaign. It is like the difference between sending a Christmas card to all your contacts once a year and sending birthday cards every day to those whose birthday it is.

Elements of both DM and EDM have existed side by side as long as recorded human history, and the basic ideas behind both are part of everyday life: for example, bringing a gift to someone's graduation—DM; bringing a gift to a pregnant mom's baby shower—EDM. The point is that we cannot separate the basic ideas of either DM or EDM from common sense.

However, we can apply a distinction on how we conduct the two disciplines. Most DM tracking, reports, and analysis are based strictly around DM principles. Catalogers, for example, select prospect lists based on buying similar products. They track offers by RFM segment. They may rarely, if ever, target offers based on changes in circumstance. Even if they chose to, their existing key codes, customer data, and tracking reports, would have to be revised to include such information. Many DM firms can and do operate profitably without using EDM principles and as a result can miss opportunities.

Tracking changes in circumstance is quite a different matter from simply recognizing that they occur. A marketer that sends a birthday card may do so without any EDM-related tracking of results. A birthday card simply goes out and, if it tracked, is given a key code and shown in the same reports as the RFM-segmented and key-coded offers. The DM marketer may know response rates, average order, and ROI of the cards sent in any given month, but see no distinction in offers to young or old, no awareness of a difference in response among young or old, and no targeting of offers based on changes in life circumstances (e.g., getting or losing a job; getting a significant job promotion—and equally substantial raise in pay). EDM is harder to do because it includes DM and builds on it.

EDM Prospecting

As we described earlier in this chapter, EDM is primarily about marketing activities based upon information available about individual current customers. That information can come from internal sources (the company database) or from external sources, such as customer lists available from other companies or from list brokers. Of course, the quality of such lists can vary. Also, this is not actually EDM since Event-Driven Marketing targets only your own customers, not third-party customers. However, if your house list is good and your outside sources are good, traditional lead generation can be useful to build your company's list of likely prospects and future customers.

One difference from traditional DM prospecting is that event-driven prospecting involves seeking out interesting leads beyond our existing clientele, based upon relevant recent or imminent events. Several such prospecting programs are illustrated in the case studies in this book. One is the "Happy Box" from Wij Special Media, a gift pack containing samples and special offers through which suppliers in the Netherlands try to establish first contact with expectant mothers. The women in question are only prospects, but activities of this kind, based on their propensity or likelihood to buy, attempt to identify them as soon as possible so that they can be turned into customers. From that point on it is possible to include them in EDM programs.

Other EDM-related Concepts

Like traditional DM and other related strategies, CRM was devoted to focusing more precisely on customer needs and likelihood to buy. In addition, based on the belief that "not all customers are equal," CRM was developed specifically to improve on the bottom line by focusing on identifying the company's most profitable customers.

One of the basic pillars of CRM is deciding exactly when dialog with the customer delivers the best results in terms of both loyalty (a feeling: the "soft" element) and retention (the customer keeps on buying: the "hard" element). The latter, in particular, also applies to event-driven marketing. Marketers should not be approaching customers when it best suits the business but when the customers are most receptive to the proposition. So there is a clear overlap between CRM and EDM, with both endeavoring to serve the customers as effectively as possible. CRM, however, has an extra dimension in that it tries to forge loyalty in addition to the retention aspects that typify EDM. Here is an authoritative definition:

> By CRM (customer relationship management), we understand the implementation of a strategy whereby a company or institution attempts to optimize customer relationships in terms of customer yield and customer satisfaction. CRM is regarded as an ongoing, systematic and organization-wide activity.
>
> —*CRM Association, 2010.*

An important corollary of CRM is that marketing occurs at every point of customer contact ("marketing is everyone's job"). Thus, it often results in organizational change, such as streamlining customer service procedures by giving cross-department access to information related to customer issues.

Like all other direct marketing-related activities, most of the signals that trigger EDM activities come from the organization's database. EDM can be the "driver" behind the sending of individual direct mail as well as individual sales calls. As mentioned previously, EDM is very much like all of the other DM-related program strategies we have discussed: bonding with the customer, creating loyalty by knowing the customer well, and by devising tailored offers and activities for each customer or group of customers. EDM is the logical fulfillment of all previous types of marketing.

Exhibit 1.3 shows EDM's position compared with related concepts. The dia-

Exhibit 1.3. Positioning of EDM-Related Marketing Tools and Concepts

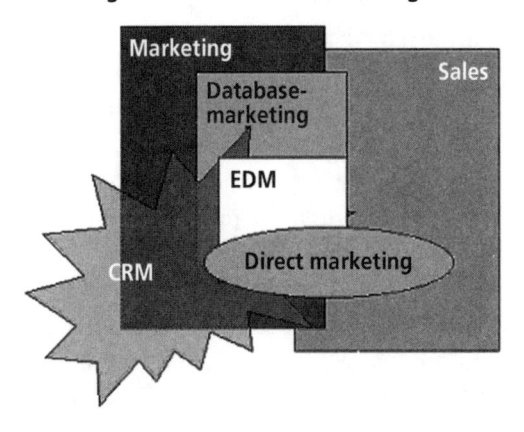

gram is somewhat simplified and generalized—the exact situation will vary from company to company—but it does reveal the following:

- CRM is not always "just" marketing, but also has a lot to do with the organization and general business issues.
- EDM is linked to database marketing: the information needed for good EDM is database-generated (but it does NOT necessarily have to be provided by the database manager).
- Direct marketing has a big overlap with database marketing and, hence, also with EDM.
- Like DM, sales are results-based when there is true multichannel thinking; actual sales are what counts, so they are in fact linked to all marketing concepts. Although the "4 Ps" and many marketers categorize sales under the heading of marketing, in reality they are still often a separate activity "alongside" the marketing department.

Exhibit 1.4. The Returns from EDM: Better Results at Lower Contact Costs per Customer

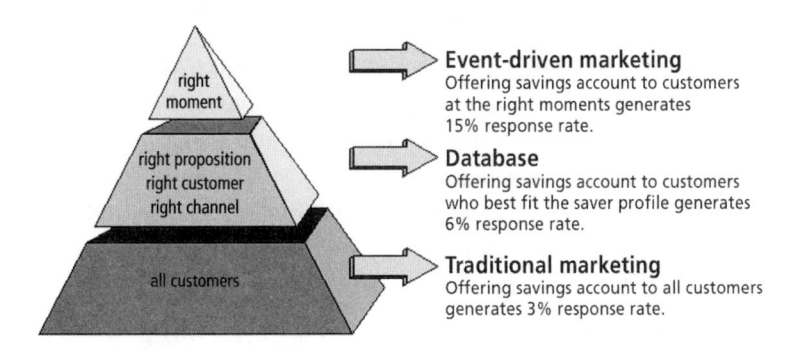

Event-driven marketing
Offering savings account to customers at the right moments generates 15% response rate.

Database
Offering savings account to customers who best fit the saver profile generates 6% response rate.

Traditional marketing
Offering savings account to all customers generates 3% response rate.

Segmentation: Old and New

This book discusses segmented marketing in relation to customer-focused marketing, such as Event-Driven Marketing (EDM). EDM occupies a prominent place in successful up-selling and cross-selling to customers. Those companies that have clearly identified their customer and the customer's needs, have good (and preferably multichannel) interaction with those customers and are able to conduct successful marketing campaigns according to the "Right 4" principle: the right message at the right place to the right person at the right time. Please note that the order here is not random! It is a logical sequence.

People have always said that companies can market themselves more efficiently by directing their products or services, channels, and communication only towards those customers who can generate the most profits for the company. Segmentation can work well in this situation, with a view to mining and developing the potential or existing customer base. But now that we can impact the customer more personally and directly with technology that enables us to follow and serve our customers very specifically, it is possible that segmentation will no longer be "in." How you create those segments is especially important. It is critical not only to know customers' behavior and situation of the customer; you must take steps to be ahead of these. More and more companies are successfully working in an event-driven manner with their customers. Segmented marketing is not "out." In the end, marketers who segment are in the position of being able to use segmentation more effectively to acquire customers from the market. Just as EDM is a logical extension of traditional DM, the new EDM-based segmentation is logical, positive extension of its predecessor.

Various banks and insurance companies have successfully incorporated an event-driven approach. Now pet food brands and travel agencies are also using this concept, with growing success. That's why these companies no longer immediately categorize their customers into rigid segments, but allow for flexibility in the process. This means that they are able to offer the exact product that the customer is waiting for.

Taking the Event-Driven Approach

EDM can be applied profitably in both business-to-consumer (B-to-C) and business-to-business (B-to-B) environments. Any organization can identify indicators like reaching a particular age, the expiration of a contract, or the passing of a set number of days after a quote is issued. However, the more advanced applications of EDM are primarily of interest to businesses that are in regular contact with their customers and so can draw upon an extensive source of information.

Four major B-to-B contact types, which may or may not overlap, are:

1. Users: People who use, consume, or install a product. Examples would include factory workers who install a component, officer workers who use software, and workers who wear uniforms or specialized clothing. Users

may not have a direct say in what they install or use, but it must be able to support their task without generating problems or complaints.
2. Specifiers: People who specify which product or service can or must be chosen. Examples would include engineers who describe exactly what a component must be, IT specialists who select software, and designers who determine colors, sizes, and fabrics.
3. Decision-Makers: People who have the authority to approve a purchase. Examples might include marketers who decide how many finished items to order (based on what they can sell), top management who are responsible for what capabilities office employees must have, or store managers who decide what they should or should not stock.
4. Buyers: Someone who actually makes the purchase, and may or may not have authority in what or how much is purchased. Examples include people in purchasing departments, bookkeepers and accountants.

Each of the four types of B-to-B customers has a different relationship with a product or service and a different viewpoint as to its benefits. A user might like the way a clothing product looks or fits, a specifier might like the fabric's color quality, a decision-maker might like the way it gives employees a polished appearance, a buyer might like that they have 60 days to pay. As a result, understanding the behavioral intent of any given customer within their B-to-B contact type can be a challenge.

EDM is best suited to organizations with easy access to data from which behavioral intent can be discerned. The organization must be able to identify purchases at the individual level—a loyalty card, for example—or must gather customer data as part of their primary business process.

A second precondition for the initiation of an EDM program is the availability of sufficient absolute profit margin or customer value. If the individual customer's potential contribution to overall profit is very limited, then there is a good chance that EDM—and any other form of customer-specific marketing—will not pay for itself. For more about this, see Chapter 6.

There are good arguments to be made in favor of a business "customizing" its customer contacts. Database marketing has been used since the 1980s as a way of trying to reach the right customer with the right proposition through the right channel. But with today's growing competition, declining customer loyalty, political developments (privacy laws) and increasing consumer knowledge and self-confidence, that is no longer enough.

EDM is a marketer organizing the means to approach customers when it best suits the customer, not when it best suits the business. The "right moment" is the time when the customer is most receptive to the proposition on offer. In other words, the *"three rights principle"* (right message, right place, right person) becomes the *"four rights"*: the right message in the right place for the right person *at the right moment.* **The aim: to optimize customer potential.** The challenge: the ability to identify customer value and customer potential.

Exhibit 1.5. From Production to Process Orientation: Where Do You Stand?

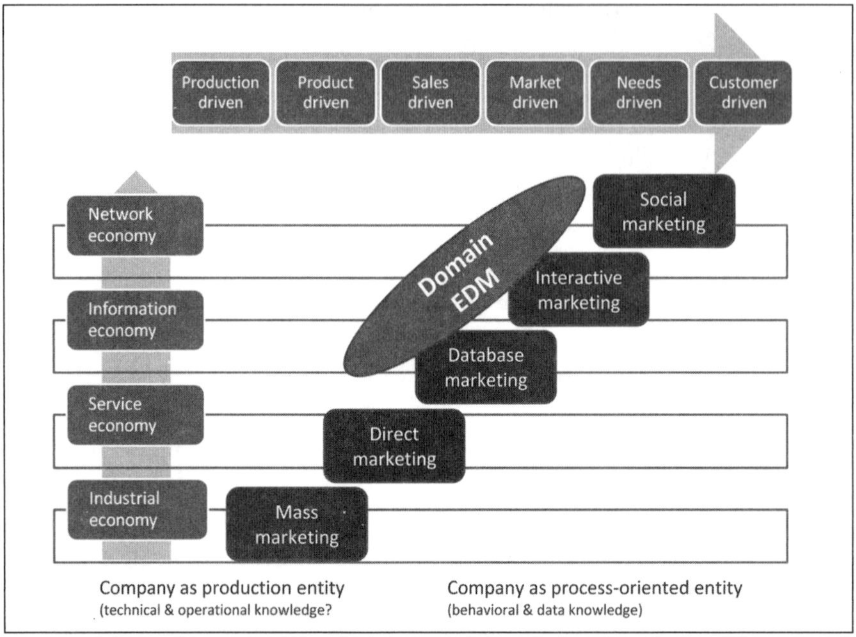

(Diagram: arrow progression from Production driven → Product driven → Sales driven → Market driven → Needs driven → Customer driven. Economies listed vertically: Network economy, Information economy, Service economy, Industrial economy. Marketing stages: Mass marketing, Direct marketing, Database marketing, Interactive marketing, Social marketing, with Domain EDM overlaid.)

Company as production entity
(technical & operational knowledge?)

Company as process-oriented entity
(behavioral & data knowledge)

Over the next few years, the technology is certain to develop in such a way that it will be able to provide current and reliable customer data for use in responding to changing patterns of need and the differentiation of customers and markets. It is important to be able to apply particular marketing tools at particular times and to vary the way in which the customer is approached according to the hoped-for results. The correct use of such tools requires sufficient knowledge and experience within the organization.

Most businesses these days are talking about all kinds of interactive marketing and customer-oriented thinking. Conferences and journals are overflowing with enthusiasm on the subject. It has become the elixir for marketing success. But don't let yourself be fooled. Stay realistic and true to yourself. Where does the average marketer or entrepreneur really stand in the midst of all this marketing innovation? See Exhibit 1.5.

It is interesting to note that some of the companies that spend the most on CRM still consistently appear on consumer organizations' "most complained about" lists. An anecdote published recently in a consumers' association magazine described the desperate efforts of a customer to reach a certain company's customer service department in an attempt to resolve a complaint. Eventually frustrated by being passed from pillar to post in the supplier's labyrinthine back office, he gave up and decided to cancel his contract. Within a week he received a personalized mailing making him an attractive new offer if he would just withdraw his cancellation: a perfectly timed example of event-driven marketing, but in a context that made the whole thing utterly ridiculous.

Exhibit 1.6. The Top Ten EDM Considerations

1.	Vision, strategy	What do you want to achieve with EDM? Can you name specific events? Can you "fine tune" your vision and strategy using new knowledge? Event-Driven Marketing and the techniques involved are evolving fast; this is a young discipline in which we still have a lot to learn.
2.	Information	Information about events sometimes becomes available too late. Or is incorrect. Then there is the phenomenon of multichannel management: through which medium do you best reach the customer in terms of effect (results) and cost? For one person that is email, for another a letter and for a third the telephone.
3.	Missed opportunity	The organization misses impulse purchases because, unlike in DM, not the entire population is called or emailed. So it is difficult to quantify how correct measurements of an EDM program's effect, costs and yields are.
4.	Time and money	Initially, huge investments of time and money are often needed.
5.	Control	In some cases, an event is easy to predict. Births, for example, which can be identified months in advance by specialized data suppliers. Particularly in this kind of situation, though, careful checks before contacting the customer are vital.
6.	Speed of response	An EDM program imposes high standards upon an organization's response times. When reacting to an event, it is vitally important to keep the interval between signal and customer contact to an absolute minimum.
7.	Communications	Both internal and with the customer: ask yourself who needs to know about the EDM campaign—from switchboard operator to sales manager (Question: "About the savings account offer...?" Answer: "What savings account offer?").
8.	Marketing and yields	EDM is not an automatic choice: it first needs to be estimated in terms of "expected result" per customer. To know and measure that, you need good experience in database marketing and—as we like to call it—spreadsheet marketing. In other words, you need to be able to calculate exact input figures based upon experience. But the danger with spreadsheet marketing is overoptimism. So stay realistic.
9.	Rollout and follow-up	Can I manage rollout without turning the organization upside down in its efforts to keep an EDM program going? Without having to put up with huge difficulties and very high costs? You need to keep the entire process manageable.
10.	To measure is to know	Taking measurements at the end of the process is vital. Ask (to guess is to miss) yourself, "Can I properly test and evaluate, and distribute the knowledge obtained through the organization (reporting) in such a way that it helps improve and adjust the EDM program?"

CASE 1: Birthday Clubs

Later in this book you will read about several case studies that rely heavily on external data gathering, elaborate contact strategies or advanced data profiling and modeling. As you will see, there's a lot to it and setting up such an Event-Driven Marketing program can be rather complicated. You might not have easy access to data, you might not have data mining staff available or maybe your average customer's value simply doesn't allow for high program costs. As such, smaller businesses often tell us that EDM is not for them. Still, not every EDM program has to be rocket science. You would be amazed what you could do with a simple piece of data like the birthday of your customers. In this chapter we'll show you how you can keep EDM simple and effective.

The Customer Connection (TCC) is a full service CRM agency in Escondido, California, founded in 1979. An area that TCC has specialized in is helping restaurants improve sales and profits by administering Loyalty/Frequency, Birthday and Gift Card programs for hundreds of restaurants and other businesses throughout the United States. TCC develops CRM technology, implements marketing tactics based on their client's customer database, provides direct mail and email services and report results back to their clients. All of this enables TCC to collect, analyze and use information about individual customers such as:

- Name, address, email address, birth date and names and birth dates of spouses and children
- Specific dining out information such as when, where, for what meal, how often, how much money they spent and much more
- How they respond to promotions
- How they chose where and when to dine
- How to communicate and motivate them to choose a restaurant when making a dining out decision

As President Judd Goldfeder explains: "We find that any communication, irrespective of whether or not there is a promotional offer, will increase visits. However, the right promotional offer to the right recipient at the right time will dramatically increase response." If that doesn't sound like event-driven marketing, nothing does.

Birthday Clubs

Over the past 30 years, The Customer Connection has created successful Birthday Clubs for over 500 restaurants nationwide. A Birthday Club is much more than celebrating "kids" birthdays. Results from all clients have shown that programs that generate the most redeemed cards and most sales increases include the whole family.

Starting a Birthday Club is relatively easy. Restaurants simply need to get their customers to join at their location(s) or on their websites. The gathered data is entered into a customer database hosted by TCC. TCC will then help their client to design, print and distribute direct mail and email communications such as:

- Birthday and Anniversary greeting cards, combined with a tailored offer like a free entrée or a money-off coupon
- Prospect invitations (for instance, TCC has found that the best 'cold prospects' are the neighbors of their existing customers)
- Other promotions that are unique to your restaurants

The redeemed coupons from the promotions are returned to TCC and entered in the database, enabling the agency to provide frequent reports on

- Redemption results for birthday and anniversary greetings and other promotions sent to members
- Number of new members who join each month in each of your restaurants
- Motivating customers to visit your restaurants to redeem their birthday "present"
- Reactivating guests who are not regular customers
- Nobody eats alone; for every guest who redeems their birthday card another person dines in the restaurant without additional gift costs
- Reinforcing top-of-mind awareness when members making a dining out decision creates visits after the birth month

For one 25-unit steak and seafood company, they offered a $10 birthday discount to 215,600 customers who filled out a Birthday Club registration card. A database was created from these registrations. The birthday card mailings, over a year, cost $90,000. 41.1% of the cards were redeemed, producing overall sales of $2.9 million dollars. Each birthday patron brought an average of 1.8 other guests for the party who paid full price.

Analysis of who redeems birthday cards has shown that the commonly held belief that people who redeem birthday cards "would have come anyway" is incorrect. In one of many tests birthday cards, offering a free entrée, were mailed to the 7,000 members of a client's loyalty/frequent diner program who had not visited the client's restaurants for over six months prior to receipt of the birthday card. The results:

- 1,600 (23%) of the members who received a birthday card visited the restaurants during their birth month:
    —880 members redeemed their birthday card to receive their free entrée
    —720 members dined in the restaurant but *did not* use their birthday card
- The 7,000 recipients of the birthday card who had not dined during the 6 months prior to receiving the birthday card dined 1,750 times in the restaurant during the *5 months following* their birth month.

- The client realized *incremental* sales of $100,000 at a cost of $7,900 for printing and mailing the birthday cards.

Flush with the success of the birthday programs, TCC created permanent Frequent Diner membership cards for restaurant patrons. In one specific week TCC mailed out 24,725 permanent plastic cards for a restaurant chain. During the week before the cards went out, these patrons visited the restaurants 1,050 times. During the 13 weeks after receiving their permanent plastic cards, these patrons visited an average of 1,400 times per week—an increase of 33%. They spent $156,000 more than they were spending before the cards were mailed.

While TCC was servicing many restaurants with their Birthday Club programs it shouldn't be hard for a small business to set up a similar program by yourself. All you need is:

- a simple database, which could be as basic as a list in an MS Excel spreadsheet
- mail merge software (e.g., MS Word) to print personalized letters with offers
- the dedication and drive to select, print and post frequent batches of letters, in this case at least weekly

Many companies have begun to register dates of birth of customers in their database, whether it's mandatory for the purchasing process or not. Some have thought about using this data for birthday offers. Very few however are actually doing this, which is a shame because the impact can be marvelous. TCC's case is just one example. In business-to-business the possible investments per customers can often be much higher.

One direct marketing company that one of the authors has frequently worked with captured the data of the contact persons at their clients in their customer database. Whenever a birthday would come up the company would send them a present. In case of inactive clients it normally concerned a playful gift like a paper chain decoration with the contact person's name printed on. For active clients the agency would have flowers and a personal message delivered. An excellent way to stay top-of-mind with inactive clients, demonstrating an innovative example of the agency's capabilities, while reinforcing the relationship with the active ones.

Points Programs

Once you have implemented a program like the Birthday Club and have found it successful, it becomes easier to add additional features to your marketing initiatives.

For the restaurant business, the next step above birthday and membership programs, of course, is points. Everyone likes to accumulate miles or points whenever they shop. Restaurant patrons are like everyone else. TCC set up an on-line real time frequency program that links a point of sale terminal and TCC computers. The process is just like a credit card verification. Whenever a member presents his plastic membership card, it is swiped through the terminal that connects to TCC's server. TCC's computers post the transaction, and send back information that is printed on the member's transaction receipt. The information includes the member's up-to-the-minute point balance, along with offers, rewards and messages tailored to the individual's past frequency and purchase behavior.

Members earn points (typically 1) for each dollar spent. They receive a reward when the required number of points are earned, while some members may also be entitled to special "soft benefits" such as priority seating, announcement of special "members only" events, etc. TCC sends their clients monthly program reports showing the status of the program, membership and the response to promotions.

This POS system has a lot of nifty side benefits for the restaurant owner:

- **Gift certificates.** These are similar to a pre-paid phone card. When a patron presents a gift certificate, it is swiped through the terminal and the meal is charged to the card. The certificate data is stored on the TCC computer, so if the card is lost, the card can be reconstructed. Cash balances can be increased.
- **Specific menu items can be tracked**. This provides the restaurant with expanded marketing flexibility for special promotion creation. It has been used for a continuity program for tracking the tasting of a variety of beers.
- **Pre-meal offers can be issued**. By swiping the member's card before he orders, he can get bonus points or special discounts on particular appetizers or desserts which might not otherwise be ordered.
- **Reception areas can have terminals**. While they wait to eat, members can swipe their own cards to get up-to-the-minute account information. This can be an opportunity for promotional messages, incentive purchase coupons or announcements of future events or upcoming promotions.

How to Join

As mentioned. guests are invited to "join the club" at participating restaurants. The registration card may include many family members with their birthdays. The form may solicit other information such as business address, dining behavior, demographics or customer satisfaction evaluation. The forms include a perforated temporary membership card that can be used immediately. The permanent plastic card with the magstripe is mailed to each member within a week. If a member shows up without his card, the transaction can be entered manually so that he gets full credit for his purchases.

Guests can also join the program on the restaurant's website, where visitors go to a special Frequency Club (or Birthday Club) page and click on the "Join" button. They are linked to a page TCC has created that has the "look and feel" of the restaurant's own website. The completed form is sent to TCC where it is added to the database, triggering a "Thank You for Joining" email and membership card mailing that are sent to the new member.

Below is an example of an online registration form.

Exhibit CS1.1. Online Registration Form

Register On-Line request Form
* Denotes required fields
*Location: Five Crowns - Corona del Mar
*First Name: ____ Middle Initial: ____
*Last Name: ____
*Email: ____
*Street: ____
*City: ____
*State: ____ *Zip Code: ____
*Phone: ____
*Birthday: Month / Day / Year
[Reset] [Submit]
We have a very strict privacy policy. Your email address and other personal information will never be shared with anyone outside of our organization.

Points on the Web

Members of the Frequency Club can also access their account on the restaurant's website by going to the Frequency Club page and clicking on "My Account". The page displays the current point balance, recent transactions and allows the member to communicate directly, via email, to TCC with questions about their account. Questions are answered within 24 hours by TCC's Member Services Department. Communicating the up-to-the-minute point balances to members through the Internet eliminates the previous cost and need for mailing monthly statements.

"They Would Have Come Anyway"

So how do points programs really affect dining behavior? A program like that of TCC really permits managers to measure the impact of their points programs in detail. Lets take a specific example:

A restaurant chain wanted to increase frequency and reactivate members who seemed to be "drifting away." TCC selected 4,000 members who had not earned any points during the previous three months. They sent them a letter offering a $5

Exhibit CS1.2. Customer Request Form

Check Account Activity

Please enter your member number as it appears on your card.
(Include all zeroes)

[   ]

Please enter your name as it appears on your card.

[   ]

[Check My Points]

Customer Request Form

* eMail Address: [   ]
(Form Processing requires a valid email address)
* Your Name: [   ]
Mailing Address: [   ]
City: [   ]
State: [▼]
* Zip: [   ]

☐ I need a new card
☐ eMail my account number
☐ Send me a statement

* Denotes required field

[Submit Query]

---

discount on dinner. The offer was good for 35 days. The letter cost $1,800. What were the results?

- **Average member visits** went from 25 per day before the promotion, to 42 per day during the promotion, and 29 per day in the 35-day period after the promotion was over.
- **Average visits per card** went from 1.18 before to 1.26 during and 1.22 after the promotion.
- **Incremental sales** were $17,100 during the promotion and $4,700 in the 35 days after the promotion was over.

In other words, by spending $1,800, this restaurant chain reactivated 599 people who were otherwise lost as patrons. The gain was not only during the promotion period, but had a lasting effect, with 147 of the reactivated people visiting the restaurant after the promotion was over. Relationship building works and has lasting benefits.

Measuring Member Satisfaction

Besides the effects on sales with the client, TCC has also measured customer satisfaction with members of the clubs by conducting surveys for two clients. TCC administers a Birthday Club for one of the clients that operates over 20 restaurants (average total guest check $50) and a Loyalty/Frequent Diner program for the other that operates 8 restaurants (average total guest check $100). Over 20% of the members responded. The surveys asked for rating 1-5 with 5 being most important:

"In considering possible future benefits of being a guest in our restaurants please rate how important each of the following would be to you":

	Score 4	Score 5	Total
Frequency/rewards/VIP card program	29%	45%	74%
Special recognition by the manager	24%	16%	40%

"Please rate the following elements of a Loyalty/Frequency program based on how much you value each element"

	Score 4	Score 5	Total
Points based reward certificates	11%	82%	93%
Birthday certificate	18%	58%	76%
Double points early dining	22%	44%	66%
Promotion bonus opportunities	25%	44%	69%
Members only events/invitations	24%	38%	62%

"Which of the following apply to you due to your membership in a Loyalty/Frequency program?

Visit more often	83%
Chose this restaurant instead of another	72%
Spend more when we visit the restaurant	61%

The conclusion is simple, not only have the Birthday Club and Frequency Club increased sales substantially; the benefits of these clubs are also highly appreciated by their members.

Event-Driven Marketing is gradually catching on in a variety of industries. Day by day we see hundreds of different businesses building their databases and finding innovative ways of building relationships with their customers that are satisfying for the customers and profitable for the companies. It is refreshing to see the proof of its success so clearly demonstrated as it is in this case by The Customer Connection.

Hospitality Technology magazine sponsors an annual survey of restaurants' use of IT/POS technology as a strategic tool. Excerpts from the CRM section of the 2008 survey:

> *Communicating with present customers, CRM, is the most cost effective way to increase profitable sales. Tactics that use a database to send personalized communications to members will build brand image and keep your business Top-of-Mind.*

> *While it seems as if hotel loyalty programs and CRM applications are catching up to those of the airline industry in terms of maturity, the restaurant industry remains a distant follower in this race. However, our market analysis indicates that the chance for success in this arena is very promising for restaurants.*

Customer-Related Terminology and Marketing Myopia

Terms matter. It is very important to know exactly what a customer is and what customer-related terminology really means. For example, there is *market share*, but there also is *customer* share or *share of customer/ share of wallet* (that proportion of a customer's total spending on a particular product group that goes to you). The notion of market share actually says nothing about your customers, but share of customer or share of wallet tells you where the money (and profit) is.It shows you how much money a specific person spends or is going to spend with you out of his total budget.

Here is an example. XYZ Company manufactured breathing apparatus, such as oxygen concentrators, masks, and portable bottles, and sold them through equipment pharmacists. The company had a 33% market share in the USA; i.e., overall sales were about 33% of the entire market for the types of breathing apparatus they offered. They sold about 11,500 through equipment resellers. They wanted to expand their market share, so they hired a marketing firm to help them find new customers.

The marketing firm confirmed what the company knew: There are about 11,500 equipment resellers, total, in the USA. Thus, XYZ had a near-100% market penetration. Virtually everyone in the equipment reselling pharmacy business was already a customer. The problem was that they had an average "share of wallet" of about 33%. It was impossible to grow the business with new customers; it was only possible to grow by selling more to the customers they already had. Needless to say, they shifted from a new-customer focus to a growth-and-retention strategy to increase share of wallet.

A simple formula shows how to use the most basic and critical component of market share:

Market Share = (Market Penetration) x (Average Share of Wallet)

Event-driven marketing is not really about achieving a particular market share. Rather, it is about preventing your customer from spending with your competitor, about improving your "share of wallet" with a specific customer and thus increasing that customer's value (see also Chapter 6). If you do that properly, you will also extend the customer lifecycle because the customers are happy with you and so become more "loyal."

> The definition of a customer: *A customer is somebody who buys from you regularly and who pays his bills on time.*

Admittedly, in the case of B-to-B markets it can be difficult to define exactly who the customer is because we are often dealing with complex decision-making unit (DMU) structures (see Chapter 1). The customer is no longer one person, but sometimes an elusive, many-headed monster. Not that this detracts from the fact that even this being has to pay your invoices. Otherwise this is not a customer.

Here are additional important terms:

- **Customer value.** Depending upon how you want to measure it, this is the turnover or the margin a customer generates during a given period–say, a year.
- **Customer lifecycle.** The period over which a customer continues to buy from you. Somebody who is in your database but has stopped buying is no longer a customer.
- **Customer loyalty.** The chance that a customer will remain faithful to you. This is a soft term for the intention to keep on buying from you.
- **Customer retention.** The hard fact that a customer keeps buying from you.

We discuss loyalty and retention at greater length in Chapter 5. In Chapter 6 we take a closer look at customer value and customer lifecycle.

The definition of customer *satisfaction* is another matter entirely, and a complex one at that. How do you quantify your satisfaction? Is it by the number of complaints somebody makes? That seems a reasonable indication, but not everybody expresses his or her dissatisfaction in the same way. Some people will complain only reluctantly and remain loyal nonetheless; others will simply disappear; they stop buying without a word of warning.

Another way to view satisfaction is through a customer's relationship with you. Do you have a high share of wallet? Do they buy a range of your products, or do they buy some items from you, and other items like what you sell from a competitor? Are their buying decisions based on price alone, or do they value unique benefits of your product, your service level and support, and do they have a relationship built on trust with you? In other words, is it worth the time and effort to them to shop and compare with competitors, or not?

Market Segmentation: From Old Economy to New?

Dividing markets into segments is a tried-and-true technique, but there are two different definitions of market segmentation:

1. As an *analytical technique*: dividing your market in homogeneous groups of customers (segments) based upon relevant characteristics.
2. As a *marketing strategy*: as a supplier, focusing upon one or more segments and tailoring your marketing efforts to them.

There are four criteria for good market segmentation:

1. Measurability.
2. Sufficient size.
3. Accessibility.
4. Workability.

The traditional objective of marketing is to serve one or more customer groups, the members of which all share the same wishes and characteristics. Unfortunately, however, today's society is difficult to compartmentalize that easily. And particularly when it comes to more expensive and specialized products, the customer nowadays expects personalized treatment.

Traditionally, once a market has been segmented, the positioning of each segment is established (see Exhibit 2.1).

Exhibit 2.1. Market Segmentation, Definition and Positioning

Market segmentation	Market definition	Market positioning
Defining the basis for segmentation of the market.	Defining the attractiveness of a segment.	Developing a positioning for each segment.
Developing profiles for the resulting segments.	Selecting the segments to be targeted.	Developing a marketing mix for each segment.

Traditional segmentation techniques are the following:

- **Geographical segmentation.** Dividing the market into different geographical units or "territories", such as countries, states, regions, counties, cities, or neighborhoods.
- **Demographic segmentation.** Dividing the market into groups based upon demographic variables such as age, sex, household composition, household lifecycle, income, profession, education, religion, race, and nationality.
- **Lifecycle segmentation.** Offering products or adopting marketing approaches in a way that acknowledges consumers' changing needs at different stages in their lives.
- **Geodemography.** Studying the relationship between geographical location and demographics.

- **Psychographic segmentation.** Dividing the market into different groups based upon social class, lifestyle or personal characteristics.
- **Behavioral segmentation.** Dividing the market into groups based upon consumer knowledge, attitude and use of or response to a product.
- **Opportunity segmentation.** Dividing the market into groups based upon when purchasers decide to buy, when they actually buy, or when they use what they have bought.
- **Benefit segmentation.** Dividing the market into groups based upon the benefits consumers are looking for in a product.

Segmented marketing is gradually going out of fashion at many companies, slowly being replaced by event-driven marketing. EDM is a prominent factor in successful up-selling and cross-selling. Those who have identified their customers and their needs accurately and who have good multichannel interaction with them can conduct successful sales activities by using the "three rights" principle mentioned earlier: the right message in the right place at the right time. Many banks and insurance companies are already successfully "event-driven," but businesses ranging from pet food suppliers to travel agencies are now applying this concept as well with better and better results. As a consequence, they no longer feel the need to divide their clientele into rigid segments. Instead, they are embracing flexibility because it allows them to offer the product their customers are waiting for.

Flexibility allows for greater differentiation. Differentiation can also be achieved by offering convenience and service. Companies should manage their business based upon the differences between customers, looking at the value and needs that that entails. As a rule, loyal customers still have to stand in the same queue as long as occasional buyers. But at the American department store Bloomingdale's, the best customers do not even have to go to the cash register. Somebody does that for them. At the Dutch cash-and-carry chain Makro, the biggest customers have their own parking spaces near the entrance. And why are the same web pages always presented to everybody? Why not differentiate them by customer group? Or, even better, by individual customer?

Put Down That Scatter Gun

Stop dividing your target group and customer base into segments and then taking a scatter-gun approach to each of them. Instead, make sure that you understand the customer's behavior and circumstances, which you can use to anticipate what they are going to do and make sure that you respond accordingly. Remember you have two ears and one mouth. The best time to talk to a customer is not when you want to speak, it is when the customer is ready to listen. Events define the times when the customer is likely to be "all ears."

More and more businesses are taking up an event-driven approach to the customer, and it is not exactly doing them harm. Segmented marketing is now long in the tooth for the time being, EDM remains confined to customers, but future development in data warehousing, data sharing and data partnerships will make them suitable for generating new business as well. Nothing works better than making the right offer to the right person at the right time. But nothing is more difficult. We still have a lot to learn.

Segmented marketing is not yet "out," but it is a strategy best suited to lead generation and prospecting programs. Once somebody has become a customer, you can better give them "bespoke" service—in other words, replace marketing segmentation with EDM.

Exhibit 2.2 shows where the "new marketing" terms are found. Have you already incorporated them into your marketing plan? How, for example, is your personal dialog with your customer structured? How have you arrived at flexible pricing? What are your customer's value and lifecycle? Can you separate the poor-value customers from the good-value ones, and do you have the courage to dump the former?

All critical questions, and if you cannot provide solid answers to them, you need to do something about it. Or resign and get yourself retrained.

Segmented marketing and event-driven marketing respectively concentrate upon leads or prospects and upon a customer-oriented approach. Using segment-based thinking, it is possible to cultivate the right leads until a customer relationship is formed. By then tracking individual customers actively–the basis of EDM–you can respond to their personal situation and needs (events). So EDM is actually the ultimate form of marketing differentiation. Prompted by a signal, the supplier can act upon the customer's needs with a direct marketing or sales activity. EDM uses the increasing effectiveness of communications to approach the customer at just the moment when our information tells us that he or she is likely to be most interested in our proposition.

This form of extreme differentiation in marketing has the advantages that less interested customers are not contacted, that cross-selling is stimulated, that individual customers become more profitable, and that the organization becomes more customer and market-focused. Moreover, it creates a lot of goodwill on the customer's part because you give the impression that you "come when called." This makes EDM a strong customer relations tool, as well as a stronger marketing tool.

Viewing from the Customer's Point of View

In the buyer-seller relationship, it is often very difficult for sellers to fully understand a buyer's motivations. The resulting "marketing myopia" is what happens when sellers, designers, and engineers look at their product only from their viewpoint rather than that of the user's/customer's point of view. This idea, more than half a century old, is still the basis for profitable product innovation and marketing. It also is the

Exhibit 2.2. Traditional Versus Event-Driven Marketing

Traditional Marketing	Event-Driven Marketing
Focus	**Focus**
"Selling the brand"	"Managing the consumer"
Emphasis on markets, (mass) production, managing the chain, promotion, branding	Focus on customer, individual demand, value and personal interests
Marketing orientation: mass marketing; linear marketing	Marketing orientation: interactive marketing, mass customization
Value proposition built around 4Ps, product value, brand	Value proposition built around individuals: time, content, (customer) values
Segments	Clusters of n=1, aggregation
Transactions	Dialog, conversations
Action-led	Process-based
Acquisition, lead getting	Retention, customer lifecycle
Market share	Share of wallet / Customer share
Value chain management	Customer value management
Marketing intelligence / data	**Marketing intelligence / data**
Market research	Behavioral data
General data about anonymous customers	Individual customer knowledge by data analysis
Knowledge about target groups	Customer insight
Pre- and post testing of advertising	Web statistics, A/B-testing, usability, behavioral data
Product	**Product**
Assortment	Individual offer, mass individualization
Product attributes, relatively tangible	Content attributes, virtual
Mass production	Mass customization
Communication	**Communication**
Mass communication, mass media	1-to-1 communication
One way traffic, broadcast	Interactive, dialog
Off-line channels; radio, TV, print	Interactive and online channels, narrow casting
Customer's awareness of the company	Company's awareness of the customer
Positioning (to larger target groups)	Profiling (on individuals)
Input—output oriented	Oriented on communicative self-directions
Distribution	**Distribution**
Mono distribution	Multi-channel approach
Pricing	**Pricing**
Standard pricing / listing / tendering	Possibility of flexible pricing
Pricing differentiation	Customized pricing on individual demands
Performance	**Performance**
Turnover, sales	Customer value and customer lifecycle
Reach, numbers	Response / conversion / value
Cost accounting	MRM—marketing resource management

basis for the notion of planning and developing from the "outside-in", a cornerstone of integrated marketing communications. Sellers are trying to make a living and look at their own products or services as something that makes them a living. This is backwards from what is needed. Buyers are trying to solve a specific problem with the product or service that may be quite different from what the seller perceives or even thinking about.

For example, consider a manufacturer of mobile phone components that offered five different families of devices. Two were digital, three were analog. Different engineering staffs were responsible for each component family, and each had a different product manager responsible for sales and marketing. The catalog manager asked for a review of the customer data to see if it was practical to put all five product families together into one catalog to save on cost. Since each component had different technical capabilities, the engineers and product managers felt they were sufficiently different to each have their own catalog. They were particularly certain that the analog and digital components should be offered separately.

Upon reviewing the data, the marketing analyst found that about 80% of customers buying one analog product family also bought another product family and that about 80% of the buyers of a digital product bought the other. In other words, there was even an 80% overlap between all analog buyers and buyers of either digital product.Then the analyst looked at how many of all the digital buyers also bought an analog product. There was a 100% match. How could that be? Digital mobile phone components are used to communicate with the towers. Thus, people speak to each other in analog sound, so digital phone components are worthless without analog components.

As a result the company has *one* catalog with *all five* components!

This isn't an aberration. A manufacturer of ice cream products had "designed" their product managers around its products. There was a chocolate manager, a vanilla manager, and even an inclusions manager for things like chocolate chips, cookie dough and sprinkles.

Then someone decided to ask moms what they wanted, or more precisely, how they looked at the company's products.They asked them to come in and sort the products in the way they thought were most logical. Every mom did the same thing. They would sort all the ice cream into one group (regardless of flavor), all the low-fat or low calorie frozen yogurts into another pile, and all the ice cream bars, cookie sandwiches and other treats into a third pile. This opened management's eyes and they rebuilt their organization around how the customer viewed their products. They now have an ice cream manager, a healthy products manager, and a treats manager.

"Stuff" and Self-Image

Particularly with consumer products, it is difficult to relate to how a customer views your product or service relative to how it affects their self-image. We tend to look at the features and benefits of a product in strict sense, such as how it performs.

Consider for example hybrid cars. It would be understandable to assume that people buy hybrid cars to get better fuel economy. As a result, engineers, marketers, and salespeople focus their offers around this benefit. A consumer, on the other hand, may buy a hybrid primarily as a statement. It tells the world they are "green" and care about the environment. They might never actually check their fuel economy or even use it in such a way to fully benefit from the technology. But they will make a statement about themselves.

People will do almost anything to bring their stuff into line with their self-image. That is particularly hard for marketers to grasp when focusing on the technical aspects of a product's performance.

Alan's Cars

Alan recounts his experience:

> "Long before becoming an author, I worked my way through college at an automobile dealership and then worked for a major manufacturer as a factory representative to dealers. Needless to say, I'm a bit of a car nut and always appreciated the mechanical or design aspects of what makes a particular car unique. But to me, a car is really either something I want to make money with or at the very least use inexpensively. Owning a car to me isn't a lot different than working with them. If I'm at point A and need to go to point B, any car might do. Working on or modifying a car can actually be fun.
>
> "People who weren't car nuts that spent far more money than I on automobiles amazed me. It didn't make sense to me that people who didn't know or care what kind of engine a car had, how it worked and why it was different or better were so much more willing to spend so much money on a car.
>
> "When I went to college, I drove a small, three-cylinder car with a 1.0 liter engine because I had a long commute and I needed a car with excellent mileage. Several years after graduating, I drove a used Jaguar XJS with a V-12. Then I found a really good deal on a used Rolls-Royce Silver Spur that was priced at about as much as a new Honda sedan. I bought it and drove it for a year, then sold it for slightly more than I had paid. My cost of ownership was very low and that was what I was looking for.
>
> "My daughter began taking horse-riding lessons and I needed something that got good mileage (the horses were a long drive away) and was something I could park near a dusty stable and not care. So I bought another little car a lot like what I had in college.

"This visibly upset my friends. Several came to me and asked if I was all right. It seemed a perfectly logical thing to do to me, but they did not see it that way. On top of that, some people (even to this day) ask me if I still drive that Jaguar. I tell them no, I sold that when I bought the Rolls. They say "you owned a Rolls?" I often remind them that that yes I did and you saw me driving it.

"The Rolls was so far away from what my "image" is that it didn't even stick in people's minds, the way the Jaguar apparently did. I also discovered people drove courteously around me when I had the Rolls. Women in BMW's would smile at me at stoplights. When I got a small car again, that changed. People often honked, women would avoid looking over at a light. Seriously—it's true.

"Then I understood what people were buying when they bought a car. It's not about the car. It's about them. How do people look at them, what does it do for their status and does it fit their image or the image they want to project."

Sales Funnel

In EDM, it is important we understand the optimal trigger points for contacting and responding to customers. In order to convert these trigger points into distinct steps we can respond to, use the well-known concept of the *sales funnel*.

In order to fully implement EDM, a simple understanding of the sales funnel is crucial. The funnel represents the steps to a sale that a customer generally goes through before purchasing (Exhibit 2.3). For many organizations, marketing is

Exhibit 2.3. Sales Funnel

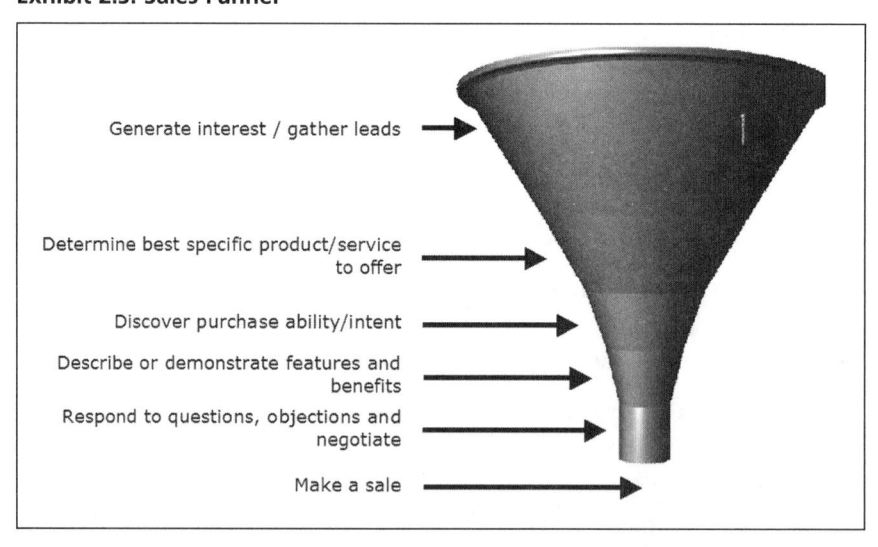

- Generate interest / gather leads
- Determine best specific product/service to offer
- Discover purchase ability/intent
- Describe or demonstrate features and benefits
- Respond to questions, objections and negotiate
- Make a sale

only assigned the task of lead generation (finding new prospects). Salespeople and stores are given the job of closing sales. Too often there are no processes, no tracking, and no thought as to the steps in between. Building a system to track, measure, and respond to the customer's journey through the sales funnel is often a start-from-scratch proposition.

Cross-Selling

When a customer buys more than one type of product or service from the same seller, it is a clear indicator they have begun a deeper relationship with a company than when they bought only one type. As with the example of the manufacturer of cellular phone components, most marketers view their products from their own point of view. A company might believe two technically different products are quite separate from one another, while a customer uses them together to solve the same problem.

Products that are used together are called complementary products (e.g., car tires and wheel alignments; eggs, flower, and milk; or pens and paper).

Consider the patrons of a symphony orchestra. They can buy season tickets, single tickets, and make donations. These offerings are all considered quite different in the symphony-marketing world and often have different managers in charge of marketing each. However, a symphony's most loyal and valuable patrons are involved in all three every season. The best subscribers of course make donation in addition to their ticket purchase. They also buy single tickets in addition to, but not for, additional performances. They buy them to bring their friends along.

Consider Exhibit 2.4, which shows the year-to-year loyalty repeat rate at a symphony by whether people were in one category or how they crossed over.

Exhibit 2.4. Analysis of Patrons of a Symphony Orchestra

	Singles	Donors	Subscribers
Singles	10%	64%	71%
Donors	64%	52%	88%
Subscribers	71%	88%	45%

Patrons who only bought single tickets returned at a 10% rate, but patrons who bought a single ticket and donated returned at a 64% rate and patrons who subscribed and bought a single ticket returned at a 71% rate. Patron who did all three (not shown on the chart) returned at a 97% rate!

The symphony had two completely separate database systems, one for donations and another for tickets. The separate systems made it even more difficult to coordinate the three managers' activities, but the challenge to understanding the customers' motivation(s) and coordinate activities is clearly worth the challenge of implementing DM when you consider the value of making sales across types.

Looking at the combinations of things people buy can get complicated quickly. A simple and effective way to measure the importance of cross-selling is to count the number of categories of things customers buy.

Consider a manufacturer of components used in hydraulic equipment. They make things like valves, switches, and fittings that can neatly be categorized by type. In total, they sell five basic types of components. All of their component types are complementary, which essentially means that most hydraulic systems have at least one of each type of component they sell. To put it another way, any customer making equipment with their components that does not buy each type from them must be buying the other types from a competitor.

Exhibit 2.5 shows how loyalty increased as customers bought more types of products.

In addition, customers buying more types of components spent more on average.

Selling a customer another type of item is clearly an important task. If the products have separate product managers it may be a challenge to build a structure that centers around the customer's point of view, but it is crucial to success.

Regulars, Buyers, and Tryers

Getting the organization to embrace EDM demands explaining it so that everyone outside of marketing can understand and embrace it as a strategy. But marketers often rush right into tactics without explaining to everyone else what the goals of these new tactics and strategy really are. We select a product we will push, select a media, then set a budget against it and off we go. On the other hand, marketers who rely on technical expertise or direct marketing experience might start with 400 segments on which to base their strategy.

For strategy to be useful, it must be simple enough to understand and explain easily. The sales funnel, with events based around a specific set of trigger points for prospects becoming new customers and a second, different set of events with different trigger points for ongoing customers, can provide the basis for developing a simple, yet easily understandable and powerful marketing strategy. The sets of event triggers may be quite different, but most important they should be useful and usable for categorizing and describing logical categories of customers. It probably is wise to divide each set into three categories: Regulars, Buyers, and Tryers (RBT).

Regulars, Buyers, and Tryers (RBT) can be defined as follows:

- Regulars: Loyal customers who provide a substantial portion (usually 80%) of sales revenue. They have bought multiple times, usually over multiple months or years and across multiple product types.
- Buyers: Buy a few things or buy occasionally, but not on a regular or consistent basis. Many are good targets to become Regulars.

- Tryers: Buy one or two things, have very few transactions and buy infrequently enough that there is no real repeat pattern. Often the majority make only one purchase and never return. Some Tryers will become repeat customers and grow into Buyers.

RBT helps us simplify our goals around customers. We can focus on who we can grow by cross selling, who we can strive to keep for increasing loyalty and how we can build a base of customers with greater worth and loyalty.

Regulars, Buyers and Tryers are often defined around the events we focus on with EDM. The reasons for moving a customer from one phase of a relationship to another can be easily understood and explained to non-marketing groups in the organizations. This gives us a strategic framework to developing and implementing EDM tactics.

Exhibit 2.5. Loyalty Rate

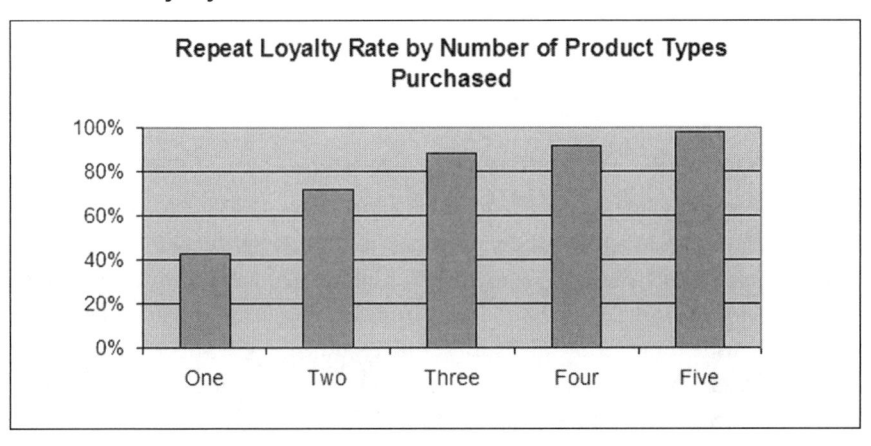

Exhibit 2.6. Average Annual Sales

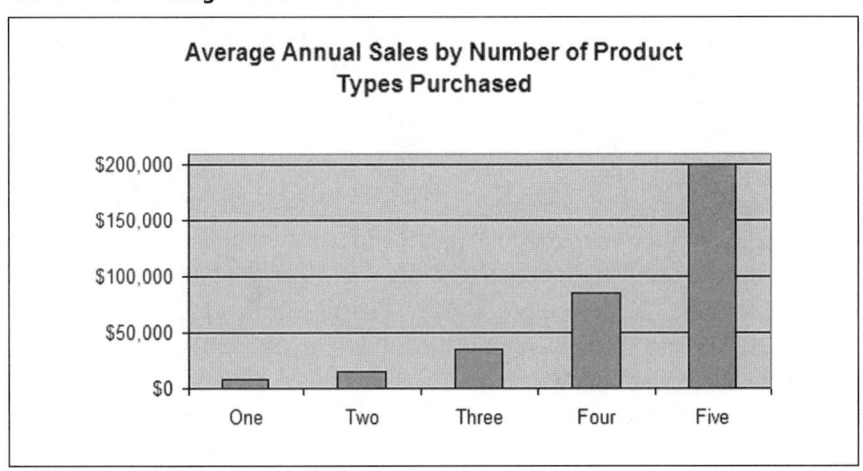

The EDM Quadrant

Event-driven marketing can be applied at four areas. This chapter introduces those levels using the EDM Quadrant. It also describes the process by which an event results in an action targeting an individual customer.

From Internal Planning to Customer-Oriented Supply

Traditional direct marketing still tends to be based upon product and (as we have seen in the previous chapter) segment-led thinking. Dutch mail-order company Wehkamp, for example, has for some years been sending customers an e-newsletter featuring a wide range of products for a broad audience. For this firm, a generic approach to its entire clientele is sufficient to achieve its sales targets. For the time being, Wehkamp is not going to change to EDM (making offers reflecting shifting customer behavior and needs). The cost of such personalization would far outweigh the benefits. But nevertheless Wehkamp does use EDM in certain cases. For example, it takes action when a line of credit is about to expire. That provides a good contact opportunity at a moment when the company knows exactly how long the customer has owned what products. In other words, this is the perfect time to make a new offer.

A financial institution or an automotive company is in a unique position to make tailored offers to its target group. After all, not everybody will want a real estate mortgage or a convertible, but people with an appropriate profile (existing customers or potential ones) might. And they can be selected from the database. But even that is no longer enough. We have to act earlier to approach customers at the right moment for them—not just twice a year when it best suits us, but at those times that is/are the best moment(s) for the customers; in other words, when they are most receptive to our proposition. In short, we need to base our thinking upon the customers' needs rather than our own planning cycle and

Exhibit 3.1. Contact Planning Steers Individual Actions

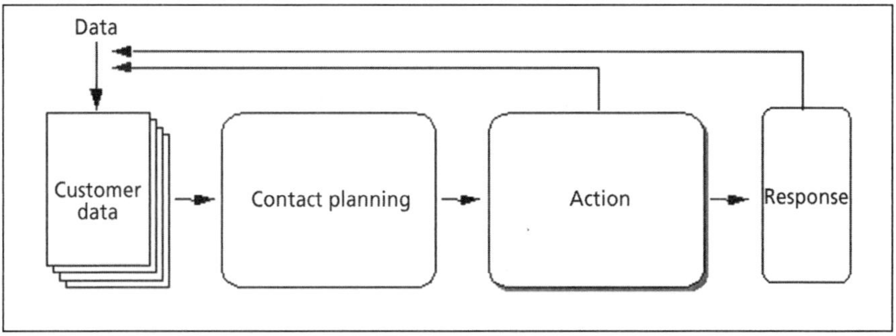

```
Data
  │
  ▼
Customer  →  Contact planning  →  Action  →  Response
data
```

logistical efficiency; in other words, we need to build our planning cycle around customers' needs and timing.

To approach each customer at the right time, our communications have to be driven by what we know about them as individuals. And the only way to do that is for the entire customer knowledge process to be steered from the database. Using individual scores, we track when and how the next contact should be made. This process is known as *contact planning*. We want to bother the customers as little as possible with things that they are not interested in, so we only offer them those products and services that the information available to us indicates they need, using arguments and contact methods (e.g., individualized mailings) they are most receptive to. Note that "individualization" goes much further than "personalization".

The costs of these marketing activities are monitored by using customer lifetime value (see also Chapter 6) as well as the customer's individual risk profile (e.g., the chance that he may not pay.) These factors are recorded on *scorecards*. The choice of the most suitable medium for the approach—direct mail, telemarketing, email and the like—is no longer linked to the product but instead based upon the **individual contact plan.**. Every new event–a response, for example, or even a nonresponse–has the potential to revise the contact plan, it is subject to change any time new information is received. Thus, contact planning is a permanent, cyclical process (see Exhibit 3.1).

Event-Driven Marketing: Choosing the Right Moment

Being able to approach each customer with the right product proposition at the right moment requires a continuous, active review of his or her account. This process requires a considerable amount of data that must be collected, processed, and analyzed constantly. Identifying a "right moment" for customer contact is a complex business, one in which we are primarily responding to changes in individual circumstances with the assumption that these have important predictive value

Exhibit 3.2. From Event to Action

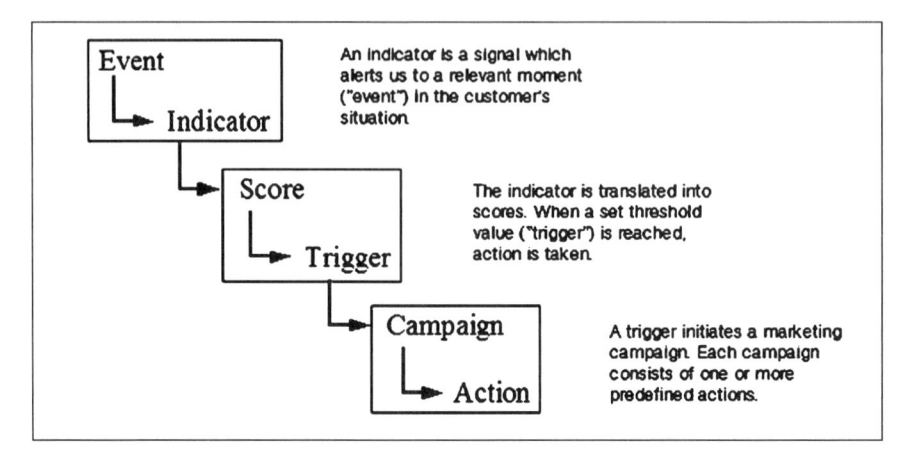

```
Event
 └─▶ Indicator          An indicator is a signal which
                        alerts us to a relevant moment
                        ("event") in the customer's
                        situation.

        └─▶ Score
              │         The indicator is translated into
              │         scores. When a set threshold
              │         value ("trigger") is reached,
              └─▶ Trigger   action is taken.

                    └─▶ Campaign
                          │       A trigger initiates a marketing
                          │       campaign. Each campaign
                          │       consists of one or more
                          └─▶ Action   predefined actions.
```

in respect of purchasing intentions. The following elements (Exhibit 3.2) play an important role.

Events are occurrences that affect the customer's own situation or the relationship between the customer and your organization and are relevant to your marketing objectives. We distinguish between three kinds of events:

- **Life-phase events.** Examples in personal life include starting secondary school, going to university, starting work, and retiring. Equivalents in the business domain are such things as setting up a company, its rapid growth, experiencing financial difficulties, and disposing of the business.
- **Product-phase events.** Personal examples here include buying a (new) car, moving house, and going on vacation. In business, they could be replacing the office furniture or modernizing machinery.
- **Relationship-phase events.** Personal examples include a customer who just opened a checking account and then adds a savings and investment account a few days later, or a previous cash customer opening a store charge account. Business examples include a buyer making a small sample-size order and then following with a large second purchase or a client manufacturer buying bolts from you and washers from another supplier starting to buy bolts and washers from you.

It goes without saying that there is no point in recording events unless they signal some kind of significant change in the relationship between the organization and the customer, a change you hope to respond to. In many cases, it is difficult to ascertain that an event is significant. We have to infer significance from the customer's subsequent behavior. This is why indicators play a very important role.

Indicators are the outward signs from which we can infer that an event has taken place. These vary considerably from industry to industry, but they could include making a payment, conducting a telephone call, or buying a product. In many cases, multiple indicators are needed to signal a particular event, sometimes in combination with historical data. Indicators may also be "hard" or "soft," depending upon the probability that they correctly signal a particular event. For a car dealer, for example, the most interesting event is the purchase of a car. The fact that somebody has borrowed money from a bank is a good indicator for that. For the bank, on the other hand, it is relevant that somebody needs money to buy a car, so it will use other indicators. Somebody passing his driving test is a harder indicator that he is likely to buy a car soon than reaching the legal driving age. But a combination of these two signals with other data could be used to trigger sending a quote for a personal loan.

We distinguish between three kinds of indicators:

- **Temporal indicators** are specific signals denoting a time-dependent situation. These can be subdivided into three types: indicators with an absolute reference, a periodic reference, and a relative reference. An *absolute reference* relates to a specific date—e.g., February 1, 2009—and usually applies to agreements reached with a customer; for example, a promise that we will call him back on that date. A *periodic reference* is a regularly recurring event, such as Christmas or the customer's birthday. And a *relative reference* is measured in time from or to another indicator; three days after receipt of an application form, for instance, or two weeks before a contract expires.

- **Implicit indicators** represent a special situation in the customer data as a result of which action is taken. The bank account going into the red, for example, somebody using the telephone twice as much as he did in the previous month or a customer's buying pattern suddenly changing significantly. Somebody who starts travelling more frequently can be offered annual travel insurance. Implicit indicators are based upon external factors, but are always considered in relation to something else: only by comparing the old situation with the new one is a signal given.

- **Explicit indicators** are external actions signaling an event to which we can respond. Examples include a request for information, a change-of-address notification or a death notice. The signal comes from outside, in many cases directly from the customer. The skill lies in linking that external signal to your own customer data.

Indicators are particularly important in triggering and steering EDM activities (see below).

Scores are the calculating mechanisms by which we convert individual indicators and combinations of them into forecasts that a particular event will occur. A score is often arrived at based upon statistical research, and these scores need to be updated on a regular basis, ideally as soon as any relevant indicator changes. Here is a simple example. Analysis by a mail order company indicates that customers

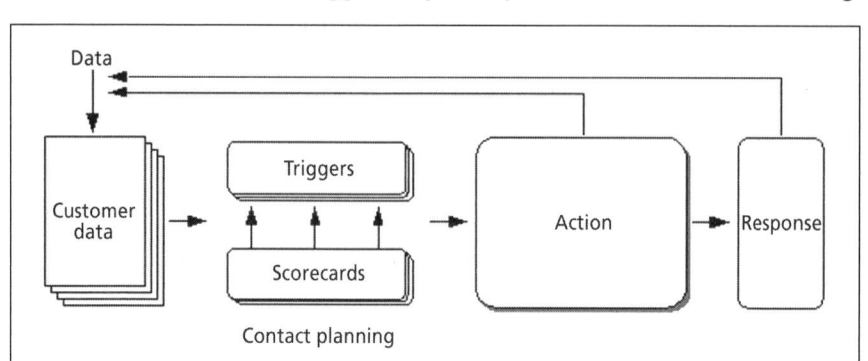

Exhibit 3.3. Scorecards and Triggers Play an Important Role in Contact Planning

[Diagram: Data flows into Customer data, which feeds into Triggers and Scorecards (within Contact planning), leading to Action, which produces Response. Response and Action feed data back.]

who fail to respond to five successive mailings are unlikely to react to any further approaches in the long term. Given our aim of only contacting customers with a suitable proposition at the right moment, we decide automatically to stop direct mailings to this group. The number of times that the indicator "no response to mailing" appears is recorded on a so-called scorecard. Once that score reaches 5, it triggers a signal to take appropriate action–in this case, transferring the customer to the "do not mail" list.

Triggers are the values a score must reach to initiate a predefined action. In the example just given, that value is 5 on the "stop mailing" scorecard. As soon as the defined value is reached, the associated marketing campaign or other action is triggered.

Scorecards and triggers play an important role in contact planning (see Exhibit 3.3). The actions to be taken in particular situations are defined in advance and then converted into scorecards with appropriate triggers. We can, for example, define scorecards for expected customer yield, for the customer's payment risk, for the extent to which he qualifies for particular products, for the number of times he has already been contacted, and so on. Here is another example: for a specific campaign by a telephony provider it was decided that a customer will be offered a new type of subscription if he meets the following criteria:

- More than three international calls in one calendar month.
- Not offered this product more than three times in the past.
- Not approached already within the past month.
- Not in risk category 1 or 2.

Campaigns consist of one or more actions, such as a mailing, a telemarketing call, or a personal visit. A campaign is defined in advance and is made up of at least one link to a trigger and one link to an action. The trigger indicates *who* is to be included in the campaign and *when* they are to be included. The action component defines *what* proposition is to be made and *where* it is to be made (i.e., the means of distribution or communication). A campaign describes what actions are to be

Exhibit 3.4. Selection of an Action: Based on the Contact Plan

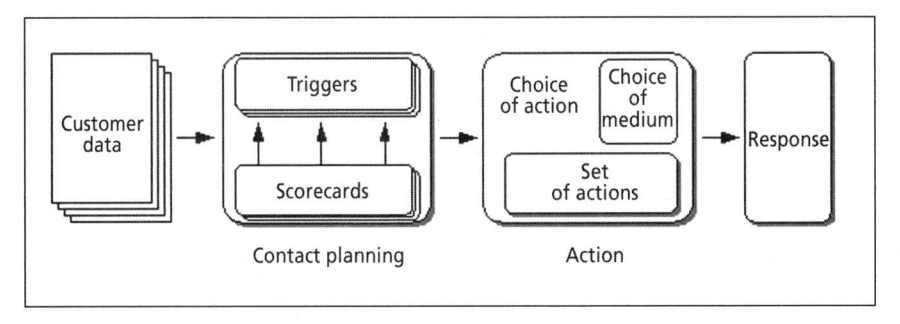

```
[Customer data] → [Triggers] ← [Scorecards]    [Choice of action] [Choice of medium]    → [Response]
                                                [Set of actions]
         Contact planning                              Action
```

Exhibit 3.5. Roles in the Marketing Process

Role	Description
1. Attract	Activities designed to initiate a relationship with a customer or to bring about a first transaction.
2. Inform	Providing information related to a specific product or service.
3. Advise	Providing advice about the use and applications of a product or service, or assistance with the choice of form and content.
4. Close transaction	Achieving a commercial transaction.
5. Provide service	Activities designed to resolve complaints, to increase customer satisfaction or to maximize customer value.
6. Maintain relationship	Activities designed to facilitate future transactions with a customer.

taken, in what order and at what interval. In fact, the campaign definition generates an indicator for next action.

Actions are the components of a campaign and are predefined in an "action library." They specify the proposition to be made to the customer and the channel to be used. As we have already seen, a campaign can also involve ending a particular channel of distribution for an individual customer. If the channel being used is "direct mail," then the associated action could be choosing a particular version of the letter and specifying the brochures or other material to enclose with it. In the case of telephone calls, the action could state which script to use. Actions can also encompass logistical factors, such as the choice of printers or telemarketing agencies.

Key Roles in the Marketing Process

The contacts with a specific customer can have a range of purposes. Exhibit 3.5 shows them.

Personal contact and direct marketing are two different ways of achieving our objectives. At each stage in the process, we can choose whether or not to employ direct marketing. When linked to events, indicators, triggers, and actions as described previously, that produces the kind of plan for a bank shown in Exhibit 3.6.

Exhibit 3.6. Events, Indicators, Actions, and Media

	Customer event	Indicator and trigger	Action by the bank	Choice of medium
Attract	Interest in investing.	Customer without investment products clicks on investment section of the website.	Signal to local bank to raise the subject of investment with the customer.	Email or letter to the customer.
Inform	Fall in interest rate.	Interest rate falls below the threshold value indicated by the customer.	Notification that "the interest rate has fallen below X, the value you indicated".	Mobile telephone, email or extranet.
Advise	Mortgage period expires.	Signal from database, X months in advance.	Invitation from bank's mortgage adviser to discuss new form of mortgage.	Letter, email, telemarketing.
Close transaction	Failed transaction.	Bank system signals failed transaction.	Offer continuous credit, with amount adapted to customer's situation.	Letter, email.
Provide service	Customer moves house.	Details submitted to account manager (database, card, in person)	Bank completes all necessary procedures and transfers customer to new branch.	Letter, email, telemarketing.
Maintain relationship	Birthday.	Tomorrow is customer's birthday.	Birthday card.	Post or email.

The EDM Quadrant

Event-driven marketing can be applied at four levels reflected in the EDM Quadrant (Exhibit 3.7).

Singular events are the easiest to work with. In fact, this is "ordinary" database marketing. In the database you record such information as rental status, guarantee terms, service periods, and so on. Not difficult! But for many companies this is the first step towards data-driven management of customer information. By working with warranties and service contracts, for example, it is quite easy to gather focused customer information. If an optician knows how often somebody uses contact lenses, he can respond to the demand for replacement sets. If a car dealer knows what mileage a customer is running up, he can predict when the customer is likely to want to trade in the vehicle. These are relevant events. But what are the indicators? How do you know when the event will occur? To some extent through experience, common sense, and logic, but the easiest way to find out is to ask. Ask your customers how they behave and record the answers in a database. Such indicators have an "absolute reference": They consist of fixed data, so they are applied only with respect to agreements reached with a customer. Since you have recorded them yourself, they indicate highly predictable events.

Exhibit 3.7. The EDM Quadrant

	High	Singular	Recurring
PREDICTABILITY	Low	Interactive	Anticipative
		Short Term	Long Term
		TIME	

Recurring events are closely related to singular ones, but either repeat themselves or succeed one another in a set order. Like singular events, they are signaled by *temporal* indicators—that is, those which describe a situation dependent upon time and predictability (although recurring events are less predictable than singular ones).

We differentiate between two types of recurring events:

- Periodic reference events.
- Relative reference events.

A *periodic reference event* is one that recurs on a regular basis, such as Christmas, a customer's birthday, a wedding anniversary or the start of an academic year. A *relative reference event* is measured in time from or to another indicator. For example, three days after receipt of an application form, two weeks before a contract expires or a month after the purchase of a new car.

The only restrictions on identifying relationships between events associated with different products and services in the recurring field of the EDM Quadrant are your own intelligence and common sense. Banks, for example, have developed a whole variety of products to serve the customer "from the cradle to the grave." In many cases, these succeed one another smoothly and logically so that they are ideal for overlapping marketing campaigns and well-timed cross-selling and up-selling. This is *lifetime marketing*: regarding somebody as a potential customer at every phase of his life and always having a product or service suited to the current phase.

Lifetime marketing strategies are used in many industries and product categories. Take, for example premium pet food manufacturers (see also Case Study 5). They provide the dog owners with regular offers reflecting their pet's age: from food for puppies, then to young dogs all the way through to "retired watchdogs." Here again, we see extensive use of such tactics as cross-selling and up-selling. Ideally, the sale of one product leads directly to more sales of a whole series of others. For every red pot, there are yellow, purple and blue lids that fit just as well.

Chapter 6 looks in detail at return on investment in event-driven marketing for the range of products suitable for cross-selling and up-selling that illustrates customer value–and hence the value of the business–most clearly. So the creative marketer looks first and foremost at what combination of products increases that value now and in the future.

The move from the singular field of the EDM Quadrant to the recurring one is fairly easy to make in one step. But to go from either of these to the *interactive* field requires a more ambitious leap. In the interactive section of the EDM Quadrant, we encounter both implicit and explicit factors. You are no longer fixing events in time, but tracking the customer in such a way that you identify and respond "interactively" to events and even changes as soon as they occur. That requires much more powerful database marketing and multichannel marketing management. And the internal information distribution processes also need to be very well organized. Webmasters, sales directors, logistics managers, and the like have to work effectively together under the command of the marketers. To put it mildly, that is one hell of a job. But get it right and it can generate a lot of customer value and hard cash.

A leading European bank closely monitors failed bank card transactions. In the event of two failures within a set period, the customer is sent a neutrally worded letter asking if he would like a small overdraft protection policy in order to avoid such disappointment in the future. Is that service or sales? In fact it is the latter, but to the customer it comes across as positive and empathetic. It actually helps the bank build up a good relationship with the customers and enhances their sense of loyalty. Many telecommunications providers monitor their customers' telephone use and respond to changing patterns by offering more appropriate subscription plans. And even if there is no need to change the plan, it is still a good idea to let the customer know. This is a service that shows you put the customer first: an excellent form of retention marketing.

The ultimate form of event-driven marketing is that found in the *anticipative* field of the EDM Quadrant. For example, say you notice that the average age of first-time mortgage applicants is increasing and that the average price of the homes they are seeking to buy is rising. Perhaps this indicates that the time is ripe for the "Generation Mortgage," a form of mortgage in which a third party (for instance the parents or other relatives) guarantees part of the loan. That is what the Rabobank discovered in the Netherlands. With the launch of this product, it successfully responded to that perceived evolution of the age indicator and managed to push down the average age of its first-time buyers, thus increasing their customer value and lengthening their lifecycle as loyal customers.

Is a supermarket chain engaged in business development if it starts putting its private label products into smaller packs for one-person households? As long as it then actively markets those products to that group, yes. We can already anticipate that the events of the future are likely to reflect Baby-Boomers growing richer, the population as whole aging, increasing obesity and young people becoming ever more critical and difficult to reach. What are the indicators, scores, triggers, campaigns, actions, and interactions associated with these events? This is the game of future events that can be planned for.

Admittedly, the anticipatory section of the Quadrant does not fall entirely within the definition of EDM given earlier in this book. That is based upon identified changes in the customer's situation and needs. Anticipation, however, implies a predictive aspect. You develop products and services in response to future events extrapolated from what is happening now. In other words, you engage in business development and business planning. The marketer prepares your organization for the future, short-term and beyond, by anticipating your customer's behavior.

Time versus Predictability

Quite unlike the singular and recurring fields, the anticipatory section of the EDM Quadrant is appealing but unpredictable. So how do the elements in each layer relate to the factors time and predictability?

Exhibit 3.8 illustrates the continuum from basic to advanced applications of event-driven marketing. The benefits of an advanced application are clear: It enables you to contact the customer earlier, thus giving you a chance to pre-empt the competition. However, predictive power (information value) requires a constant flow of data because the accuracy of information declines rapidly as indicators age and become vaguer. Few organizations have the resources available to them. From the criteria presented in Exhibit 3.8, every organization should be able to work out its current position and what is ultimately feasible for it.

Exhibit 3.8. Application Levels of EDM

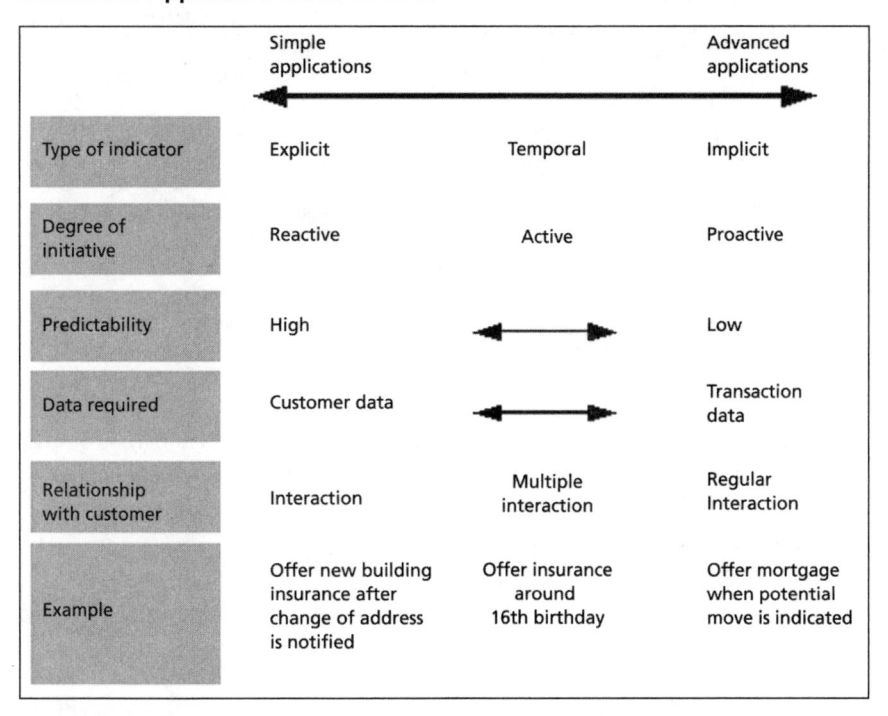

	Simple applications ←——————————————→ Advanced applications		
Type of indicator	Explicit	Temporal	Implicit
Degree of initiative	Reactive	Active	Proactive
Predictability	High	←——→	Low
Data required	Customer data	←——→	Transaction data
Relationship with customer	Interaction	Multiple interaction	Regular Interaction
Example	Offer new building insurance after change of address is notified	Offer insurance around 16th birthday	Offer mortgage when potential move is indicated

Exhibit 3.9 Examples of Different Applications of the EDM Quadrant

For an insurer.

		Singular	Recurring
PREDICTABILITY	High	• Expiring contract • Opportunity to end insurance • Life insurance	• Beneficiary's birthday • Purchase date of car • Interval X after policy is taken out • Development/growth of child
		Interactive	Anticipative
	Low	• Increased claims • Change of address • More staff (large company) • Switching behavior • Certain questions about products and services • New beneficiary on policy (birth)	• Political developments in respect of legislation, deregulation or "open borders" • Social and financial developments • Population growth and composition • Aging
		Short Term	**Long Term**
		TIME	

For an automotive business.

		Singular	Recurring
PREDICTABILITY	High	• Expiring loan • Warranty period	• Birthday • Purchase date of car • Annual car inspection
		Interactive	Anticipative
	Low	• Visit to showroom or workshop • Damage • Mileage	• Economic or political developments • Changes in behavior/lifestyle
		Short Term	**Long Term**
		TIME	

EDM in Mobile Telephony

Let's see how the EDM Quadrant can be applied to the telecom market. Winning customers in the market for mobile telephony is difficult and costly. And one of the biggest challenges is retaining customers once they have been recruited. The industry suffers a huge rate of customer churn. In the US, the average annual rate of churn stands at about 18 percent. Even worse, Vodafone UK once reported that it had lost no less than 30 percent of its customers in one year.[1]

Such churn represents a huge drain on resources. On the one hand, the lost customers no longer generate revenue or ROI and therefore have to be replaced

---
[1] Vodafone Group PLC, *Preliminary Announcement of Results—Year Ended 31 March 2003.*

quickly in order to maintain income levels. On the other, the investments made in acquiring those customers–e.g., a free handset or introductory offer–may not have been recouped before they depart. Recruiting the average new customer can easily cost in excess of $300, after which they generate about $60 a month in turnover. And from that amount operating costs need to be deducted. So it is easy to imagine how long it takes to recover the acquisition costs.

In a market where the consumer is now used to changing providers and those firms' services are looking more and more alike, making products increasingly generic commodities, it is vital to find ways to increase retention rates. There are various possibilities to achieve this aim:

- **Increase caller satisfaction.** Look at things from their perspective so that you make relevant propositions. In an interview with the magazine *Emerce*, the marketing director of T-Mobile once said, "If people make 300 minutes of calls at the weekend, we can offer them an off-peak discount."
- **Recruit the right customers.** Target acquisition activities at those who are less likely to change provider. The proposition made at the time of acquisition plays an important part in this. A price-based offer will attract price-sensitive customers, and there is a much greater chance that they will move on quickly. The same is true for premium-based offers.
- **Monitor customer behavior.** Identify events and respond to them effectively. See the next section for some examples.
- **Make the customer an appealing new offer.** Do this before his current contract expires, so that he is encouraged to extend it.
- **Win back lost customers by making them a good offer.** For this, it is usually better to wait until their contract with your competitor is approaching expiration (event). But remember that the customer left you for a reason. Identifying and dealing with that should take priority over winning him back.

Earlier in this chapter we discussed the four quadrants. In mobile telephony, there are usable events within all these quadrants. Examples for each quadrant follow.

Singular Quadrant

- *Contract expiration date.* This is a point at which many customers are lost. Offering customers—profitable ones, at any rate—an attractive incentive or superior service can stem this tide.
- *Expiration of a competitor's contract.* Anything you can do with current customers, you can also do with prospects and former customers. US provider BellSouth discovered that there was no point trying to win back lost customers until eleven months later because that was when their new contract was approaching its end.

Recurring Quadrant

- *Young people who reach a certain age.* The age at which children want a mobile for their birthday is falling all the time. By making them or their parents an offer at the right time you can acquire a new customer.
- If you are able to identify a consumer's *holiday plans*, you can offer him a so-called "roaming" plan for calls made abroad. This is a cross-selling opportunity.

Interactive Quadrant

- *Change of job.* If a user has a company phone, there is a chance that he will want to take out a new subscription if he changes jobs. This could be a business contract through the new employer or a private one if that new position doesn't come with a company phone.
- *Changed calling patterns.* If a customer with a prepaid subscription suddenly starts making a lot of calls, it may indicate that he is using up his credit before transferring to a competitor. A sudden fall in use could also signal a problem: perhaps the customer has bought a second phone from a competitor. Identify such patterns in the marketing database and respond to them swiftly and appropriately.
- *Cancellation of fixed-line subscription.* More and more people are giving up their landline phones altogether in favor of mobile-only use. Cancellation of a fixed-line subscription could provide a sales opportunity for the mobile network.
- *International calls.* If a customer makes or receives a lot of calls when abroad, it might be worth offering him a different subscription plan.

Anticipatory Quadrant

- *Media interconnectivity.* Hardware is becoming easier to interconnect, producing a range of combined applications. Mobile telephones linked to route planners and PDAs is just one example. Create relevant packages by analyzing events to establish what combinations are suitable for whom and when. Then skim this market.
- *Co-marketing.* Find partners who are willing to share events, triggers, and indicators that you could not identify yourself but which might provide you with good opportunities to sell unique products. International partners can help you serve "roaming" callers better by offering cheaper connections than your competitor. For example, you could even link this to the products offered by tour operators.

4

Process Management and the Implementation of Event-Driven Marketing

This chapter goes into a number of important operational aspects of direct marketing in general and EDM in particular. Amongst the topics it addresses are business process management (BPM), campaign management, customer-related concerns, and the demands made by EDM of the operational marketing organization and the supporting IT systems. If there is one concept in which marketing and IT come together in a perfect love match, then it is Event-Driven Marketing.

As well as highlighting challenges and points for attention, this chapter also provides a number of concrete tips for transforming an EDM strategy into actual EDM.

The Customer Comes First

Consumers' heterogeneity and unpredictability are increasing. It is becoming more and more difficult for businesses–and for retailers in particular–to predict what an individual customer is going to buy tomorrow. Those that have responded most successfully to this problem have adopted an approach in which the customer really does come first, adapting the whole structure of their business to customer interaction. And making that interaction manageable has prompted a trend towards greater control over the entire commercial process.

Putting the customer first, and hence being able to act immediately in response to his wishes, actions, and conduct, implies that the business processes are actually steered directly by the customer. And allowing that means that you first need to have a firm grip on things yourself.

It is therefore vital to invest now in the management of those processes that, like Event-Driven Marketing, are concerned directly with the customer. That goes much further than mere marketing, communications, and sales (the front office). Finance, logistics, and other back-office functions also need to be tackled.

Companies should have their entire business process in order. Especially in large companies, the IT department needs to work with marketing, logistics, and sales to place more emphasis upon the customer and upon customer-oriented processes. All parts of the organization should be directed from a single process management system that oversees the entire business process and can handle all kinds of database, financial, logistical, and front-office (customer contact) systems in order to be able to sell the right product to the right customer at the right moment. The customer is king and has to be treated as such, not with marketing activities aimed *at* them, but through an interactive process *with* them.

In the recent past, people expected the web and e-business to give the customer more power. They gave prospective buyers a fast and full overview of what was being offered and allow them to make simple price comparisons. With the web, distance is no object. Any company that ignored the Internet would eventually lose out. That was what they said. But now we can see that things have not worked that straightforwardly. Most web sellers have already disappeared; those established companies that invested in e-business, often on a huge scale, are licking their web wounds. Only a few have actually introduced it successfully. But the trend has been set. It is essential to be ready for your customers. Ready to answer their questions, ready to respond to their complaints and, increasingly, ready to allow them to influence your range of products and services.

One of the key challenges of the web, as with all new technologies, is that we begin using it to solve an old problem and wind up using it to solve new problems. For example, an old problem marketers face is fulfillment cost–the cost of taking, filling, and delivering an order. A small US manufacturer of switches used in specialized equipment sold the bulk of its products to a few equipment manufacturers but found that most of their orders were to equipment owners buying one item for a small amount. It cost them more in time, effort and money than it was worth to take small orders over the phone, so they set up a web site to take small orders in order to lower their fulfillment costs. The only way to place a small order is online, which saves the company a great deal of manpower and money.

Funny thing happened, though. They started getting larger orders of thousands of dollars from manufacturers they had never prospected or even heard of before. It turns out that a lot of other US component manufacturers had moved their production to Asia, which caused longer lead times in ordering their product. Desperate purchasing managers searched the web when they were short on components and found them on the company's site. It opened a whole new market.

So being ready is more than just being ready to solve the problem you set out to solve. It is being ready to find out what new problems can be solved, and being flexible enough to take advantage of them.

Marketing and IT Merge

Companies that want to respond to what we want can no longer simply deliver "off the shelf." The customer today expects to be waited on hand and foot, to be offered reliable products tailored to whatever he wants to buy—be it a holiday, a new home, insurance, a mortgage, or a computer system. From working with web sites, many companies are already practiced in dealing with interactive customer queries and orders. Now offering a flexible, tailor-made product has to be embedded in the management process. That calls for more than just a technical and organizational change of direction; it requires a complete overhaul of the way entrepreneurs think. Those who manage to achieve that quickly gain an edge over the competition:

> All the experts agree: the consumer has never had so much power as now. Together, the rise of information technology and self-awareness are giving buyers unprecedented influence over what the manufacturers and service providers offer. Suppliers are falling over themselves to wrap the customer in cotton wool, countless numbers of them mindlessly parroting supposed marketing truths without ever pausing for a moment to look at what is really happening. If they did, they would see that things are far less rosy. Forget the idea that all these firms are responding to the wishes of today's demanding consumer. For the most part, they feel much happier sheltering behind the protective barricades of impersonal mailings, call centres, labyrinthine organizations and silence to keep the customer at arm's length. Turnover is great, but they would much prefer to generate it without having to have customers.
> —*Jan C. Bezemer*[1], freelance consultant and publicist.

In the past, it was not uncommon for the implementation of ad-hoc systems or off-the-shelf information systems packages to result in chaos and loss of control. And the bigger the system, the greater the potential for disaster. For example, many companies have introduced new enterprise resource planning (ERP) systems in recent years. In many cases, firms build temporary solutions to streamline current processes with a view to arriving at a sound, yet flexible, final situation. The result is a complex interplay between marketing and IT, not to mention finance and logistics, in order to strike a balance between what is desirable from the marketing point of view and what is actually feasible technically, economically, and organizationally. That requires marketers who think beyond brochures and IT people who think beyond bits and bytes. Perhaps a new kind of employee, who can engage in discussion with the entire organization and who, as well as understanding processes, is able to manage them.

Traditional industrial processes, in many cases still based upon principles like those posited by Frederic Taylor[2] in the early 20th century, are too functional in

---
[1] PIM Marketing Trend Report 2004
[2] Tayor, F. W. (1911), *Principles of Scientific Management*. New York, Harper & Row.

their structures for today's world. The laws of big numbers and cheap mass production are outdated. In a highly heterogeneous market, the economies of scale derived from large and standardized batches have disappeared. A better response to that heterogeneity and its accompanying unpredictability would appear to be a business structure based upon processes steered by the customer. But that is no easy thing to achieve, since heterogeneity has a major impact upon how a business is managed: it forces us to control the business processes down to the finest detail.

Remember two things when setting out to build an ERP system—or any other system, for that matter:

1. If you cannot understand and define it logically, you cannot program it
2. If you cannot do it manually, you cannot automate it

Any system should begin with the customer. What are their wants and needs, how do they want to interact with the organization, and how do we facilitate that with systems?

It's important to remember that the stakes are high. ERP and corporate-wide CRM systems can cost into the tens and hundreds of millions. Depending who you ask, most (or at least a substantial portion) fail to achieve any result.

For example, a major wholesaler of communication equipment set out to install an ERP system based on a technical (as opposed to customer) focus. Several years and 50 million dollars later, they had no results to show. As a result, the entire management team–the president and every vice president–was swept out and replaced by the parent company's management. A "build it and they will come" technical focus won't just doom the system. It could doom careers.

The consumer has ever more choice and, even though companies like Unilever may have slashed their portfolios, more and more products are available. And every new one further complicates the supply chain, with a direct effect upon the ability to achieve economies of scale in the supply.

The FBC Formula: Faster, Better, Cheaper

Industry is constantly striving to improve its efficiency with just one simple aim in mind: to be faster, better, and cheaper than the rest. If you can achieve that "triple play" after all, then you will beat all your competitors hands down. Yet that drive for efficiency seems to be totally negated by the complex IT systems mentioned above and by miscommunication between marketing, sales, IT, finance, and logistics. Meanwhile, the customer stands by and looks on—and is not helped.

Of course, desperate attempts continue in this more complex world to improve efficiency so that enough money can be made again. The typical stated strategy is to make processes "manageable." Initiatives like electronic data interchange (EDI), enterprise resource planning (ERP), and business process redesign all try to eliminate costs from the business chain on a large scale. But all are actually mere variations on established themes; although they might be able to stretch the elastic a little further, it will always snap in the end. The only true way to create more value is to respond better to what the customer wants, which means gaining a much better understanding of customer wishes and actually tailoring processes to meet them. In practice, that involves making the right offer to the right customers, responding effectively when they have queries or want to place orders, delivering the goods properly and quickly, sending clear, accurate invoices, and having your administration in order.

In our view, the often not entirely successful SAP and Siebel implementations that a lot of businesses have under their belts are proof enough that in many cases only lip service is being paid to the mission of efficiency. In fact, what they are looking for in systems of this kind is a high fence behind which to hide from the customer's view. "We have put our house in order," they can say. "We have invested in a big way. So if things still don't work, then that must be the customer's fault." But sorting out difficult processes internally and giving them customer focus should first mean mutual agreement among the departments concerned, then involve the customer and only after that address the systems—a logical-enough order, but one that all too often is reversed.

FBC from a Customer's Perspective

Just as businesses seek efficiencies, customers seek efficiencies. However, the customer is setting out to solve a completely different problem than the seller. The product or service will be used in some way to solve a problem, either by itself or in combination with other products. He or she looks at cost as what he gives up to get something, which may be more than just money. For example, the cost of obtaining a product or service can be made up of:

- Money
- Time
- Physical Effort
- Mental Effort
- Risk

Sellers tend to focus on price but consider the other factors. Let's say that you are planning to go to the grocery store and notice you are low on salt. So you put salt on your list.

When you get to the store, you see there is a raffle in the aisle where the salt is, and a crowd of people waiting for a number to be drawn. Would you wait five minutes and then get the salt, or just forget about it on this trip and get it next time?

Let's say that ground salt is not available that day, but they do have it in blocks. You've got a hammer at home. You could buy the salt block and, with a few minutes of intense pounding, could have salt crystals. Would you beat the salt into submission, or just forget about it on this trip and get it next time?

Just for fun, on this trip, you try a different food store that sells items for people who have moved from another country and speak a different language. You don't recognize any of the brands, don't know the right word for salt, and aren't sure which type is which. Do you try to cross the language barrier and figure it out, or just forget about it on this trip and get it next time?

What if you arrive at the salt display, you find someone who clearly works for the salt company. He tells you that they are doing research, and in exchange for your detailed personal information, you can have the salt for free. You worry about your privacy and are naturally reluctant to give information out that could harm or embarrass you. Do you accept the risk and take the "free" salt, or just forget about it on this trip and get it next time?

All kinds of things can play into the customer's perspective of the cost of the relationship, which can be quite different than what a seller imagines. The non-monetary costs of the relationship demand that some products simply have to be sold with no hassles, or they literally aren't worth buying.

Don't Just React, Anticipate

Being receptive to the customers' wishes and prepared to interact with them requires entrepreneurial courage, money, and vision. And here lies a paradox: on the one hand, costs have to be pushed down by streamlining processes, but on the other value creation is linked to what each individual customer wants. In more traditional times, your local carpenter would come to your house and build a kitchen to your particular specifications. Now we buy factory-built kitchens from home improvement specialists and wait for delivery—with a good chance that something will go wrong. We could still go to the local craftsman, of course, and in fact the price of his hand-built kitchen will be much the same as the factory-produced version. So why do we have all those factories, and what is the added value if the end product is no cheaper?

Because selecting from a few factory-made alternatives is easier than creating something fully customized. The buyer doesn't have to work with the custom craftsman on each aspect of what he wants, when it can be done, etc. It requires less physical effort, since it can be decided in one trip to the store and installed with one delivery to the home. It also takes much less mental effort, since he doesn't have to consider every possible choice. And there is less risk, since he knows what he will get, can see and touch examples exactly like it and knows that the manufacturer has probably already eliminated potential bad choices.

It is much the same set of choices that drive different buying behaviors of people buying cakes. The grandmother buys the ingredients and bakes a cake from scratch. The daughter buys a cake mix and bakes it. The granddaughter buys a cake. As society becomes more consumer driven, the convenient "do it for me" choice becomes more popular.

Another related problem facing entrepreneurs is that customers are becoming ever more difficult to segment. Where once we saw reasonably homogeneous, well-delineated groups, such divisions are increasingly difficult to pin down. Consumer attitudes and behavior are more and more fluid, demanding a lot of flexibility from the marketer trying to segment them. On top of the greater choice of products already mentioned, the multicultural society, and wide variety of lifestyles now practiced are making it harder to identify what items will be bought tomorrow. Marketers are living in volatile markets.

You need to anticipate that "tomorrow" in the right way. You have to overcome the fear of not being able to supply everything that people want. Trying to satisfy all the demand out there has simply become too expensive.

As Chapter 7 will show, you can anticipate what is going to happen by correctly analyzing the buying patterns of particular customer types and groups. You are no longer working reactively, in response to today's actual demand. Instead, you are preparing your organization for tomorrow's likely demand.

Rather than trying to anticipate demand with complete products, another option is to leave their configuration to the customer. Dell has been doing that for years with the sale of PCs on its web site (www.dell.com). But it also works well with travels, insurances and cars. Stop assembling the end product yourself and let the customer do it as far as possible.

Once assembly and delivery are out of the way, it is not uncommon for modifications to follow (e.g., the structure of insurance or investment products). Allowing customers themselves to make those changes not only saves the provider a lot of money, it saves the customer a lot of time. It even enhances customer loyalty: The supplier is perceived as "looking after" the products owned by the customer, who always has access to them.

This is not new: Insurance companies and internet-based investment firms have been doing it for years. But this form of "self-modification" is set to take on many new forms, in everything from B-to-B to retail.

Although we stated in the introduction to this book that a gradual trend such as increasing individualization is too general to be of much use to us, that particular phenomenon is leading to greater heterogeneity, and that, in turn, is making things more unpredictable. Ultimately, more technologically advanced planning systems do not offer a solution; all they do is increase costs. A different and more radical answer is needed: anticipation rather than reaction, a proactive approach to heterogeneity. Instead of offering predefined choices, offer the chance to define choices. To that point:

> The emergence of business process management (BPM) is the culmination of a decade of the evolution from the workflow market and is now having a major impact on businesses. Holistic process automation across the entire modern business enterprise is now a reality, and not just a "blue

sky" concept. BPM's ability to manage complex processes and to facilitate electronic channels of communication makes it an ideal solution to many of the issues that enterprises are facing in this area. It is no wonder, therefore, that enterprises everywhere are looking at the potential that BPM can offer in making their processes more efficient and manageable.

—*Kendal Hunt*[3]

Keep IT Simple . . .

The harder you make it, the more expensive it becomes and the bigger the risks you run. There no longer is money to be made from exploiting what customers have in common.

Segments these days contain only a few customers each and are changing all the time, so, as we saw in Chapter 2, the end of segmentation as a marketing concept or method is in sight. The value now lies in spotting the differences between them, and being able to respond to them or, even better, to anticipate them. And customers are becoming time-specific. When exactly does somebody want something, how much trouble and expense is he prepared to go through in order to get it at that precise moment? The same consumer who goes out of his way to buy a frozen pizza from a particular store in the morning because it is ten cents cheaper there will pay many times as much that evening to have an identical pizza delivered hot to his front door.

Everything is a process. Whatever happens, a process is under way, and when processes are not "understood," what that actually means is that unwanted complexity has crept into them, often at unjustifiably high cost and with a risk of other dangers to boot: loss of time, loss of focus, loss of direction, and so on. Managing processes and understanding them is called process management, but process management should never become the aim itself. All too often, companies, departments, and people get hopelessly entangled in the process itself without ever achieving the intended results. What we then see is the rise of the meeting culture, a situation in which nobody dares to assume responsibility.

When assessing the "costs of complexity," managers are often astounded at where those costs have come from and how big they are. A common excuse is that the complexity has "slipped" in, which is all the more reason to keep an eye on your processes all the time and to remember that the goal is at least as important as how you get there (the process).

Part of the challenge is that we need to change the way we think about marketing, so that instead of seeing complexity we can find simplicity. For example, although it has been around for barely 100 years, an assembly line is logically simple. Each product receives the components it needs, at the time it needs it, as it progresses down the line.

---

[3] Management Tools, Kluwer 2004.

There may be hundreds or thousands of components, but each is brought in at the right time. By looking at the customer's process of become more and more familiar, and hopefully dependent on the company, we can devise a logically simple way to react to customer needs at different points in their individual journey.

Today's commercial processes are not adequately tailored to heterogeneity, at least not at an acceptable cost. To satisfy demand from a customer, business functions need to be organized into an effective "chain" (process) so that the product being asked for can be supplied. In current structures, these functions are managed from above, as "columns" in a top-down organizational model. But as unpredictability increases, companies organized in this way are running into problems. Unpredictable demand leads to an explosion in the number of different orders passing through the hierarchy. So either the speed of transmission needs to be stepped up to deal with them all more quickly or parallel structures have to be put in place so that more messages can be handled simultaneously.

The Customer: In the Driver's Seat

In an unpredictable world, you can only react to the customer's behaviors. This implies that it is the customer who is in control of the process or, at any rate, who decides what route to take through the processes and activities. So the process chains need to be extremely flexible. Sometimes a customer will want to skip a step. Sometimes he will want to choose from a number of alternatives. The process has to be organized as a "solution space" full of activities for the customer to navigate through his own way.

While sounding complex, it is similar to building products with different optional components on the same line. Some get the digital panel, some get the push buttons, but all travel the same path. The difference is in what is requested, and how we respond (Exhibit 4.1).

If the process is organized in this kind of dynamic way shown in Exhibit 4.1, the number of product variants no longer holds us back, and it does not matter that we do not know the customer demand in advance. If every process acts as a

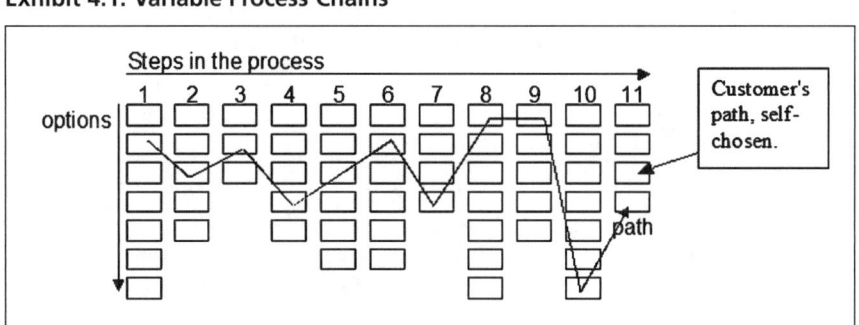

Exhibit 4.1. Variable Process Chains

Exhibit 4.2. The Event-Driven Marketing Cycle as a Variant of the Direct Marketing Cycle

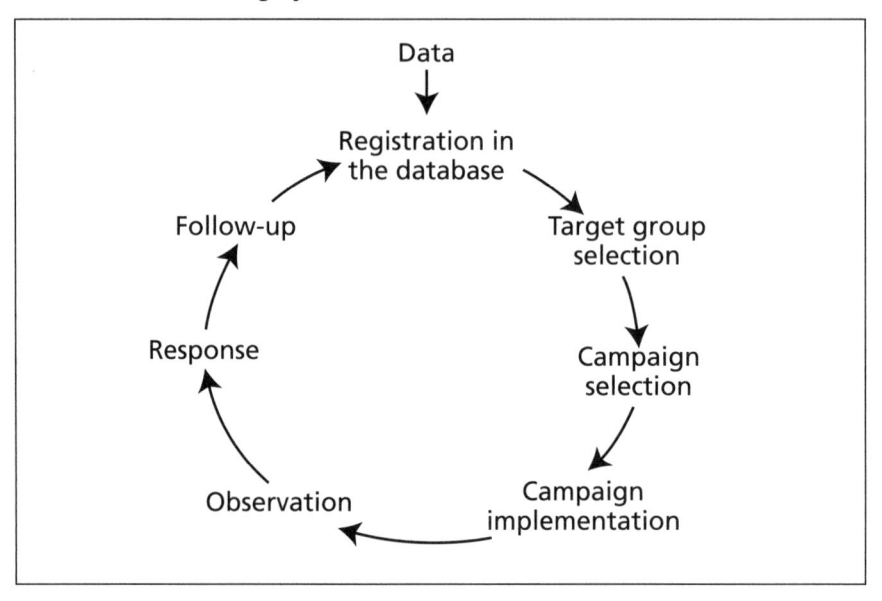

```
                        Data
                         ↓
              Registration in
              the database
      Follow-up  ↗            ↘  Target group
         ↑                        selection
         |                          ↓
      Response                   Campaign
         ↑                       selection
          ↖                       ↙
            Observation   ←   Campaign
                              implementation
```

loop, the "traffic" will find its own way through—with the customer at the wheel at last without incurring unacceptable additional costs.

Campaign Management and the Event-Driven Marketing Cycle

The process of Event-Driven Marketing shown in Exhibit 4.2 is based on Paul Postma's Direct Marketing Cycle®. Comparing the two, what first strikes us is that our cycle is data-driven rather than marketing objective-driven. This may seem strange at first sight, but the reason is that in EDM we have already translated those objectives into customer groups, customer needs, and the associated campaigns. The customer's behavior is tracked and turned into data that is being analyzed constantly to see if the moment has come to approach the customer. It should also be noted that the cycle has "shifted" one phase forward as a result of it being data-driven. We will now go through the phases in the event-driven marketing cycle one by one.

Phase 1. Registration in the database

The process of event-driven marketing is being monitored and steered from the marketing database on a constant basis. By collecting relevant behavioral information, we are able to signal events in the customer's life. A telephone company's database, for example, can recognize somebody who has started making more international calls or has increased the usage of his mobile phone. This information can then be used to initiate appropriate action. Therefore, it is extremely important that we possess essential basic data at the individual customer level.

It is not necessary that your organization itself makes all the observations used. You can also draw upon external sources, such as a list of everybody who has moved house recently (see Case 2). The downside with external sources is that there can be problems with the recency and reliability of the data, so always check them thoroughly before using them as the basis for a marketing program.

Multiple sources of external data can be used when data accuracy is crucial. For example, people with a specific job description listed in one external data set may be only partially accurate. If the same person is listed with the same or similar job description in two data sets, it is much more likely to be recent and accurate. This is why business will often look at data from magazine lists, web sites, trade shows, and other sources simultaneously.

Out of the stream of basic data coming in, we distill that information deemed relevant as an indicator of changes in the customer's pattern of needs. The next step is to define indicators in the database (see Chapter 3). This has to be done in a structured way. In practice, it is very likely that an indicator will reflect an aggregate of underlying transaction data; in the case of a bank, for example, the number of times a month that a customer withdraws money from a cash dispenser. This is an aggregate of all the individual withdrawals because it may be that a subsequent indicator uses a different aggregate of the same basic data, such as the fact that a customer usually uses cash dispensers at night. It is advisable that, as far as possible, the basic data itself be recorded in the first instance. This makes it easier to compile a range of aggregates from it.

Particular focus on the behaviors of our own customers is the most crucial. Without a full and complete understanding of each customer's relationship with us, external information may be useless or misleading. "Forgetting" what a customer has done with you often leads to offers and responses that simply alienate them.

This is actually the last phase as well as the first. The cycle begins with incoming data, but it also ends with registration of the results achieved. So this is also the point at which to evaluate those results and, if necessary, to revise scorecards, triggers, campaigns or actions accordingly.

Phase 2. Target Group Selection

Event-driven Marketing is all about responding to the customer's particular situation or to changes in it. The basic principle behind this is that customer behavior is a better indicator of needs than any other information available. Of course, the correlation between the "event" and the new "need" has to be investigated thoroughly in each situation.

Target selection can often be better described as target de-selection. Marketers often start from the standpoint of "we'll talk to everyone about everything." That drives much of the waste in marketing. We simply can't get ourselves to "not do" something, especially when we've "always done it."

EDM isn't about using more marketing resources, it is about using marketing resources more wisely. With EDM we add the challenge of hitting it at *precisely the right time.* That includes the inverse of the challenge: Doing things at the right time also means not doing them at the wrong time, or too often.

It is extremely important, therefore, to determine exactly what events will initiate an EDM activity. We then look for *indicators* that will enable us to *observe* that event. If a customer is unhappy with the quality of the dog food he has been buying, then it is a good moment to make him an offer linked to an alternative brand. But if he does not tell you of his dissatisfaction, you cannot exploit that event. So it is important to find a means by which you are informed at the right moment. Hence the fact that in the previous phase so much emphasis is placed upon gathering the right data. Ideally, there is 100 percent correlation between event and indicator. For our purposes, however, it is sufficient to achieve a "reasonable degree" of accuracy. To achieve that, we generally use statistical techniques like regression analysis (see also Chapter 8). These translate combinations of indicators into a score revealing the probability that a particular event will take place. We store the resulting profiles in the database.

In Phase 1, the incoming data is combined with that already recorded. This new data set is then compared with the stored profiles. Once the new combination of data (score) pertaining to a customer meets the criteria for a particular profile (trigger), the customer is selected for the relevant marketing campaign. This process is discussed in detail in Chapter 3.

Phase 3. Campaign Selection

In the previous phase, all the customers who satisfy the criteria for a particular campaign have been selected. In the simplest case, campaign selection takes place at the same time, and we can move straight on to the implementation phase. The customer may be at a phase in their relationship when we are seeking a timely repurchase in order to keep them. They may be at a phase when we are seeking to cross-sell them a product that fits with other products they are already buying in order to grow them. We may be seeking customers that "look like" our best customers to try us in order to get new customers. Building campaign tactics down from the strategic goals allows us to stay within a simple enough framework that complexity doesn't become overwhelming.

More complicated situations are also possible, though, so it is worth looking at campaign selection in a little more detail. One quite feasible scenario is that the ratio of fixed to variable costs in a marketing campaign is such that it can only deliver worthwhile returns if, say, 1,000 customers are approached at once. In that case, target group selection may have taken place, but the actual campaign is delayed. For efficiency reasons, each campaign, therefore, has a *waiting list*. This is used to "gather in" a number of customers before the campaign is actually put into effect, thus preventing costly activity being initiated for each individual subject. The waiting list specifies the minimum number of customers needed for implementation, as well as the maximum time that they can be held on the list. Once that period expires, they are removed from the list. We can imagine this as a train waiting at a station platform; every new customer who matches the profile can board, but the train will only depart when it has at least 1,000 passengers.

This brings us to the next issue. It is not inconceivable that newly received data results in customers qualifying for more than one marketing campaign. In our metaphor that means that they could board more than one train at once, so choices have to be made in the campaign selection phase. Do we direct the customers to the train scheduled to depart first or to the one likely to generate the biggest returns? Or do we opt to target them with more than one campaign at the same time?

Phase 4. Campaign Implementation

A campaign can consist of one or more actions. For example, a direct mailing followed a week later by a second letter. And then a telephone call to nonrespondents after another three days. The campaign begins as soon as the first action is carried out. If that is a direct mail activity, details of the selected customers and the texts of the letters are submitted to the organization responsible for sending them out. With a suitable marketing database system in place, in theory no human intervention is required. The address, signature, and personal variables can be inserted automatically. Meanwhile, the individual customer's marketing history is updated in the database.

A similar approach applies to other channels of communication. In the case of telemarketing, the relevant customer details and a script are sent to the call center. For personal selling, lists of customer data are given to the salesperson. Ideally, the local sales system is populated automatically with information about the customers to be approached.

Phase 5. Observation

Galileo once said, "Observation requires knowledge. But that alone is not enough, it is but one of the three elements of success." We experience the world through the observations made by our senses. On the one hand, they reveal objective physical properties (the ball is round); on the other, we often attach meaning to an observation that is not directly related to any sensory perception (that is the ball used to score the first goal). The term *reach* is often used to describe how many people have seen or heard a message, but that says nothing about its communicative value or its impact upon individual recipients. So there is now a growing trend in favor of measuring the quality and positive effect of messages rather than simple numbers. Regardless of how accurate our senses are in making observations and even the subconscious aspect of sensory perception, what matters is whether your message hits home. And it has a good chance of doing that if you use the Poiesz Triad model. This identifies three values:

1. Motivation: the recipient's interest in the message and willingness to receive it.
2. Ability: the extent to which the message is understood (mental capacity).
3. Opportunity: the timing of the message.

This model exactly defines the three conditions for successful EDM: the right message to the right person at the right time.

Phase 6. Response

Prompt registration of responses is an essential part of event-driven marketing, not just because they are what we were trying to elicit in the first place but also due to the vital importance of timing in our approach. In a marketing campaign, we can link actions to whether or not the customer responds; for example, by making a follow up call after a week. This makes it important to record responses immediately, not leave them lying around for a week. A response can also serve as an indicator of other events, thus triggering different campaigns. So good response processing is far more critical in EDM than it is in traditional direct marketing.

For example, marketers don't often consider the lag-time between when a customer event occurs and when they actually respond to that event.

Exhibits 4.3 and 4.4 (from two different nonprofit organizations) show the donor's time between their first gift and their second gift. In the first example (4.3), the organization follows up with a repeat request relatively quickly.

The most common times to send the second gift appear to be in the first 6 or 7 months, with a spike at their one-year anniversary, then tapering off. Quite a few repeat gifts occur in the first 60 days.

In the second example (4.4), the nonprofit organization kept all new donors off mailing lists for 45 days, which means it really took about 60 days for them to get their second offer.

By waiting to follow up, the second nonprofit appears to miss out on nearly all second donations for the first sixty days. Not surprisingly, the overall retention rate for the first nonprofit is much higher than the second. It appears that losing a repeat response due to poor offer timing often equates to losing a customer. Looking at it from the customer's point of view is critical. Remember that marketing is really based on simple human relationships. Let's look at it from outside of marketing for a moment.

Marketers often forget that when customers continue to buy, it is because they are having a positive relationship. Yes, it is certainly possible to stalk them, or intrude on them, but as the relationship becomes more familiar, customers expect, and welcome, relevant and well-timed communication.

Exhibit 4.3. Response Example A

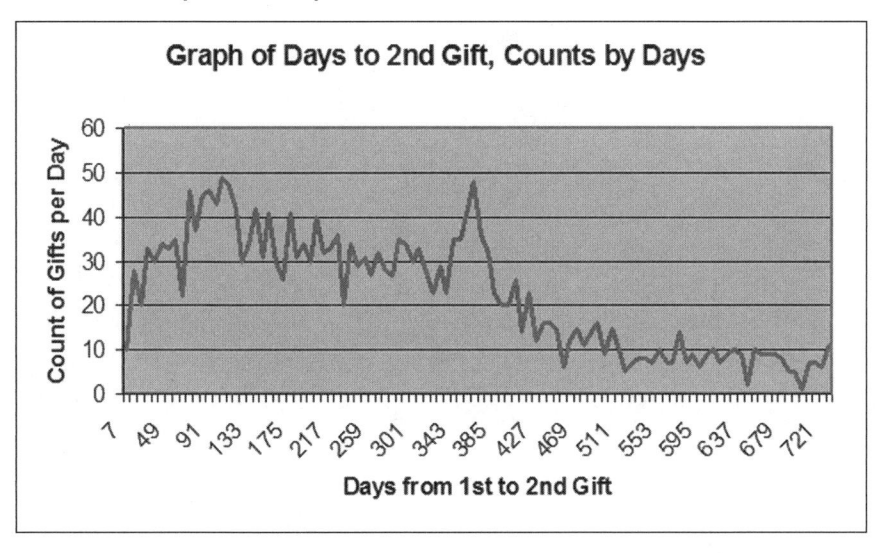

Graph of Days to 2nd Gift, Counts by Days

Count of Gifts per Day vs *Days from 1st to 2nd Gift*

Exhibit 4.4. Response Example B

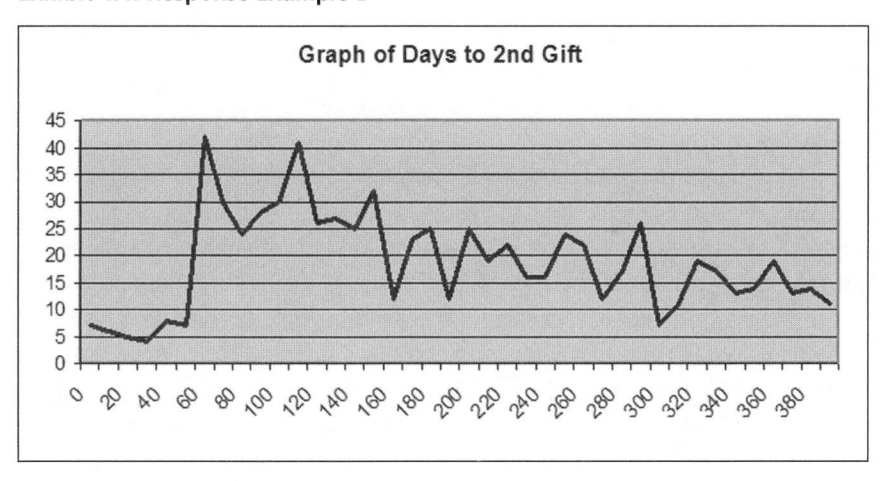

Graph of Days to 2nd Gift

Phase 7. Follow-up

Much the same applies to the customer follow up. Actually doing what you promise the customer is the key to success in direct marketing, but in EDM it is—if that is possible—even more critical. Having taken so much trouble to select exactly the right moment to approach the customer, it is essential to maintain the momentum. From the long-term point of view, every contact builds upon all previous ones. The fact that we have recorded all of them in a database makes things easier for us.

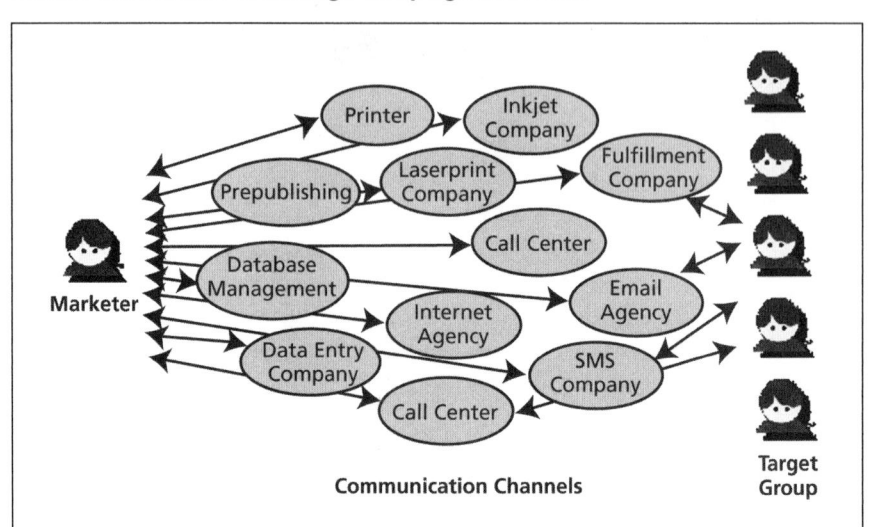

Exhibit 4.5. Difficult-to-Manage Campaign Execution

EDM Execution

Even before we add EDM to the mix, the world of business and marketing is already challenging enough. Advances in communications and database technology are multiplying the possibilities in direct marketing. Yet even more is needed. Customers, prospects and your own management are proving all the time that they can change their patterns of expectation with surprising speed.

Multichannel, multiwave and even *multilingual* communications—fine terms that just hint at the complexity underlying the average direct marketing campaign. Using a variety of channels of communication has been common practice in recent years, partly for reasons of effectiveness and efficiency and partly in response to customer preferences. What all successful multichannel campaigns have in common is the careful coordination of message, channels, and timing. The marketer faces the challenge of having to manage all of this at the same time as a whole raft of other tasks simultaneously screams for attention: analysis, strategy, and so on. It is not uncommon for people to "drown" in the operational management of their campaigns.

Another complicating factor lies in the fact that many companies and organizations use the services of many different suppliers in their campaign execution. Since marketing is often vendor driven, as opposed to customer relationship driven, it can be a challenge to coordinate these efforts.

Together, these firms ensure that the right message reaches the customer at the right time and through the right channel and that responses are received, recorded, followed up, and reported. As the complexity of marketing campaigns increases, so does the importance of co-ordinating the activities of and communications between all those involved. This is a need only enhanced by the likely incompatibility of the supporting IT systems used by each.

Exhibit 4.6. Marketing Campaigns Versus EDM Programs

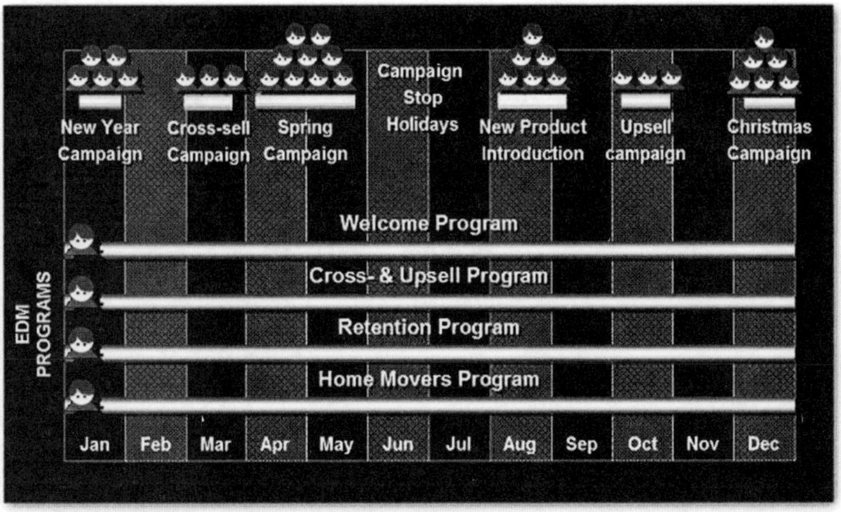

The Impact of EDM Execution

Executing direct marketing campaigns effectively can be difficult enough in itself. And things are certainly not made any easier if you then decide to let events in individual customers' lifecycles guide when and how you communicate what to them.

Campaign Versus Program

It is important to realize that EDM is not a finite campaign with a beginning and an end. Rather, it is a continuous program—what we call *cyclical*. With EDM we want to respond immediately or in a timely fashion to every customer event predefined as relevant. Marketers and their suppliers may well not know what communications will need to be sent tomorrow or next week. In the case of temporal indicators with an absolute reference (see Chapter 3), such as a customer's birthday, it is possible to plan roughly what the daily volumes will be, but that is virtually impossible with more complex forms of EDM involving implicit and explicit indicators. All this is in total contrast with direct marketing, where the necessary resources, stocks, and budgets can be planned weeks, or even months, in advance (Exhibit 4.6).

Complexity

EDM execution is highly reactive in nature. Indicators signal events on a daily basis and, in most cases, trigger communication with the customer.

In theory, this is best kept under control by limiting the number of customers, events, and triggers. Once you have thousands of customers, dozens of events and multiple triggers, the complexity increases exponentially (Exhibit 4.8).

64 ⤳ Follow That Customer!

Exhibit 4.7. The Complexity of EDM

EDM's complexity

Communications are <u>constantly</u> being triggered by the customer's <u>individual</u> behavior!

Time>

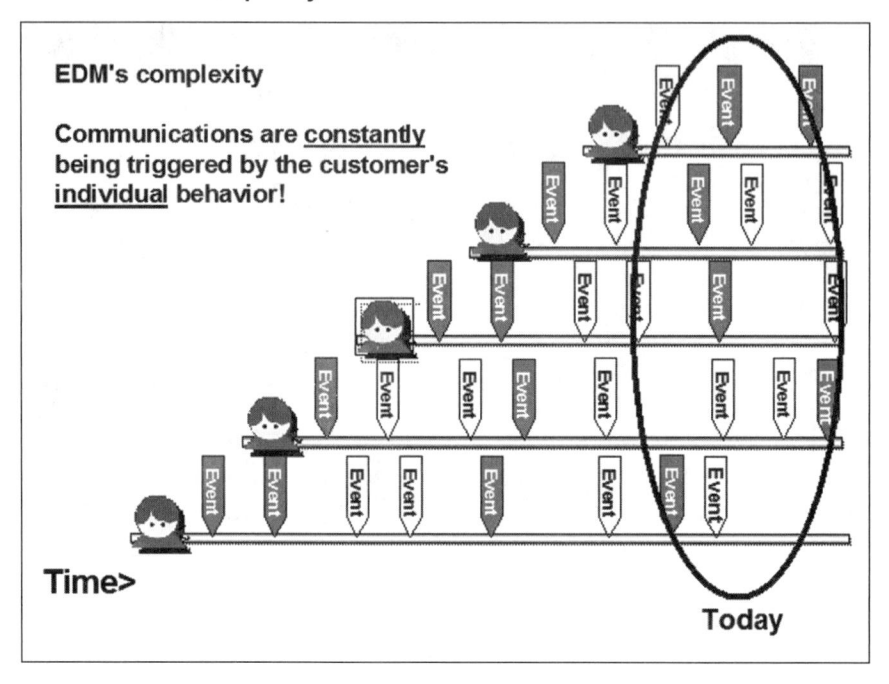

Today

Exhibit 4.8. From DM to EDM: Increasing Complexity

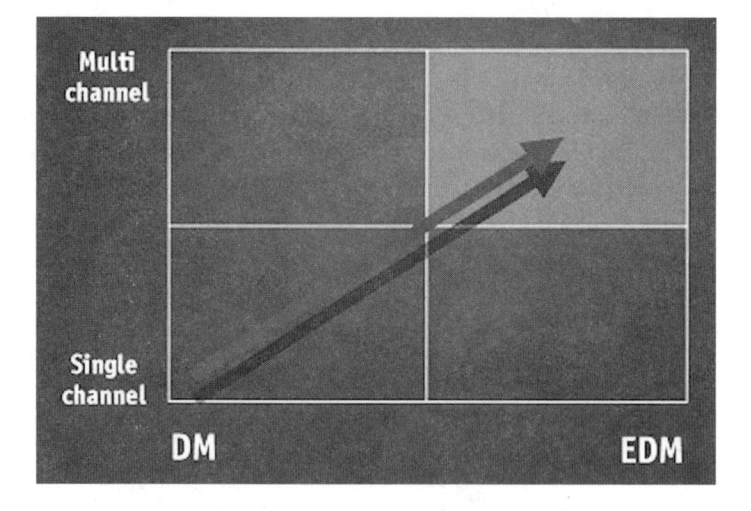

Even more than in traditional marketing and DM campaigns, it is an absolute prerequisite of EDM execution that the process throughout the chain be properly designed, implemented, tested, and managed. This requires a high degree of coordination, preferably automatic, between all the IT systems in the chain.

Is that not just a matter of linking up those systems? Unfortunately not. In most cases, things are not that simple in practice. Even where it is technically possible, most IT managers are unwilling to give outsiders direct access to their systems and the information they contain. Instead, there have to be planned document exchanges between all the IT systems in the execution chain, resulting in multiple import-export operations each day, complete with all the risk of errors that they entail.

Campaign Management

Campaign management systems can help reduce the complexity to governable proportions. Quite rightly, they seek a solution on the organizational side. More and more marketing departments now employ dedicated campaign managers charged with defining, implementing, supervising, and analyzing campaign processes, both internal and external. This can make complex EDM and DM processes manageable by channeling all the communication flows. It also becomes possible to record, steer, and monitor campaign and program processes centrally, along with all the triggers.

Chain Integration

If all the parties involved in execution can integrate themselves into an effective campaign management system, then you have taken the key step towards creating a well-oiled EDM execution machine. Chain integration–merging process elements and standardizing data-exchange protocols with a limited number of suppliers, the more extensively the better–considerably reduces the chance of errors occurring and can deliver big efficiency benefits.

CASE 2: Folksam's Moving Birds

Chapter 3 looked at the EDM Quadrant. The first case in this book discussed the relatively straightforward event of birthdays, a good example of the recurring section on the EDM Quadrant (high predictability and long-term timing). Things get a bit more complicated when predictability is low and timing is short, like with events in the interactive section of the Quadrant. You will depend on explicit or implicit indicators to run your program. A good example of innovative ways to deal with this challenge is the following case of Folksam's Moving Birds program.

Folksam, a leader in the Swedish financial services market, analyzes the world around it, looking at the lives of consumers. What drives human behavior is important to the company, which insures every second person, every second family home, and every fourth car in Sweden. Folksam has a long, successful heritage dating back to 1908 and consists of two mutual insurance companies: Folksam sak (non-life) and Folksam liv (life). Folksam's customers are also its owners. Its profits don't go to shareholders; instead they remain within the company to benefit everyone. The company is closely connected to the cooperative and trade union organizations in Sweden. There are 3,300 employees working for Folksam and the company provides a range of financial products in the areas of insurance and savings and loan products to suit its 4 million customers' every need. Every year, Folksam settles 600,000 claims. It also is one of the largest investment managers in the country. In recent years the company has found itself operating in an increasingly complex marketing environment with new marketing channels, growing numbers of market players, and more discerning customers who are increasingly open to switching suppliers in search of the best value for service.

Business Drivers

Since 2003 Folksam has had an ongoing Customer Relationship Management (CRM) initiative to ensure that company culture and processes are truly customer focused as well as to effectively meet customer needs in order to win and retain more customers, improve loyalty, and maximize the value that is derived from customers over the course of their lifetime. This project includes Enterprise Marketing Management (EMM), Sales and Customer Service. In addition to the CRM initiative, Folksam used advanced customer analysis, including studies of customer demographics, buying habits, and the impact of different life events. Folksam noticed it needed to better identify changes in clients' individual needs.

In 2001 the company came up with a clear wish list of what they wanted to do regarding CRM and Event-Driven Marketing, and a goal was set for 2008.

During this long period it was discovered that many events needed to be included in a client's life, from marriages to births to moving a residence. These occurrences had an effect on the client's own situation or the relationship between the client and a given company, which were relevant to the marketing objectives of that company. Folksam identified more than 60 different events where the company needed to meet objectives to take care of its customers' changed needs. To gain a better perspective on these changing needs, Folksam conducted a loyalty research study of Service and Relationship Marketing focusing on customer-switching behavior.

For any company, loyalty of existing customers is important. Three things can change this loyalty, explains Staffan Magnehed, CRM Manager for Folksam in Stockholm. "The individual situation of the customer changes. This is a life event, or the consumer is influenced by another company or the expectation of a customer is not in line with his experience. These three triggers can make customers look out for another insurance company." Of these three reasons for disloyalty, the change in the individual situation of the customer is the most important one (40–45 %) to come out of the research. Folksam also divided the events into different categories (an event that depends on the agreement between Folksam and the customer or an event in the customer's life). Then the company determined whether or not an event presented a business opportunity or a threat and then defined when the company would need to know that the event took place in order to act on it as efficiently as possible. It did this for every event.

There are several examples of events that affect the relationship between a customer and Folksam. One, when Folksam is at the point of customer payment (a claim compensation), the claim manager will offer the customer a free financial advisor. They also do this when Folksam is about to disburse a capital insurance or a pension to the customer. Another example involves parents of newborn children. In Sweden, insurance companies are not allowed to do any marketing activities geared toward new parents until a child is six weeks old. Instead, Folksam offers parents free pregnancy insurance, together with an email newsletter. Additionally, Folksam has partnerships with most of Sweden's trade unions and offers their members home insurance. If a member leaves the union, Folksam contacts them and offers them an individual policy. However, perhaps the best example of Folksam's Event-Driven Marketing is its "Moving Birds" initiative.

Moving Birds is a way to describe people moving their home. Folksam is aware of the downside of these events, but they also present distinct possibilities and benefits. Magnehed says, " For Folksam when customers move house it presents an opportunity to sell, cross- sell, keep on selling or, conversely, lose the customer. So it is a business driver.

Moving Bird

Sweden is one of Europe's biggest movers in terms of numbers: 700,000 households (of a total of 4.5 million households) relocate every year in Sweden. Before using Event-Driven Marketing, relocation was the highest reason for customers to cancel their life insurance with Folksam than any other reason. Magnehed says, 'This percentage is so high for several reasons. Customers are advised by their real estate broker to go with a different insurance company. These brokers have a partnership with another insurance company, or the bank, which provided the mortgage advice with another insurance company. Or customers simply take the same insurance company the old house owner had.' According to Magnehed the time-to-market is also an important business driver. "When do we know that a customer is moving house? Is it before this event happens, during or after? Previously we knew too late, far after the customer had already moved, and had also moved insurance company. And the question is how do we get the right information to act on?"

The Swedish government knows when people are going to relocate. Sweden's postal service has a subsidiary company called Addresspoint. On the website, addresspoint.se, people who want to relocate must enter their phone number, old and new address, number of house members that are going to move, etc., in order to receive their post at their new address. Folksam arranged that on the site of Addresspoint people are asked: "Are you a client of Folksam?" This gives Folksam a message that they are going to move. If the customer is with Folksam the company knows that he is a 'moving bird.' Folksam is then made aware of 60–70 percent of such customers three to eight weeks before they move.

Solution

To reap the maximum benefits from its improved understanding of life events, Folksam planned to accelerate marketing activities. Campaigns needed to be triggered by individual customer life events and also needed to incorporate multiple steps and marketing channels—call center, email, web, and direct mail. To reach the customers who are moving house Folksam uses cross-channel methods: telemarketing, email and direct mail. The most efficient way to reach the customer is by telemarketing. Magnehed: "By phone you get to know the most about a customer because you can ask functional questions. It is a complex file. But it is done manually and takes a lot of time." First customers are called by Folksam's contact center, then they get an email, and if they still aren't reached, they receive a letter by post. It normally took a week to be able to reach the customer.

A customer file is made and put in Folksam's data warehouse. "These files are complex and in the past, compiling them was a manual job, which took a long time and much manpower—about four hours per segmentation." This is where Aprimo became involved. It was clear that new technology was needed to cope effectively with the greater demands on marketing. Aprimo could deliver this technology and insight, which accelerated the marketing productivity of Folksam and the ability of marketing to document effectively its own performance.

Moving Birds is a multichannel campaign consisting of telemarketing, direct marketing, and email marketing. Aprimo automates the whole campaign. Aprimo streamlines Folksam's campaign to simplify the process of defining and selecting data segments for marketing campaigns, improves cycle times for planning and execution and provides an all-around view of customers as they come into contact with different marketing channels. This increases speed and efficiency. Folksam's sales force system (Epiphany) can define, via customer processes, the needs before and after the moving event and the system takes care of the gap. First, they get the address of a customer from Addresspoint and send it out to all the channels: telemarketing, email and direct mail. This information is put in the data warehouse overnight; the database is updated by the next day. Folksam built a centralized data warehouse to replace many, separate, old databases. This centralized warehouse included automated file making, which consists mainly of analyzing the files and comparing the new information with the existing customer data. Is this customer really a customer of Folksam? Is it the right address? This means a lot of analysis. Now this analysis is done in three or four steps and on the same day.

According to Magnehed: "In which channel should the customer be included or what is the next step to reach the customer? Campaign Management has become much more precise by automating it. For example, if a customer sells his property, should he stay in the same campaign? Why are customers moving, what triggers them? Is there an addition to the family or did the customer lose his or her job? And if so, what is the next step Folksam should take, in which campaign program should this person be included." Since introducing Aprimo's solution and Event-Driven Marketing, Folksam is able to make more effective use of its customer knowledge. Again, Magnehed: "Identifying, analyzing and targeting customers is now much easier, as well as facilitating a more holistic view of customer histories. This all used to be done manually."

Essentially automating this process makes Folksam able to see what its customers truly need: Which insurance do they need? What campaigns should they be offered?

Implementation

The approach was to implement the Aprimo Marketing suite in order to best enable the significant change in marketing activities that Folksam was seeking. Folksam started out with Doubleclick in 2004, which was taken over by Aprimo in 2005. Magnehed: "As in every implementation period a few problems occurred but these were small. Aprimo used to work only with B-to-B companies, so they had to get used to a company that does business with consumers. With B-to-C everything happens at the moment you meet the customer. Leads don't lie down for months, so the Lead

Management is also different from B-to-B. Aprimo understood what was required and they were determined that this was something they could accomplish."

Learnings

According to Magnehed, users should be involved at an earlier stage in the implementation process because they are the ones who have to work with the new system. But more importantly they are the ones who know the bottlenecks of the old system and the old tricks with this kind of data. A shorter learning curve should be achieved. "The response of a customer to an event should be acted on right away and then the ability to proceed further should be made possible. This is inherent in Event-Driven Marketing. You have to act much faster to get the right response back from the customer. If you do this right, you can maximize the benefit from the customer potential."

Results

For Folksam there have been many benefits to using Event-Driven Marketing and Aprimo's automation. When a Folksam customer migrates to a new home, the company contacts this customer before he moves. Since August 2004 Folksam has contacted over 300,000 "Moving Birds."

Because the Aprimo solution is integrated with the Folksam data warehouse and customer management software Epiphany, they are capable of maintaining an up-to-date all around view of how individual customers are being targeted, together with their responses. Hereby, Folksam has 50 percent higher selling and a 15 percent higher Return On Investment (ROI).

The Lifetime Value went up by 11 percent. Magnehed: "This is actually quite good. The Lifetime Value is a calculated value in relation to Folksam. How long does a customer stay with Folksam and how much profit does the customer bring in for Folksam every year? This Lifetime Value went up due to the Folksam "rescue team." If the company's customer service workers discover a customer with triggers for leaving Folksam, a special team within the call center will contact the customer to make sure that he or she stays, that is, if they have a positive lifetime value prognoses. Certain parts of the segment might have a higher potential to buy advance insurances than the average. Aprimo's tool ensures that every seller has optimal customers to work with and it ensures that the best channel handles these customers based on the customers' Lifetime Value.

Benefits

Comparing Event-Driven Marketing with an ordinary campaign provides good insight into how beneficial it is.

Retention

Folksam knows more about more customers than ever before, which allows the company to conduct better campaigns now and in the future.

Interactions with customers are 25 percent longer. Magnehed: "This is not something bad, because, in addition, our administration needs have gone down. With a phone call we get to know more about the customer and his or her needs and we can focus on what we can offer to the customer. For example, does the customer need home insurance or car insurance. Hereby, 38 percent more living insurances and car insurances were sold. Moreover, Folksam had 35 percent less annulations, so loyalty went up tremendously and we can conclude that Event Driven Campaigns are effective."

Brand

The well-developed program with the Addresspoint partnership has helped Folksam's brand. Folksam now exceeds customer expectations so well that it gains several new ones simply by word-of-mouth, just by offering the telemarketing service. "Surprisingly, with Addresspoint, people started to click in the box that they were a Folksam customer when they actually were not. They were pleased with getting a call from telemarketing that they didn't expect, which had analyzed their situation to make sure that their need for security were met by good solutions. This spurred people to say they were client of Folksam and to tick the box on Addresspoint. Therefore, Folksam now has another check box if you are not customer: Do you want receive an offer from Folksam?" says Magnehed. Now, 20 percent of all the leads are from noncustomers stemming from the tick box. These noncustomers want to get advice on how they should take care of their needs for security after they move. Magnehed says: "The most important thing about a brand is would I advise a friend to use it? This [word-of-mouth] is the best and cheapest advertising you can get and works surprisingly well for Folksam."

Future

Folksam now works with 9 life events with Moving Birds the most important one. However, the company has 30 more events it wants to take on sooner or later. It is a business secret, which specific events it is talking about, but for these 21 other life events Folksam has a business case of five years. During these five years Event-Driven Marketing will evolve as well. "Before 80 percent of the campaigns were batch-driven, which meant telemarketing had to discover what insurance customers lacked and also find out with which customers we wanted to work. Only 20 percent was Event-Driven Marketing. Now we are moving towards doing it the other way around with 80 percent comprising Event-Driven Marketing," says Magnehed.

Advice

Magnehed says you have to know several things if you want to implement Event-Driven Marketing. "Who are your customers and which customers do you want? What kind of event is most important in their lives and which customers and events are most important to your business? Start simple!"

CASE 3: Product-Phase Event Driven Contact Strategies

In this book we discuss several event-driven marketing programs that rely heavily on gathering external data, like birthdays of pets and babies. But sometimes external data can be hard to find, expensive, or even nonexistent. Too many companies decide not to implement EDM because of the lack of data that can enhance their own databases. And that's a shame really, because most of them have very valuable information available in their basic transactional data. As we've seen in Chapter 3, some events are not so much linked to happenings in the life of a customer (life-phase events) as they are tied to the purchase of a product (product-phase events) or movements in the customer's lifecycle (relationship-phase events). Events can therefore be as simple as buying a product, starting the use of a service, or the nearing end of a contract. Most businesses have data on these events available in their back office systems and should be able to put it to use. This case looks at two examples of companies that have done so and have built successful customer contact strategies around such data.

Example One: How Travelers Retains Their Best Customers

Long-term loyal customers are more valuable than other customers. They generally buy more often, they buy higher priced options, they have a higher retention and referral rate, and they are less costly to serve. Any company with a database can measure the difference and prove to themselves how valuable long-term loyalty is.

But, how do you get customers to be loyal? How do you organize your company and your channels to foster and reward loyalty and to discourage the other kind of customer? Most organizations are set up for acquisition. Few are organized for retention. That is the problem. This is the story of how Travelers Property Casualty Company worked through their independent agents to build profitable relationships with their insurance customers.

Home and automobile insurance is a tough business. Because of vigorous competition and high acquisition costs, it takes several years before an automobile insurance customer can become profitable. If the customer leaves a year or two after being acquired, the company loses money. Travelers knew this, but was not able to do much about it. They work through thousands of independent agents who handle insurance for many different companies. Then Alison Bond, Director of National Agency Sales and Operations, working with Customer Development Corporation (CDC), hit on a system that really paid off. She designed a series of customized communications with insurance customers designed to build a relationship with them so that they stayed with the company for a lifetime.

From her previous experience, Alison knew that:

- All similar programs attempted at Travelers had failed.
- Customers want communications. They like to hear from their insurance agents.
- To be effective, the communication should come from a local agent, not from a national headquarters.
- A 1% increase in the customer retention rate would be worth millions of dollars in increased annual profits to Travelers.
- To get this type of increase in retention, she would have to get 15% of the agents covering 25% of the customers to buy into her plan.

To begin, she had to sell the program to the independent agents. She met a lot of resistance. They were not convinced:

- that a retention program was valuable to them.
- that direct mail would work.
- that communications could affect when or whether a customer will defect.
- that the program would have an adequate ROI.
- that Travelers knew anything about their customers that they didn't already know.

She also had to deal with CDC experience that suggested that the corporate headquarters should subsidize communications programs and with Travelers management that said "make the agents pay for everything." She followed her management's policies, and they worked very well.

What she developed was a retention program, built from a customer database, which provided a systematic program delivering high-quality communications at a very low cost. The messages were from the local agent. Despite this, she provided the agents with a turnkey operation that was simple to buy into, and required almost no work on the part of the agents themselves.

She developed five annual "touches" that varied with the type of insurance that the customer had, and the length of time that the customer had been with Travelers. The five were:

Within 60 days of renewal	An annual review of the policy
Within the 1st quarter	A thank you card
Within the 2nd quarter	A cross-sell postcard
Within the 3rd quarter	A newsletter
Within the 4th quarter	A seasonal greetings card

This is a good example of using a temporal event (see Chapter 3) like the renewal of a policy (a periodic reference) and use the number of days since this event (a relative reference) as triggers to start certain communications. In the EDM Quadrant this program would be placed in the recurring section since policy renewal is a recurring event that can be used long-term and is highly predictable.

Alison learned that for each customer, she had constantly to determine the appropriate message, the frequency of messages that the customer wanted, the desired channel, the timing of the message, and the likelihood of defection. She was armed with statistics that showed that 65% of the customers who defected never talked to an agent before they left. But 80% of the customers who talked to an agent during the year did not leave.

What do customers want from their independent agents? A Customer Retention Survey for Personal Lines Customers conducted by the Independent Insurance Agency Association showed that:

- 52% of insurance customers describe themselves as a relationship buyer.
- The customers want an annual review of the coverage of their policy.
- They are looking for an agent with integrity who has a stable business.
- They want information about their policies and coverage.

Repetition is not necessarily a bad thing, she learned. Why? Because the average customer gets 1,186 mail pieces in a year. Families get more than 5,000 pieces. The five communications from the Travelers agent need to get noticed in all of this clutter. Customers tend to remember the message from their local agent, whereas they would forget a letter from a Travelers VP.

The program was based on detailed analysis of the customer database. Alison used database data and modeling to determine who was staying and who was leaving. She determined customer profitability and lifetime value. She used these to drive her segmentation and retention strategy. Overall, she came up with a measurement of customer desirability. Now that she knew who Travelers wanted to keep and what they were worth, she could develop and execute a program to modify customer behavior through communications.

To get the agents to sign up for the program, she had to make it easy for them. She sent them a kit describing it. She gave them an 800 number to call and recommended a standard package. She provided a website for them to review the status of their program and provided regular reports. To sell agents on the program today, she shows them what happened to agents who bought the program in past years, versus those who did not. Agents who did not participate in the program lost 17.3% of their customers in the first year. Participating agents lost only 12.2%. She could prove with numbers like this that there was a good return on the agent's marketing dollar.

So what did her program accomplish? To measure her success, she compared the retention rates of participants and nonparticipants. For auto insurance customers, she was able to increase the retention rate by 5%. For property insurance, the increase was 4% (see Exhibit CS3.1).

Exhibit CS3.1. Effect of Travelers' Retention Program

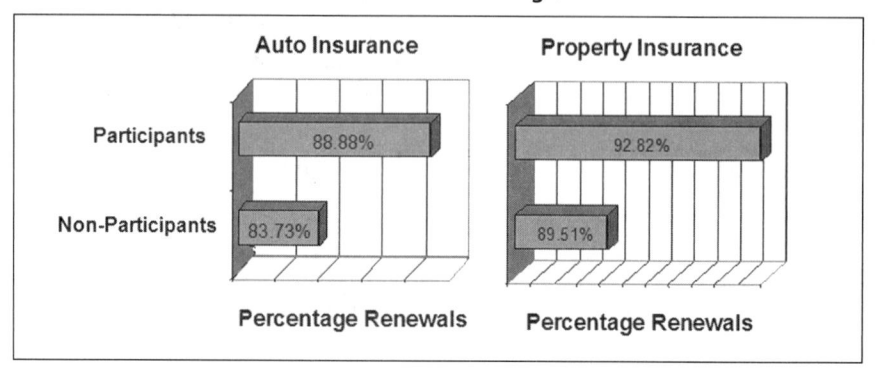

	Auto Insurance (Percentage Renewals)	Property Insurance (Percentage Renewals)
Participants	88.88%	92.82%
Non-Participants	83.73%	89.51%

Why did her program succeed whereas the others had failed?

- Her program was not centrally subsidized.
- In prior programs, the agent risked nothing.
- In her programs, the agent was risking his own money. He wanted it to succeed.

Alison's program is a great example to the rest of us of what can be done to build profitable relationships with customers. It has all the right attributes:

- It is based on a customer database with purchase and response history.
- It is based on measuring customer profitability, lifetime value, and retention.
- It creates custom communications from an agent that people know.
- It was sold to the agents, involves them, and enlists their enthusiastic participation.
- It makes customers happy, and Travelers profitable.

Later in this book, in Case Study 6, you will find another example of how a provider of financial services applied many of these same elements when developing an EDM program.

Example Two: Boosting Retention through Targeted Communications

Let's look at another case in which customers are retained through the use of event-driven communications. In Chapter 3 we already used the telecom business to illustrate the use of the EDM Quadrant. Here's an example of how a company from this sector has put EDM to use with successful result by combining it with predictive modeling.

What do you do when you have a defection rate of almost 40% and falling revenue per customer in a highly competitive industry? This was the problem faced by a large Fortune 50 telecommunications company. They knew that they had a problem, and management was willing to devote the resources to correcting the problem. They turned to a team of marketing and technology experts at KnowledgeBase Marketing, Inc., in Chapel Hill, NC.

KnowledgeBase Marketing's first step was to take 90 days to assess the situation, identifying strengths, weaknesses, opportunities, and threats. They interviewed customers and employees. During this time, they developed a cost-effective plan to solve the problem. Before KnowledgeBase Marketing arrived, the client company had a customer contact strategy that involved five event-driven communications per year:

- A welcome message
- A "how are you doing?" cross-sell piece at 90 days
- A retention piece after 6 months
- A referral piece after 9 months
- An anniversary piece after 12 months.

Everyone got the same communications. They cost an average of $7.38 per customer per year. The customer satisfaction indexes showed very high satisfaction, but 4 out of every 10 of these satisfied customers were leaving every year—most of them to the competition. One of KnowledgeBase Marketing's first steps was to build a customer *dissatisfaction* program: find out who is unhappy and work to decrease the dissatisfaction.

The company had no marketing database, so KnowledgeBase Marketing set about creating one to meet the needs of an enhanced program. They included both current customers and those who had dropped the service during the past three years. The new databases included calls to customer service and sales, and responses to marketing efforts broken into negative, positive, severe, and mild. They also appended demographic data, including age, income, education, and home value. Using this database with billing history going back for several years, they built predictive churn models that rated customers by likelihood of dropping the service.

A Risk/Revenue Matrix

Once KnowledgeBase Marketing had the database in place and had run the churn model, they developed a current value algorithm and created a risk/revenue matrix that looked like the chart in Exhibit CS3.2.

Exhibit CS3.2. Risk/Revenue Matrix

Value to Company	Likelihood to Leave		
	High	Medium	Low
High	Priority A	*Priority B*	*Priority C*
Medium	*Priority B*	*Priority B*	*Priority C*
Low	*Priority C*	*Priority C*	*Priority C*

The basic principle of this matrix is to determine which customers you should work to retain, and which you don't need to bother with. Those in Priority C were either of low value to the company or had a low probability of leaving. Don't waste money on these folks. Concentrate your resources on the valuable people (Priorities A and B) who might quit the service. This matrix reduced those customers included in the retention program from 100% to 44% — a tremendously cost-effective technique.

To determine the value of customers to the firm, they determined everyone's current lifetime value and their potential lifetime value based on their demographics. For example, a woman in her twenties might be currently using 1,200 minutes per year. Looking ahead, as her family expanded and her income grew, her potential might expand to 1,800 or more minutes per year. These calculations were built into a program that stored LTV and Potential into every customer's database record.

Now that they knew which customers they needed to retain, KnowledgeBase Marketing had to devise a communications and reward strategy designed to keep their loyalty. Essentially, the retention program was composed of four principles:

- Customer care—have good customer service and communications
- Problem detection and intervention—the dissatisfaction program
- Relationship marketing—determining the most valuable customers and building a relationship with them
- Rewards—working to modify customer behavior, and support those whose loyalty was important to the company

A Customer Contact Strategy

The relationship marketing element of the retention program consisted of a series of two-way (survey and response) communications from zero "touches" up to eight per year, depending on the priority of the customer and their personal preferences and demographics. For those people in the retention program, they devised a customer contact strategy that included the same elements the client was already mailing:

- a welcome package
- an anniversary package
- a retention questionnaire
- a cross-sell package

In addition, KnowledgeBase Marketing introduced a rewards program for a very select group of high value customers.

Once they had determined the appropriate communications, KnowledgeBase Marketing had to test various combinations to be sure that they would be effective

Exhibit CS3.3. Communications Testing Matrix

	Communication	Incentive	Components
Control	None	None	
Test A	A	A	ABCD
Test B	A	A	ABC
Test C	A	A	ACD
Test D	A	A	ABD
Test E	A	A	BCD
Test F	A	None	ABCD
Test G	A	B	ABCD
Test H	B	A	ABCD

in modifying behavior. To do this, they created a communications testing matrix, which they tested on a relatively small number of customers. Senior management agreed to test four communication components: A, B, C, and D. There were three types of incentives: none, a few free minutes, and a lot of free minutes. Each of the test programs was compared with the behavior of a control group that received no communications at all.

One of the things that the team discovered in the testing phase was that the number of minutes given as a reward had little impact on behavior. People responded just as well to a few minutes as to a lot of minutes. The rewards were scaled back to just enough to make a difference. They also learned that the creative didn't matter either. They tried two different creative approaches, one expensive and one inexpensive. Both worked equally well, so they retained the less expensive package.

With the testing completed, they were ready for the rollout, comparing always the behavior of the customers they were trying to retain with those of control groups that received no retention-building communications at all. The results were very gratifying.

The Results

In the first place, they were able to reduce churn. Overall churn went down by more than 1 percentage point annually (over 3% drop in defections), which meant a $2 million annual increase in the bottom line.

Within the target groups, churn reduction was even more dramatic. The overall rate of churn in the control group of the four priority cohorts (A and B) was 24%. Of those in these cohorts who were mailed the retention program, the churn rate was 18%; a decrease of 25%. Most of the retention packages called for a

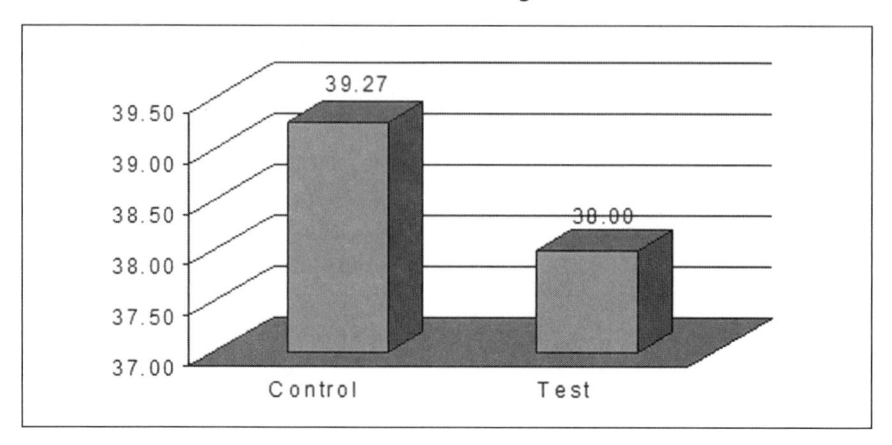

Exhibit CS3.4. The Effect of the Retention Program on Churn

[Bar chart: Control = 39.27, Test = 38.00]

response from the customer. Of those who responded positively, the churn rate was 9%; this is the same churn rate for those customers who responded *negatively* but were able to have their dissatisfaction resolved by customer service. But response was not essential to reduce churn. The churn rate of the non-responders was lower than the churn rate of the control group that received no communications.

Increased Annual Revenue

Besides reducing the churn rate, the program also had a positive impact on phone usage and revenue.

The average annual revenue from those in the retention program was 5% higher: $707 as compared to only $678 from identical people in the control group that did not receive the retention communications. The phone usage for the targeted groups also increased by 15%—from 1,300 minutes per year to 1,500 minutes per year.

Perhaps most surprising of all was the reduced cost of the communications. Previously every customer got five mailings per year for an average cost of $7.38. With the new retention program, the number of people mailed dropped by 56%. The highest value, highest risk customers received eight messages a year, while most other customers received less. The overall cost per customer of the communications, however, came way down in the third year to $1.38 because they were concentrating their messages on the 44% of the customers who were most valuable and most likely to churn.

KnowledgeBase Marketing's program shows what can be done by taking the principles of database marketing and applying them rigorously with test and control groups. To sum up what KnowledgeBase Marketing accomplished here, several key elements can be listed:

Exhibit CS3.5. The Effect of the Retention Program on Revenue

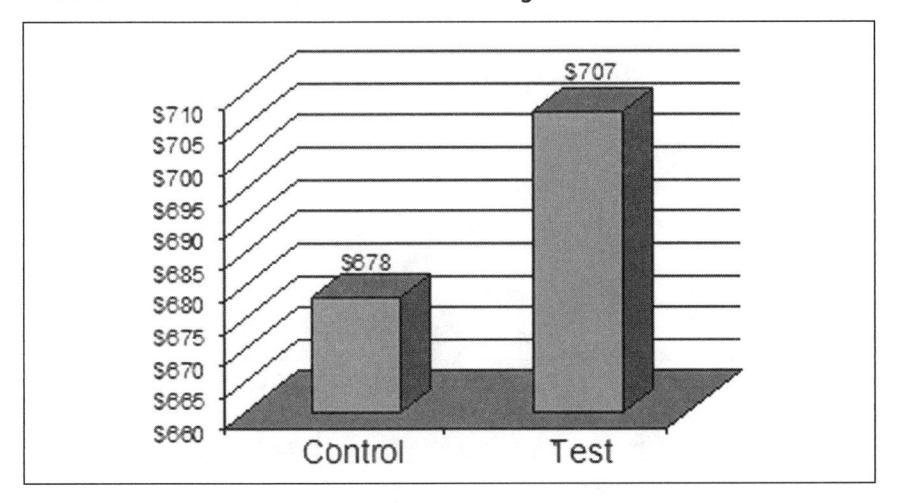

Control	Test
$678	$707

Exhibit CS3.6. The Effect of the Retention Program on Phone Usage

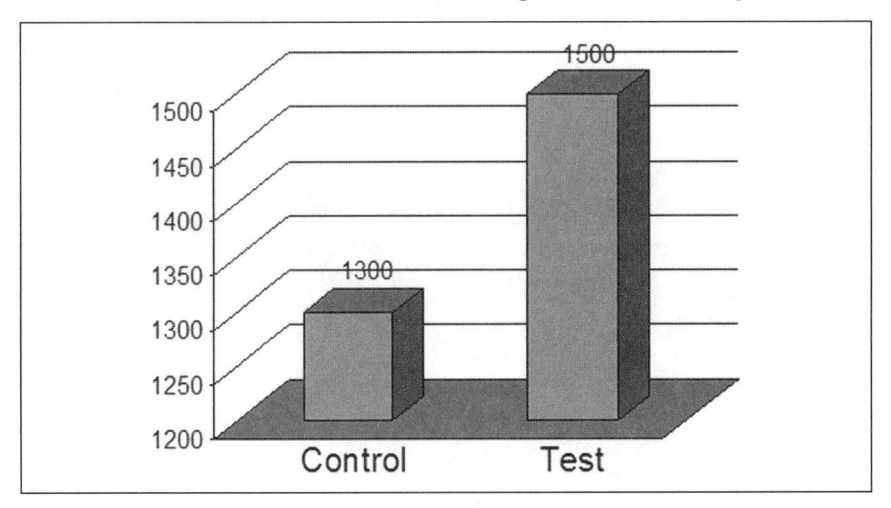

Control	Test
1300	1500

- Interviewing customers and employees to come up with a plan that would work in the circumstances.
- Building a database that contained enough data so that they could determine two things: likelihood to churn and lifetime value to the company.
- Running a churn model and determining lifetime value and potential value.
- Creating a risk/revenue matrix that was used to focus attention on only those customers who were most valuable and most likely to churn.
- Developing a winning series of event-driven communications designed to modify the behavior of the target groups.

Exhibit CS3.7. The Effect of the New Retention Program on Costs per Customer in 3 Years

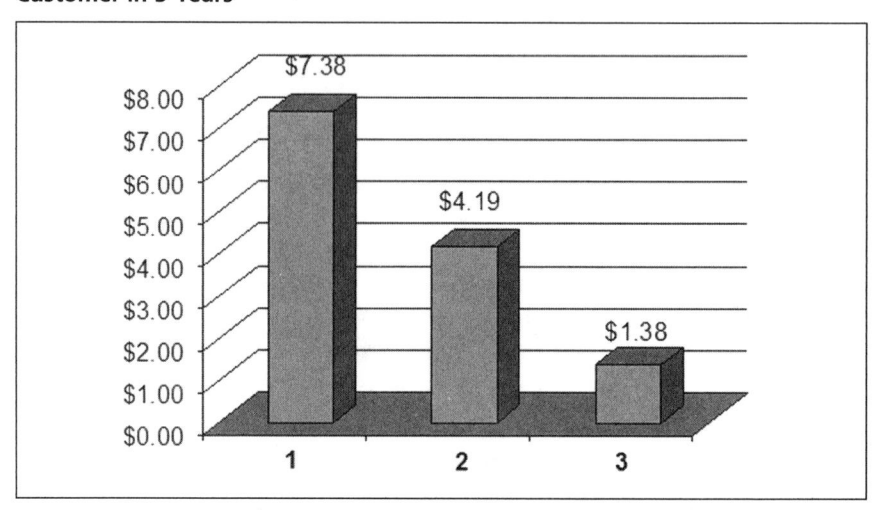

[Bar chart showing: Year 1: $7.38; Year 2: $4.19; Year 3: $1.38]

- Testing those communications against a control group so that they were sure of what they were doing.
- Measuring their success every step of the way against control groups so that they knew what was happening to churn, to usage and to revenue.

This is professional database marketing of a high order.

This case was a big inspiration to a provider of financial services when developing a product-phase-driven EDM program. At this telecommunication company they also decided to implement a risk-revenue matrix. We will elaborate on their program in Case Study 6.

5

Loyalty Versus Retention

In the previous chapters we have demonstrated how event-driven marketing is an excellent way to encourage customer retention. But that is not the same as the popular notion of customer loyalty. This chapter explains the difference between the two and why concentrating upon retention is a more realistic option than striving purely for loyalty.

The Goal of Marketing

The goal of marketing is to fundamentally shift an organization's orientation from the product to the market and the customer. This is often in conflict with corporate culture, which often is oriented to products. The way an organization views its products may be completely different from the way customers view its products. Organizations tend to focus on how their products are built, designed, or distributed. Customers are interested in benefits and how or when a product is used.

Consider the example of a company making heating, sensing, and temperature-controlling components that go into laboratory equipment and HVAC (heating, ventilation & air conditioning) systems. It's difficult to imagine a situation where all three are not used together, yet the organization had three sales groups, one for heating, one for sensing, and one for controls. Why? Because they had three plants, each making a different thing. As a result, most customers only bought one type of component from them, and the other two from competitors.

The Focus of Marketing

Ideally, the focus of marketing is homing in on what the customer desires. Two factors are important in this respect: customer loyalty and customer retention. Loyalty is a term widely used in marketing. When we read phrases like "customers must be more loyal to us," "we need to make our customers loyal," and "customer loyalty has to be rewarded," they say nothing about the customer's actual demand for the product or about whether that customer is going to keep buying—and in what volumes.

Measuring marketing performance as it relates to customer demand can be broken into three main components:

1. Market Share: Of the *total sales* within a given market, what percentage does an organization capture?
2. Customer Share/Market Penetration: Of the *total buyers* within a given market, what percentage does an organization capture?
3. Share of Wallet: Of the total spending within a given market *of a specific customer*, what percentage does an organization capture?

Certainly, retention of profitable customers is crucial to marketing success. Perfect retention alone, however, is not total loyalty: 100% retention and 100% "Share of Wallet" is perfect loyalty. So even though a customer may come back regularly, they may not be perfectly loyal.

For example, a customer that buys frequently and in large quantities is often a sophisticated buyer who maintains several sources of supply. Whether it is a factory that buys a lot of bolts, a mom with teenagers that buys a lot of milk, these "heavy users" may be good customers but not necessarily loyal.

Looking at customers by both retention and share of wallet gives a better picture of loyalty. In the heating/sensing/controlling example, customers buy only heating from the Example Company and sensing and controlling elsewhere. Would you consider them loyal? If a customer is buying one product from you regularly, but not buying another product they could buy, are they really loyal?

A manufacturer of fluid and motion control devises in North America sells four basic devices, which are valves, fittings, filters, and pumps. If customers buy one, they generally need them all. If they don't buy an entire line from one manufacturer, they must be buying from a competitor. The manufacturer found their attrition rates drop by half each time they can sell customers one more line. In their case, increasing share of wallet through cross-selling is key to improved retention.

Doing business is all about keeping customers and maximizing profit. This is why we see more and more modern marketing plans dropping the "soft" loyalty components in favor of "hard" measurements built around keeping and growing customers.

Loyal People Don't Exist, So Neither Do Loyal Customers

The dictionary defines *loyalty* as a "feeling of friendship or duty" to somebody or something but also "faithful to," which implies a reasonably unconditional and lasting mutual bond.

Are we humans a loyal species as a whole? Many people vow to remain true, but more than one in three marriages ends in divorce. And that says nothing about the quality of the rest. Every one of us can cite an example of a broken friendship. We have all done less than totally loyal things in life. Lifelong relationships can be destroyed for the sake of a few pennies in business as much as in personal life.

Few relationships these days are built upon "traditional" values like intellect, mores, and character. The most important factors now are economics and aesthetics: money and looks. Our modern Western society tends to judge everything and everyone in those terms.[1] Truth and objective value have given way to subjective taste, depth and quality to superficial appeal. "Does it appeal to you?" "Do you get along?" More and more relationships are based upon "getting along." Your looks and your lifestyle are what say the most about you, if not everything, which is why so much importance is attached to the aesthetic embellishment of the sensual body. The permanence of relationships often has an economic base. They are a "deal": What do we get out of one another?

Now we shouldn't paint too negative a picture of humanity. Just a realistic one. Loyalty is about the reasonably unconditional maintenance of a relationship for better or for worse. And loyalty is mutual. Of course, the loyalty in a customer-supplier relationship is different from that between friends or relatives. The basic notions of permanence and mutual respect are the same, though.

In the business world, we encounter the concept most often in the sense of "customer loyalty" and its inevitable derivative, the "customer loyalty program," which tends to involve a lot of fooling around with loyalty cards and points schemes. All very one-sided and supplier-led, yet these programs continue to appear—and often fail. If we kept all the cards we have ever been given, they would burst our wallets:

> You would be shocked by how disloyal you are as a customer! And that despite all those air miles, bonus cards, freebies, regular customer discounts and free tickets, and even that expensive event your supplier has just organized for you. You slap him on the shoulder, say "That was great!" and then go off and buy from his competitor. For strategic and tactical reasons. After all, it is not a good thing to put all your business eggs in one basket.
>
> —M. Hoetmer, SalesQuest.

Just as in our private lives, the trend in business relationships is towards economic and aesthetic considerations and away from traditional values. Of course, it is many years since we took out our insurance policies with a particular company just because our parents did, but as the pace with which new brands appear steps up, so does the speed with which we switch between them in search of new styles

---

[1] Borel, F. *Le vêtement incarné. Les métamorphoses du corps.* Mesnil-sur-l'Estrée.

and forms. This has long been the case in fashion, but now it applies just as much to cars and holidays, and those brands see an opportunity to penetrate markets much more quickly than in the past. You could almost say that building an image around your brand no longer matters as much as responding quickly to trends or even anticipating them. *Shaping* is a term being used more and more in this respect: You "shape" your own market.

Loyalty and Switching Costs

Certainly we can agree that customers will do whatever it is customers want to do. However, we should consider all the reasons a customer might want to keep going back to the same place, same products, or same services:

1. Switching is work. Thinking is work. Considering alternatives is work. If we don't give the customer a good reason to look elsewhere, they can use their time and mental space for other things.

2. Known good is good. Risk is bad. I know super glue will work. I know I will like Haagen-Dazs. I don't know, at least from my own experience, about a new or another product. So why risk a glue that won't hold, or ice cream I won't like? A brand is a "mark of assurance" that tells me what I will get. A good brand to a buyer reduces their risk—they know exactly what they will get every time.

3. Known buying process. A customer knows where to get it and already has a convenient way to pay for it. No account to set up, no new authorizations or delays.

These things may seem trivial, but they are not. If your house is good enough for now, would you like to move? Unless you really need more space, less space, or a different location, it hardly seems worth it. But even something as trivial as table salt is hardly worth the bother to consider. Is another brand of salt so much better it is worth the time and consideration to buy it, perhaps then to test and compare? Or would you rather just grab the usual salt and go on thinking about something else?

Switching costs often have nothing to do with products, but everything to do with relationships. Marketing has to focus on how customers interact with the product and with the organization to find ways to make it so easy and convenient it isn't worth thinking about alternatives.

Things go wrong more often than they succeed, but those companies that do succeed are the ones that respond to market and customer developments—the ones that think about more than just their image. Brands are soon exposed as too "soft" if they only work on their image and do not invest in building up a relationship with their customers in good interaction and information exchange. Only then can they develop new products and services effectively. Only then can loyalty start to outweigh direct economic principles.

Why not just say, "We don't need to know anything about you, but you can ask us anything at any time"? At least then you find out what questions the market has, which is most of what you need to know. Place an advertisement in the newspaper NOW with a telephone number that people can call with their queries. Write them down and read them carefully. For a tenth of the cost of market research, you gain a great picture of what matters to your market. And don't forget to answer the questions. Otherwise you'll be questioned about that. . . .

About Retention

According to the dictionary, *retention* means "the act of keeping something in one's possession"—a term with legal overtones But in marketing, retention refers to a supplier's desire to keep the customer.

From this definition, we can see that some of the examples given in the previous paragraph are more about retention than about loyalty. But whatever we call it, what we mean is, "I want your money."

The terms *loyalty* and *retention* tend, wrongly, to be used interchangeably.

In fact, retention is very different from loyalty. Retention is not based upon the principles of loyalty at all; rather, it is about keeping customers. All sorts of arguments can be used to do that: lower prices, better service, higher quality, faster delivery, high trade-in value, and so on. Retention counters *churn*, the number of lost customers as a percentage of the total. Particularly in the telecommunications industry, churn is now a hot topic.

What Is Churn, and What Is Its Significance?

To use a definition from the telecommunications industry, "Churn is the rate at which customers disconnect or are deactivated from their wireless service and can be voluntary or involuntary (due to nonpayment)." The churn metric is reached by taking the number of customers deactivated and dividing that by the average number of customers on the network. Churn is expressed as a monthly percentage for a given measurement period.

> A low churn rate reflects customers' satisfaction with their current service provider and that carrier's ability to attract quality customers. High churn is costly to a carrier because it signifies lost investment from acquiring a customer, lost future revenue from that customer and increased investment to acquire a new customer to replace the lost customer.
>
> —*Telecombrief*

Loyalty no longer exists. The statistics are right. Companies nowadays lose half their customers within five years, half their employees within four years and half their investors within one year. It looks as if the future will consist either of opportunistic transactions between people who do not know one another or focused, event-based ones with customers you know extremely well.

Loyalty Versus Retention

Loyalty is about consistent involvement. Customer loyalty means staying faithful to your supplier. Retention, on the other hand, is about maintaining and preserving. In marketing terms, that means turning a one-time customer into a regular customer, one who keeps on coming back. It also means turning a one-product- line customer into a customer that buys across the product range.

Loyalty is a sense of attachment to or affection for a company's people, products, or services. But what does that say about future behavior? In fact, absolutely nothing. Past results are irrelevant to the future. Loyalty is the customer's intention, after evaluating a particular service, for use again in the future. So it is an attitude and, therefore:

- It cannot be measured objectively.
- It is an unreliable predictor of customer behavior.

Do we base what we do upon past behavior or upon expected future behavior? In other words, should we reward those customers who have been very loyal in recent years or those from whom we expect a lot in the future?

"Being loyal" is a relative concept. There is a difference between "true" loyalty and "routine" loyalty (repeat purchases).

A disconnect in loyalty between marketers and customers is that marketers want customers to think or feel a certain way about a product or service, yet customers would rather not think about what brand of salt they should buy and don't care to probe their feelings about salt while pondering salt alternatives. They just do things out of habit and use the time and mental space for better things. In such a case, "thoughtful loyalty" is not what the customer wants, and "habitual loyalty" is what the marketer should hope to achieve.

Are satisfied customers loyal?[2]

Exhibit 5.1. Loyalty Versus Retention

	Loyalty	Retention
Interpretation	Scope for different interpretations	Unambiguous interpretation
Psychology	Feeling or intention	Behavior
Measurability	Not unequivocally measurable	Unequivocally measurable.
Money	No direct relationship to turnover and profit	Direct relationship to turnover and profit

---

[2] Here, "loyalty" is defined as the intention to buy again.

Exhibit 5.2. The Causes of Low Retention

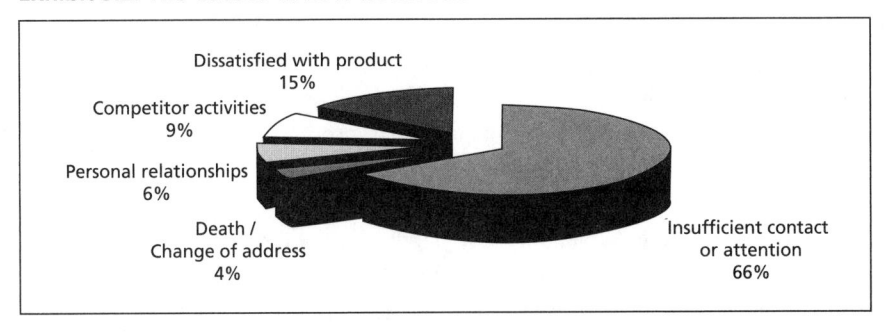

- Dissatisfied with product 15%
- Competitor activities 9%
- Personal relationships 6%
- Death / Change of address 4%
- Insufficient contact or attention 66%

- In practice, 10–15 percent of satisfied or very satisfied customers are not loyal.
- There is often little correlation between satisfaction scores and repeat buying behavior

Do loyal customers complain less?

- Customers do not complain; they go away. Those who don't complain are 10–30 percent less loyal than those who do.
- Loyal customers are probably more inclined to complain because they feel more attached to the product or service and believe that it is worth complaining since they expect the problem to be solved satisfactorily.

The reasons behind the trend towards retention programs replacing loyalty-based activities are as follows:

- They can be defined and implemented in a specific way.
- They are measurable.
- Their results, in profit terms.

Also, retention programs are usually more cost effective and efficient to carry out than loyalty programs. Often associated with CRM, loyalty requires large investments in IT and organizational development.

A lot has been said and written about CRM. As we saw in Chapter 1, it stands for *customer relationship management*, that is, managing the relationship with the customer, not managing the customer himself. All too often, it is assumed that CRM is only about "the customer," but it is not. Describe the relationship you want with your customers, and use that as the starting point for your interaction with them. That is the basis of CRM, but it is the most difficult thing to do because it involves so many parts of the organization and so many of its staff.

Seventy percent of CRM implementations fail. Psychologist Gijsbert Willenborg, who has researched consumer loyalty at the University of Groningen, believes that companies are too quick to think about relationship marketing in terms of CRM, and those that want to use relationship marketing to generate customer loyalty are too easy in their thinking about dealing with consumers. The phenomenon of relationship marketing, according to Willenborg's research, involves businesses trying to retain their customers by entering into a permanent and loyal relationship with them. But, he claims, there is actually little point in contriving marketing plans to keep consumers loyal to a particular product or service. "People are already less and less loyal in important relationships like those with their partner or employer," he writes, "let alone in commercial relationships when money comes into play." According to Willenborg, companies think too casually about how they relate to their customers. "They decide that they have to enter into relationships with customers, without bearing in mind that the customers have to join in, too."

So what is that consumer culture? If we go by broader trends, such as the consumer becoming more critical and better informed, then it involves openness and making sound arguments for people to become and remain customers. IT systems like marketing databases and analytical tools should not be used to target customers with all sorts of loyalty-based activities, but to find out why consumers start buying and carry on buying. To answer a simple question: "What do I have to do to make you happy and keep you happy?"

The consumer culture requires looking at the relationship from the customer's point of view. Consumers are benefit seeking, not product, production, or engineering focussed. The consumer culture is all about the company having an enterprising, customer-oriented attitude.

Don't Give the Customer a Reason to Leave

The only way to make sure customers stay, and stay happy, is to use a retention strategy. That means always knowing how they can be kept satisfied based upon persuasive, customer-oriented benefits—not just saying "we love you," but delivering on the promises customers want. In times like these, when we have to watch the pennies and consider every investment carefully before we make it, it has become vital to make deals with customers based upon solid arguments. Whether you are in banking or retail, it is all about reaching mutual agreement with the customer. That is why we see retention thinking and programs taking over from loyalty schemes and CRM. Communication will become more direct, telling people exactly what deal you want to strike with them.

Companies that constantly pump their promotional budgets into the same media and activities without knowing what effect it is having, companies that still think in terms of mass communication, are on the wrong track. Success lies in establishing a good relationship between direct marketing, public relations, and customer service—not in isolation but in harmony, to communicate in the right way who you are and why you want to reach what agreements with the customer.

In times like these, DM, PR, and service are an excellent combination, unlike the combination of DM and thematic mass marketing.

Not that any of this detracts from loyalty. Quite the contrary, in fact. By employing a good retention strategy whereby you keep your promises and behave as a valued partner to your customers, a "good feeling" that looks an awful lot like loyalty will form automatically: gilt-edged friendship. And that is just when CRM can work.

Loyalty and Branding

Brand thinking and brand profiling are important preconditions for loyalty. I know of only a couple of brands able to forge a kind of unconditional loyalty: Davidoff cigars, for example. But they are simply good—a strong brand with its own band of smokers, a club. This is a phenomenon you come across elsewhere, too; it is difficult to do, but giving the sense of "belonging" to a club is one of the strongest ways to generate loyalty. Once upon a time, the English aristocracy would only ever be seen driving a Rolls Royce on the road and a Land Rover off it. And everybody who wanted to be part of that elite club would spend whatever it took to acquire those products. Or take Harley-Davidson—another indestructible brand. A hundred years old, but only burdened with a marketing department for the past ten. No Hell's Angel would ride anything else. Not even if you put a gun to his head. You can count examples of loyalty that strong on the fingers of one hand.

The question, of course, is how long it can last. For years the tough and independent Harley brand has been suffering erosion from wimps who only take their bikes out of the garage for Sunday afternoon spins. It is only a question of time before brands fall. Land Rover has already lost its English shine, and Rolls Royces these days are no more than souped-up Volkswagens with an extravagant radiator grill.

Branding is fashion work. It is tied to time and place. Almost all today's powerful brands will disappear eventually. Branding is going to become a snapshot of products, customers, and offers—not the foundation of a long-term mission. As in the music industry, a lot of brands are going to be built just to make a short but effective impact.

There is less and less time for the customer to build up a relationship with a brand. Only a few "institutions" will continue to benefit from a customer loyalty strategy in their marketing; most brands will not have long enough to "bond" with their customers. Success will come to those entrepreneurs able to satisfy customer needs quickly. Larger businesses will have to deal with short product lifecycles and retention characteristics of both an emotional and a rational nature to make the right offer to the right person at the right time. At which point business development will have become a permanent process in marketing.

Organizing a Customer Retention Strategy

How do we starting working towards "retention"? First of all, by putting down on paper exactly what we want to achieve: our objectives. Retention is about solid arguments that can always be expressed numerically. For example:

- Spending a particular amount within a particular period.
- Buying a minimum number of products in one go.
- Buying a particular combination of products.
- Achieving a particular response rate for customer-oriented actions.

For more on this, see Chapter 6 on EDM and return on investment (ROI).

In recent years, many companies drifted away from their (original) primary function. A lot of effort was put into activities that are not part of the core business, often with the intention of creating loyalty and attachment to the organization as the preferred supplier, but those days are truly over! Companies that do not realize that the market, the customer, and the competitive arena have changed and that they need to adapt to that are missing the boat. Any organization, large or small, derives its right to exist solely from being the only body creating unique value by optimizing the primary function and by communicating that by stating precisely why the organization deserves a place in the market, providing arguments why somebody should become and remain a customer: clear choice, clear focus, and a clear story. In other words, not being "all things to all people" but concentrating upon one thing for a carefully chosen customer or market segment.

Survival of the Fittest

Marketing is all about survival of the fittest, by which is meant not the strongest or cleverest, but literally the "most fitting": the best adapted. The strongest and cleverest are long dead or dying.

The most successful companies are those that have adapted to customer demand, that know exactly what their customers are asking, what they need, and offer the right product in response. Do you know what your customers are asking?

6

Customer Value and Profitability

A basic operating principle: In return for costs, you get benefits. Before launching your EDM program, before even presenting your plans, you need to make some thorough calculations about how profitable it is going to be in relation to the cost of carrying it out. Specify the benefits before making the investment.

The previous chapters have talked a lot about Event-Driven Marketing and how it differs from other forms of marketing, about its technical and organizational aspects, about the difference between loyalty and retention and about the role EDM can play in all of that and about how EDM enables you to communicate with your customers at the right time in the most relevant way. But what we have hardly considered up until now is how much it all costs and what the returns are. After all, you will invest a lot of time and money in setting up an EDM program and its ongoing operational co-ordination.

On the other hand, EDM can earn you a lot of money, but the operative word here is *can*. EDM is no guarantee of fantastic results. Its success depends upon many factors.

A few years ago, when customer relationship management was all the rage, there was a fascinating and heated debate in an online CRM forum. One CRM addict was convinced that its ultimate aim was to "pamper" customers, to make them feel happy and comfortable in their contacts with the company, product, or brand. But not everyone agreed. Of course, it is important that the customers "feel good" about you, but in the end only one thing matters: making more profit. The underlying objective of CRM as a business strategy is to increase the value *of* the customer by adding value *for* the customer. And, yes, sometimes that means using technology to give customers the same feeling as when they used to buy at the little grocery shop on the corner, from the man in the brown coat who knew them by name, who knew their personal preferences by heart, and who had memorized

93

their whole family's birthdays. However, gathering personal information in order to "pamper and charm" the customer is not a requirement with CRM. Many companies are better off without it because the "cuddling costs" are so high that they outstrip any increase in returns.

An excellent example of an attempt at CRM in which the benefits never covered the costs is provided by an American manufacturer of meat seasonings that decided to identify its customers and post them a regular newsletter packed with tips on how to use its products in a whole range of dishes. Its culinary-minded customers loved the ideas and did indeed start using more of the firm's seasonings, as it had hoped. What it had not taken into consideration, though, was the fact that a jar of herbs has an incredibly long shelf life and a very low absolute margin. So the increased yields from the additional sales to the average customers fell far short of the huge cost of identifying those customers, recording them, and sending them regular direct mail. Customer pampered, at great loss for the company.

What exactly is profitability in this context? Fundamentally, it means nothing more than the returns on a program exceeding its total cost, and in most cases those are reasonably easy to establish. Total up the amount of all the invoices from suppliers involved in carrying it out, add your own regular operating costs, and you are pretty much there. But calculating the returns can often be a lot more difficult—if you do not have access to the transactional data pertaining to individual sales of your product to the end user, as is usually the case when you sell through retailers or other intermediaries. You probably do not even know who your ultimate customers actually are. And even if you do, you have no details about when and where they purchase your product. After all, the consumers buy from and pay the retailer, not you.

Even if you hold transactional data, it is not easy to calculate the returns on a marketing program. Some of them could occur in the future because the program indirectly fosters loyalty and so allows you to hold on to customers for longer (retention). Those yields cannot be seen in your current invoices.

To calculate the profitability of an EDM program effectively, you first need to understand the term *customer lifetime value* and the factors that determine it. Once you have done that, you will examine the five different methods of determining profitability, which we will discuss in this chapter. A number of cases will illustrate this. On top of this, we'll provide you with some case material so you can practice these calculations yourself.

The term *customer lifetime value* is being used more and more in in marketing and marketing plans, but this raises some critical questions. Are we all talking about the same thing, and do we understand what the term actually implies? Customer lifetime value has become a buzzword that people like to drop in order to show how customer-oriented they have become. Combine it with such expressions as *customer relationship management* and *customer intimacy,* and, so the CRM consultants assure you, you will automatically join the crème de la crème of customer-oriented organizations.

It is a shame that so few companies really pay attention to customer value (and intimacy and relationships) and take time to study the factors that influence this customer value so that they can influence it. In these times where products are becoming more and more homogeneous, propositions are looking increasingly similar and consumers have taken off their rose-colored glasses with respect to branding. More is clearly needed than just developing a product and trying to put this product on the market. The focus will have to shift from market share (the percentage of users in the market that use your product or brand) to share of wallet or customer share (the percentage of a consumer's sales that is covered by your brand or product). Or, getting what you can out of the customer.

This theory is not new. Leading database marketing experts in the US have adhered to it for at least 20 years. An increasing number of companies are scratching themselves on their heads and beginning to wonder whether this approach has a better chance of success than the classic marketing and sales approach with the difficult-to-measure results of mass media spending, sales promotion, and sales staff (and no one really knows what these people do anyway).

The Elements of Customer Value: Acquisition, Development, and Retention

Customer lifetime value can be defined as the net present value profit derived from the (average new) customer over a set period. The total value of a customer database is the sum of the individual customer lifetime values or of the values of specific customer groups.

To understand the factors that affect the value of the customer database, we can use the "customer value cube" (Exhibit 6.1). Widely used by consultants, this shows us that the full potential is a product of the maximum number of customers, the maximum profitability of each customer, and the maximum length of the relationship with them. This means that, in principle, there are three ways to maximize the value of your customer database: acquisition, development, and retention. We will briefly discuss each of these in turn.

Moving to EDM is a strategic decision that is then followed by many tactical decisions. In order for a strategy to be a success, it must be simple enough to easily understand and effectively communicated. As Einstein said, "If you cannot explain something in such as way a child can understand it, you probably don't understand it yourself."

Strategy is based on priorities, and, as someone once said, if you have more than three priorities, you probably don't have any. Fortunately for marketers, we only do three basic things we can build our strategy around:

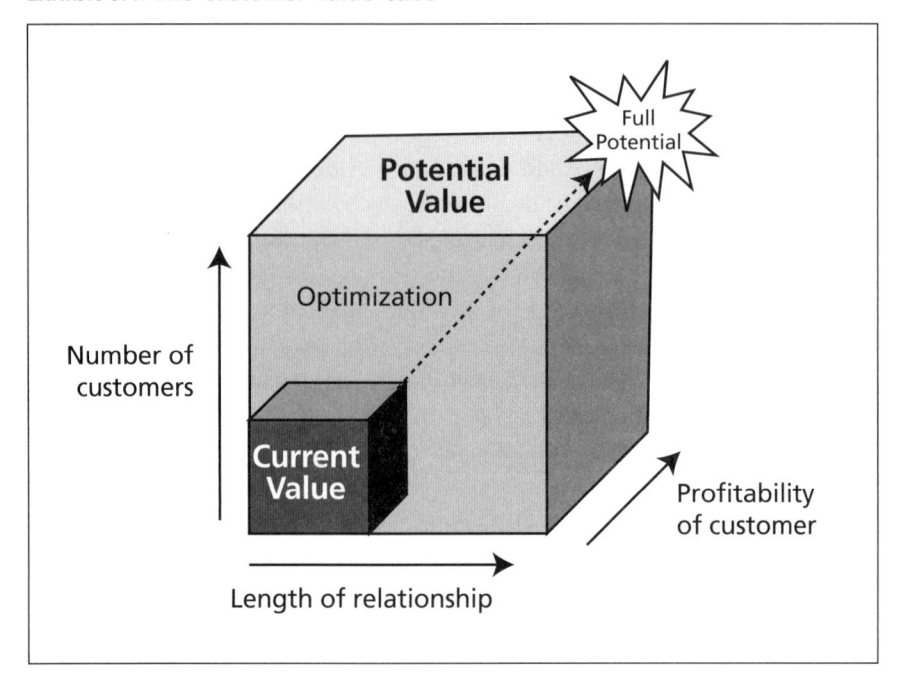

Exhibit 6.1. The Customer Value Cube

The Customer Value Cube: a three-dimensional diagram with axes "Number of customers," "Length of relationship," and "Profitability of customer," showing a small "Current Value" cube nested inside a larger "Potential Value" cube, with "Optimization" between them and "Full Potential" marked at the far corner.

- Get Customers.
- Grow Customers.
- Keep Customers.

This easily translates into three fundamental marketing activities:

- Acquiring new customers (prospecting).
- Increasing customer spend (share of wallet, cross-selling, up-selling) and/or profitability.
- Improving loyalty (retention).

These three priorities and these three fundamental marketing activities are where segmentation and target selection should start. Simple enough to be understood and communicated direct enough to drive tactics, let's look at these fundamentals in a bit more detail.

Acquisition is the recruitment of new customers. Traditionally, most companies have concentrated their efforts in this dimension of the cube without sufficient consideration of the fact that customers also have to be developed and retained. If that does not happen, the chance remains that acquired customers will not prove profitable or will soon go elsewhere.

Development is about ensuring that the customer makes the biggest possible contribution to your profits. This can be done in a number of ways:

- By making sure that the customer buys multiple products from your range (cross-selling).
- By encouraging the customer to buy products with a higher margin than those with which they were originally acquired (up-selling).
- By repeatedly selling the same product—usually a consumable—to the same customer (re-selling).
- By lowering marketing and distribution costs through the use of the most efficient and effective channels of distribution and communication for the customer.

Retention, as we have seen in Chapter 5, is about keeping customers; in other words, extending the length of the relationship with them. As such, retention is linked to re-selling. Retention is not the same as loyalty. Nevertheless, most programs focus on encouraging loyalty through a range of savings schemes, privileges, and the like. On the other hand, retention cannot be detached from acquisition, and development. If, for example, the wrong customers are acquired, retaining them can be extremely difficult. Between 15 and 20 percent of all customers are so-called "transaction buyers," who are lured primarily by low prices or special offers. They disappear as soon as the competitor makes a better offer. Retention works best with so-called "relationship buyers"; these are people who are not necessarily worried about every last penny, but instead are looking for a reliable supplier offering good and fast service.

The link with development is also important. Undoubtedly, there are customers with whom development does not bear the fruits hoped for: customers who turn out not to be profitable. In this case, the retention budget is best spent on customers who do generate profit.

By definition, Event-Driven Marketing focuses upon existing customers and hence upon development and retention. Acquisition is the domain of the event-driven prospecting programs mentioned earlier in this book. As already stated, it is a good thing that more and more businesses are devoting themselves to development and retention, but this does not mean that they can ignore acquisition completely. There will always be customers who, for whatever reason, defect to the competition or simply won't have a need for your product anymore. It is, therefore, essential to bring in new people to keep the "number of customers" face of the cube up to strength. It is important to always be aware of customer value and retention:

> When establishing the value of a business, accountants rarely consider intangibles like brands, customers, and employees. This is because their worth is difficult to express in monetary terms. On the other hand, not only is it perfectly possible to value a customer database, it is essential to do so. Marketers have for years been suffering under the yoke of account-

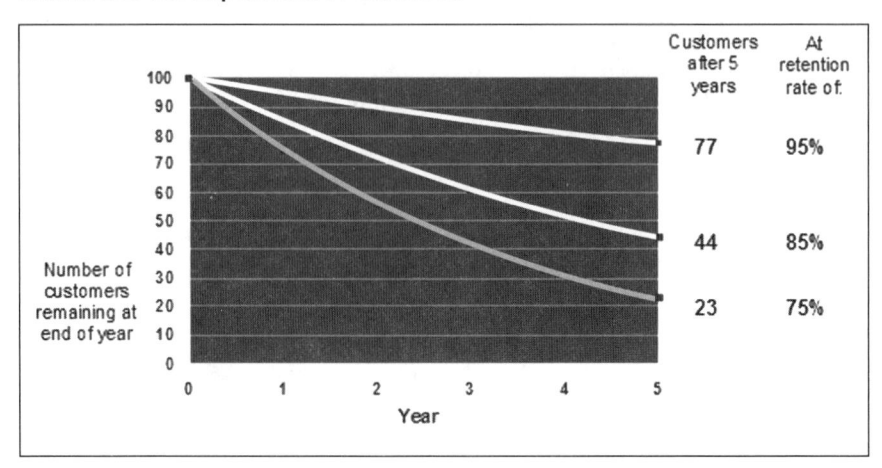

Exhibit 6.2. The Importance of Retention

	Customers after 5 years	At retention rate of:
	77	95%
	44	85%
	23	75%

ability: everything they do has to be expressed in hard figures, to several decimal places. However annoying this may be, it is quite proper. After all, their performance in branding and customer retention is a decisive contributory factor to the worth of their employer.

Ultimately, it all comes down to what the customer actually puts in the till. Now and in the future. For companies operating in a mature or saturated market, that is not so difficult to work out: all things being equal, future cash flows can be forecast based upon current ones. But companies in new markets have little or nothing to make the comparison with. Establishing the value of the business is pretty much a shot in the dark. A group of academics at Columbia University have dedicated themselves to calculating the values of the customer databases at various companies. In essence, their method is to look at what each customer spends, extrapolate that far into the future and add up the results. Applying this approach to five businesses, they discovered from the calculated customer values that an improvement of 1 percent in retention, margin or acquisition costs increased a company's value by 5, 1 or 0.5 percent respectively. A result that more than underlines the comparative value of customer retention.[1]

Five Methods for Calculating Profitability

The ability to measure ROI is essential to marketing success, and understanding the mathematics of ROI is the key to that ability. Marketers often debate what it is they should measure. Marketers that have Profit and Loss (P&L) responsibility generally are measured against a goal of contribution to profit and overhead. For

---

[1] Source: *Journal of Marketing Research*.

this reason, we will discuss marketing measures that reflect marketing's contribution to profit and overhead.

Where appropriate, we will review fixed marketing costs, such as creating or designing materials, and variable marketing costs such as printing or placement. We will not, at least not in this text, consider corporate overhead such as executive salaries and the like.

Someone once said that all work is work, so the challenge is not finding work that is fun, it is putting fun into the work you have to do. Once you see the power marketing measurement can have, you might find the fun in it!

Types of Evaluations

Understanding how effective any given marketing effort is in terms of return on investment (ROI) is a crucial goal, but there are several smaller goals marketers must reach along the way. We will look at marketing efforts in five different ways, each with it's own case study. We'll even offer some variations to each scenario, so you can get a chance to work with the formulas and really understand how they work.

The five basic measurements we will cover and the reasons we will cover each one are:

1. **Break-even:** An evaluation of the minimum response required to cover the fixed and variable costs associated directly with a given marketing offer; in other words, the point at which one offer or campaign breaks even and starts making money, usually in terms of a response in percent or revenue per contact on an individual level.

2. **Profit and Loss by Campaign:** Used to answer the question, "How much money will it make?" How much is a campaign expected to contribute to profit and overhead after all sales revenue, fixed costs associated with the campaign, and variable costs associated with the campaign are tallied?

3. **Profit and Loss for a Multistep Campaign:** A business-to-business version of P&L by Campaign, which reflects the fact that most B-to-B sales take a series of contacts over some length of time before completing.

4. **Lifetime Value:** Helps answer the question, "How much is a customer worth over time in today's dollars?" Useful for both customer management and prospecting, it is also a helpful way to compare long-term opportunities.

5. **Payback Period:** Marketers are often given a goal of recovering all the costs of a marketing effort within a specific time, or try to maximize effectiveness by minimizing the amount of time it takes to recover marketing expenses; in other words, how long it will be before a campaign is expected to make a return. For a customer acquisition campaign that might be run at an initial loss on the first sale, how long before enough repeat sales are made that acquisition becomes profitable?

Each of these basic measurements is presented in a case that demonstrates the fundamentals of what should be measured. Since businesses have such a wide variety of offers, including products, services, tangibles, and intangibles, they often benefit from some level of customization for any given business or situation.

Some of the calculation methods work better in certain circumstances than others. Break-Even and Profitability by (Multistep) Campaign work well with one-off purchases. Lifetime Value and Payback Period take future business with customers into account and work well for products that are consumed frequently. Nondurable goods such as food or clothing that is purchased relatively frequently work fine with these methods, but durable goods like houses or automobiles, where purchases are years apart, do not.

Technical Terms

In order to be consistent, we need a set of terms we can use the same way in each evaluation. They include:

- **Average Order:** They average sale amount seen (or expected) with a given marketing effort.
- **Returns, Cancellations, or Bad Debts:** Rarely do 100% of all sales go perfectly, and returns, cancellations, and bad debts give us a place to allow for sales that don't complete or that come back. Lumping returns and cancellations together is of course an oversimplification, especially in areas where returns are significant and merchandise can be resold. In addition, some merchandise that can be resold may lose some of its value. Our experience has been that people tend to ignore returns and cancels altogether if they can, so to encourage you to use it, we keep it simple in these calculations and will assume that goods returned or cancelled can be put back in stock and resold.
- **Gross and Net Sales:** Gross sales is *before* returns, cancellations, or bad debt; net sales is *after* returns, cancellations, or bad debts.
- **Cost of Goods Sold % (COGS):** COGS is often an estimate. We will use COGS, rather than profit margin, consistently. In all examples, COGS is calculated over *net* sales, assuming that goods returned or cancelled can be put back in stock and resold. For the sake of simplicity we will use the same term for services; COGS can also refer to the costs of providing a service.
- **Fulfillment Cost:** The cost of taking and making the sale. It includes bags, boxes, labels, picking and packing, shipping, etc., and normally is treated like a fixed cost per order. The DMA estimates that most direct marketers have a fulfillment cost of around $7.
- **Net Margin per Order:** The net sales minus all costs related to the order, like COGS and fulfillment. This is the actual absolute amount of profit we make per order.

- **Design of Advertising:** A fixed cost to design the first ad, letter, etc. It does not change or increase unless we revise or redesign the advertisement.
- **Printing or Placement:** Variable costs to run, print, or mail an advertisement, This is an aggregate (total) amount, not a "per unit" like cost per reach.
- **Cost per Reach:** Traditional media measure of cost per reader, viewer, or listener; e.g., a newspaper with 10,000 readers and a cost of advertising of $1,000 has a 10-cent cost per reach.
- **Response %:** Number of responders divided by number reached. If 200 readers from the newspaper with 10,000 respond, the response rate is 2% (200/10,000).
- **Cost per Name:** The sales per person reached. $ per name is generally more important than response rate. If the 200 buyers from the newspaper with 10,000 readers spend a combined $5,000, the $ per name is $0.50.
- **Time Value of Money and Risk Discount Factor:** A percentage, much like an interest rate percentage, that we use to discount future earnings because a dollar today is worth more to us than a dollar we may earn in the future.

Method 1: Understanding Break-even

The purpose of a break-even analysis is primarily a sanity check. It doesn't tell us how much we will make or how much we might lose. It simply tells us at what point we will come out ahead. By weighing performance against break-even, we can determine if marketing efforts are making sense.

Break-even is generally used to set a minimum standard for contacting customers because it often costs more to make the first sale to a prospect than is earned on that sale. The intent with prospecting is usually to gain a new customer and make money on future sales. With existing customers, however, we rarely benefit from efforts that are below break-even.

Let's look at a simple example. A restaurants that keeps a database with personal details of their customers sends out a simple direct mailing, costing $1 per piece, to couples who have their anniversary (= event) within two weeks. The mailing includes an offer for a 20% discount with every two-person meal, the offer being valid for one month.

Customers celebrating their anniversary normally spend $120 on average on a two-person meal at the restaurant. The expected response for this event-driven campaign is 10%. Costs for cancellations and bad debts are estimated at 1%. Normally the COGS is 40%, but the costs have to be increased with the incentive of the 20% discount (after all, the discount is based on the net sales, not the gross sales). The costs of reservations being $2 can be considered fulfillment costs in this case.

Exhibit 6.3 shows the calculation of the break-even point. As you can see, the break-even point for this promotion is 2.2%. Since the restaurant owner expects a 10% response he should not hesitate to run this campaign.

Exhibit 6.3. A Sample Break-Even Calculation

Category	Amount
Average Order	$120.00
Returns, Cancellations or Bad Debt	1%
Net Sales (1)	$118.80
Cost of Goods Sold %	40%
Incentive Costs (20% discount)	20%
Fulfillment Cost Per Order	$2.00
Net Margin per Order (2)	$45.52
Advertising Cost Per Reach	$1.00
Break-Even Response % (3)	2.2%
Break-Even $ per Name (4)	$2.61

The formulas explained:

1. Net Sales = Average Order − Returns, Cancellations or Bad Debt
2. Net Margin per order = Net Sales − Fulfillment Costs per Order − Cost of Goods Sold per Order − Incentive costs
3. Break-Even Response % = Advertising Cost per Reach/Net Margin per Order
4. Break-Even $ per Name = Break-Even Response Rate × Net Sales

Note that the $ per Name is really (Net Sales per Order × Break-Even Response Rate). Because marketers can often increase response by lowering prices, response rate alone is a poor indicator of success. For this reason, you will generally be more successful focusing on $ per Name than just response rate.

Note: break-even calculations as shown above only work for a one-step sale. It does not work where repeated contacts are made and is not useful for gathering names into a sales funnel.

Please refer to Appendix 2 for a case to practice this calculation.

Method 2: Understanding Profitability by Campaign

Another relatively simple calculation is calculating the direct profitability of an EDM campaign, for example, the purchase of a new car after starting a family or using the services of a removal firm just after buying a new house. These are durable goods or services that are unlikely to be bought again in the short term.

Disregarding any speculative effort made to retain these consumers so that they do buy the same product from the same provider the next time they need it, several years from now, this is a matter of achieving direct return on investment. The money spent on the marketing program has to be recouped right away.

Profitability by campaign describes how much money a campaign made (or lost) and the contribution to profit and overhead. With profitability by campaign, we are looking at customer sales in aggregate. This is different than how we looked at break-even because with a P&L by campaign we separate our fixed and variable costs out, as opposed to using a set "cost per reach."

The desire to create a P&L by campaign is obvious, but there are a few caveats. First, you need to know or estimate the average order. It is simply the net sales divided by the number of orders. That will allow you to know or estimate fulfillment cost correctly.

Design of advertising is a fixed cost. It is also a "sunk" cost that does not change based on the number of items you print or the number of times you run an advertisement. You will see from the example cases that design of advertising fixed costs often make larger marketing efforts much more practical than smaller ones.

Take the example of a removal firm that buys addresses of people who have indicated that they plan to move in the near future from a broker, at 50 cents each. Each address is sent a direct mailing, at a cost of $2 per piece. The remover's average order is $1,000 and his COGS is 70%. Of those contacted, 10% request a quote (*response rate*); this costs an average of $50 to prepare, mainly in labor costs. Three out of 10 quotes (30%) result in an actual order, which is what we call the *conversion rate*. In this example we do not take returns into consideration.

Based upon 1000 addresses contacted, the calculation is as shown in Exhibit 6.4. In the example in Exhibit 6.4, the program is indeed profitable.

When making such a calculation, be careful not to overlook certain costs. For example:

- Buying addresses.
- Print work for the mailing: letterhead, envelope, and brochure or leaflet.
- Laser printing of a personalized letter and final preparation of the mailing for posting.
- Postage (often not quoted by agencies).
- Response-handling costs, including those of a free return postage address and data entry.
- Response follow-up costs, including those of a sales visit, telephone calls, and sending additional information.
- The costs of coordinating the program.

A few words about the last two bullets: You regularly hear marketers claim that staff costs should be disregarded in ROI calculations. This, of course, is utter nonsense.

Exhibit 6.4. Profitability by Campaign Calculation

Number of Mailings	1,000
Response Rate	10%
Requests for Quotes	100
Conversion Rate	30%
Orders	30
Average Order	$1,000
Net Sales	**$30,000**
COGS%	70%
Total COGS	**$21,000**
Cost per address	$0.50
Cost per mailing	$2.00
Total Mailing Costs	**$2,500**
Cost per Quotation	$50
Total Quotation Costs	**$5,000**
Total Costs	$28,500
Profitability	**$1,500**

Note to Exhibit:
Requests for Quotes = Number of Mailings x Response Rate
Orders = Requests for Quotes x Conversion Rate
Net Sales = Orders x Average Order
Total COGS = Net Sales x COGS%
Total Mailing Costs = (cost per address + cost per mailing) x Number of Mailings
Total Quotation Costs = Requests for Quotes x Cost per Quotation
Total Costs = Total COGS + Total Mailing Costs + Total Quotation Costs
Profitability = Net Sales – Total Costs

Just like plant and premises, people represent an investment that needs to be recouped. On your profit-and-loss account, staffing costs are among those deducted from the gross margin in order to arrive at net profit. So when—unlike with general overhead costs—all or part of a person's work can be ascribed to a particular marketing program, the costs involved need to be considered part of it as well.

When you send a sales rep to follow up a customer's response to a marketing approach, that is part of the same program, so the costs of the visit should be deducted from its gross revenue. If a product manager spends 50 percent of his time coordinating the program, then you have to add 50 percent of his labor costs to the costs of the program. After all, otherwise you would only need a part-time product manager, or your full-time manager could devote half of his time to other activities.

Say the moving company in our example "forgot" that the firm's secretary spends 25 percent of her time printing the letters and another 25 percent answering telephone inquiries prompted by the mailing—activities that would otherwise have been outsourced and would have resulted in out-of-pocket expenses. It now becomes questionable whether the staffing costs involved do not outstrip the $1,500 the program originally seemed to generate. In this case, let's assume that these "hidden costs" were not forgotten but were included in the $2 per mailing.

What also needs to be considered is how many extra customers the program actually delivers. If 20 of the 30 customers in the example would have chosen us anyway, even if they had not been sent the direct mailing, then the picture changes completely. In this case we calculate only the "lift"—the additional business generated and the income from it.

We will recalculate the campaign's profitability taking the following into account:

- We don't know which 20 of the 1,000 people receiving the mailing would order anyway. The mailing volume and costs therefore do not change.
- We will deduct the net sales of the 20 regular orders from the campaign's result, only calculating the net sales over the lift of 10 orders.
- We will reduce the quotation costs with the cost for the 20 regular orders.

Now the program looks like money wasted. So . . .

- Calculate all the costs of the program, including those of the dedicated staff involved.
- Calculate only the revenues from additional orders.

Exhibit 6.5. An Example Profitability by Campaign Calculation

Mailing	1,000
Response Rate	10%
Requests for Quotes	100
Conversion Rate	30%
Orders	30
Regular Orders	20
Campaign Lift	10
Average Order	$1,000
Net Sales (lift)	**$10,000**
COGS%	70%
Total COGS	**$7,000**
Costs per address	$0.50
Cost per mailing	$2.00
Total Mailing costs	**$2,500**
Costs per Quotation	$50
Quotes for Regular Orders	20
Quotes for Lift	80
Total Quotation Costs	**$4,000**
Total Costs	$13,500
Profitability	**-$3,500**

Often the exact "lift" of a campaign is uncertain. This can result in discussions with managers who claim that business would have come without the campaign anyway. You will therefore need proof of the effect of your campaign. This can be obtained by using a control group that does not receive the mailing. If the characteristics of control group and mailed group are identical, you will be able to measure the order rate in both groups. The difference between the two is the added effect of your campaign. Note, though, that a lot of statistical requirements come into play when using control groups. This would be a chapter in itself to explain. We therefore urge you to consult other direct marketing literature about using control groups before you implement them yourself.

Please refer to Appendix 2 for a case to practice this calculation. The Appendix case demonstrates another structure for calculating profitability per campaign.

Method 3: Understanding Profitability of Multistep Campaigns

The examples presented thus far are relatively "simple," with customers either buying or not, based on a single marketing effort (whether including a quotation round or not). In business-to-consumer advertising, measuring based on a single contact method is usually appropriate.

However, in B-to-B, sales usually occur as the result of a process that requires several steps or contacts. Business prospects are acquired and then followed through a sales process over time. If a business marketer were to simply look at the first call, first contact, or first trade show meeting, they might falsely conclude that their prospecting efforts were not effective. In fact, it may take weeks or months and multiple contacts to make a first sale after an initial contact. In order to fairly determine if the overall effort is working, multistep calculation is required.

The current case assumes that the prospective customer could buy after any contact. In some cases, prospects must move through certain selling steps before they can buy at all. This is especially common when multiple decision-makers, such as engineers, purchasing agents, and approval committees, form "decision hurdles" that must be crossed before a sale can be made.

Here's an example. A provider of financial services developed a marketing campaign for a relatively complex product with a very specific target group of companies with over 20 million in annual turnover. Using the sales force to cold call on these customers would be an expensive affair because of expected low response rates, high costs of the sales force, and the aversion of the target group against cold calling. The company therefore decided to take a tiered approach in which direct mail and telemarketing follow up were used to funnel prospects to an actual visit by the sales force. This way a large group of prospects could be approached at relatively low costs, and those responding would be the ones most interested with the highest conversion. Therefore the sales force can be used more effectively since they only visit "qualified" leads.

A total of 2,000 prospects were selected from a database. The creative agency that developed the direct mailing charged $15,000 for campaign development and production management. The costs for production, printing, and fulfillment of the mail package (including postage) were $10. For the sake of simplicity we will ignore the costs of processing responses in this case. The expected response rate for the mailing is 4%.

A call centre followed up the non-response to the mailing at $7 per call. The expected extra response from this follow up is expected to be 6% of those called.

The respondents to the mailing and telemarketing calls are visited by a sales manager, an expensive communication channel at $500 per visit for this company. After the first sales call, 5% normally convert to a contract. Another 45% requests another sales call. After the second sales call another 10% converts to a contract. Another 40% of customers visited the second time request a third sales call. Of those a final 5% converts to a contract. Contracts have an average net present value profit of $50,000. (See Exhibit 6.6.) We will explain the term net present value in more detail shortly.

Imagine the following conversation:

> A: "We measured the results from the trade show, and found we didn't sell to enough new customers to justify the expense."
>
> B: "Did you gain any new prospect names you will follow up with?"
>
> A: "Yes, we gained quite a few. But we didn't make enough sales there to justify it."
>
> B: "When you mail or call prospects you gained at trade shows, is that profitable?"
>
> A: "Yes, we recontact prospects for as long as we can profitably. We always sell a few each time, it seems."
>
> B: "How long do you follow up with a prospect?"
>
> A: "We recontact all prospects for at least a year after we get their names."
>
> B: "And each segment of prospects, up to a year or so old, is generally profitable to follow up with each time?"
>
> A: "Yes, they are. We find we can contact each segment at a profit until they are about a year old, then we stop."
>
> B: "So you expect to make sales, profitably, to the names you gathered at the trade show for some time?"
>
> A: "Yes, we will."
>
> B: "Did you consider that when you said the results from the trade show didn't justify the expense?"
>
> A: "No. . . . but I see what you mean!"
>
> B: "Let's look at sales to prospects that we follow up, and see if the trade show results met your financial goals for acquisition or not."

Exhibit 6.6. A Profitability by Multistep Campaign Calculation

Campaign Design	**15,000**
Reach Mailing	2,000
Costs per Mailing	10
Total Variable Mailing Costs	**20,000**
Response% Mailing	4%
Response Mailing (1)	80
Reach Telemarketing (2)	1,920
Costs per Call	7
Total Telemarketing Costs	**13,440**
Response% Telemarketing	6%
Response Telemarketing (3)	115
Prospects to be visited (4)	195
Conversion% Sales Visit 1	5%
Conversion Sales Visit 1	9.8
Requests% Sales Visit 2	45%
Requests Sales Visit 2	88
Conversion% Sales Visit 2	10%
Conversion Sales Visit 2	8.8
Requests% Sales Visit 3	40%
Requests Sales Visit 3	35
Conversion% Sales Visit 3	5%
Conversion Sales Visit 3	1.8
Total Visits (5)	318
Cost per Sales Visit	500
Total Sales Force Costs	**159,088**
Total Campaign Costs (6)	**207,528**
Contracts (7)	20.3
Gross Margin per contract	50,000
Total Gross Margin	**1,015,040**
Result Campaign (8)	**807,512**
Return on Investment (9)	**389%**

Some of the formulas explained:
1. Response Mailing = Response% Mailing x Reach Mailing
2. Reach Telemarketing = Reach Mailing – Response Mailing
3. Response Telemarketing = Response% Telemarketing x Reach Telemarketing
4. Prospects to be Visited = Response Mailing + Response Telemarketing
5. Total Visits = Prospects to be Visited (1st time) + Requests Sales Visit 2 + Requests Sales Visit 3
6. Total Campaign Costs = Campaign Design + Total Mailing Costs + Total Telemarketing Costs + Total Sales Force Costs
7. Contracts = Conversion Sales Visit 1 + Conversion Sales Visit 2 + Conversion Sales Visit 3
8. Result Campaign = Total Gross Margin – Total Campaign Costs
9. Return on Investment = Results Campaign / Total Campaign Costs

This conversation points out another common mistake made in business-to-business: judging activity purely on the direct results without taking all of the spin-off business into account. Calculating the profitability of multistep campaigns—with the trade show simply being the first step in the process and the business resulting from following up the gathered leads the next step—works very well in these situations as well.

Please refer to Appendix 2 for a case to practice the calculation under comparable circumstances.

Method 4: Understanding Lifetime Value

Even though the profitability by multistep campaign takes the spin-off effects from marketing and sales activities into account, it doesn't really look into the future at the potential profit from these customers. Even if a (multistep) campaign is not profitable immediately and does not break-even, this doesn't automatically mean that it's a bad idea, especially in cases of consumable products, repeat purchases, and expected cross-sell opportunities the previously discussed calculation methods fail to take into account. It might well be that the initial campaign through which customers are acquired is not profitable but that initial loss is quickly recouped by near-future business. Not executing such a campaign would then be a mistake.

As shown in Exhibit 6.7, the initial contribution of a customer is normally negative because of the acquisition costs involved. In this example a customer is not profitable yet in year one and the profit of year 2 only compensates for the original acquisition costs: The customer only becomes profitable in year 3. Elements like cross-selling, referrals, and cost savings eventually add to the profitability of such a customer.

The next two calculation methods, lifetime value and payback period, take these factors into account, and they even are useful in estimating how much you can afford to spend to get a new customer and what they could be worth if contacted more effectively.

When marketers talk about customer ROI, they most generally mean lifetime value. What is special about this calculation method is that it calculates the long-term effects of marketing programs, event-driven and otherwise, taking all important factors into consideration:

- The acquisition of new customers.
- The development of existing customers so that they buy more products and/or generate higher margins.
- The retention of existing customers.
- The direct costs associated with the sales, such as the cost price of the product (COGS).
- The costs of the proposed marketing program.

Exhibit 6.7. Customer Value Structure

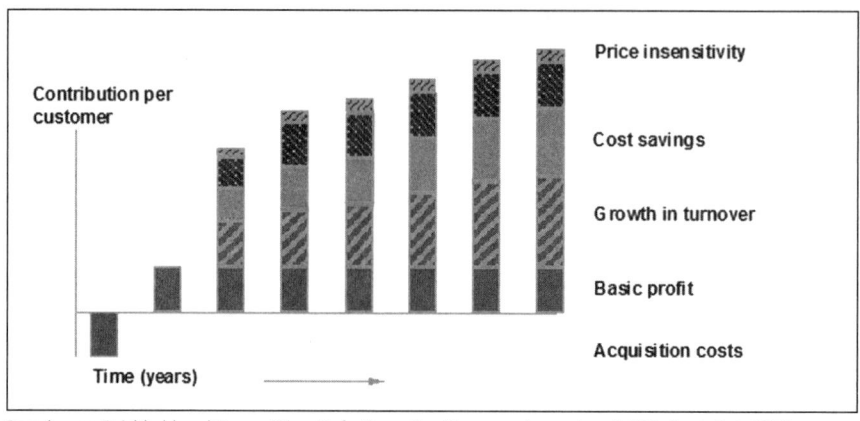

Based upon Reichheld and Sasser "Zero Defections: Quality comes to services," HBR, Sept–Oct. 1990.

Arthur Hughes explains the LTV model at length in his excellent book *Strategic Database Marketing*. Here is a brief summary.

Recently, Wal-Mart determined a typical customer might spend $200,000 over their lifetime at Wal-Mart. While interesting, that is not lifetime value. The definition of lifetime value is: the net present value of the profit derived from the average new customer over a set period. This can be calculated with the aid of a number of factors.

- **Retention rate:** The number of customers who bought in both the current period and the previous one, divided by the total number of customers in the previous period.
- **Average spend per customer:** Total turnover divided by the number of (retained) customers buying during the period of calculation.
- **Variable costs (COGS):** All of the costs that increase as the number of customers increases. These include the cost of the products or services supplied, but also the cost of customer service. Variable costs can be expressed either as an absolute figure or as a percentage of average spending.
- **Acquisition costs:** Those costs incurred in "recruiting" a new customer. These could include the costs of a marketing campaign, complete with new-customer premium, or those of a field sales team. Lifetime value was originally conceived as a tool to value existing customers. In the example we will use, it is also a useful prospecting tool. It tells us how much we can spend to acquire a new customer. To use the formula for existing customers, simply make the initial acquisition investment per customer zero. Since they are already acquired, there is no expense to acquire them!
- **Net present value and discount rate:** It is an economic principle that money you hope to make in the future is not worth as much as the cash you have in

hand right now. Profits earned 20 years from now are worth far less to us today than today's profits. A future spend of $200,000 might be worth a few thousand or even only a few hundred dollars today, depending how far into the future it may (or may not) occur. You therefore have to "discount" such future revenues. Dividing the future value by a discount rate gives you the so-called net present value. The discount rate for a particular year is calculated using the following formula:

$$D = [1 + (I \times rf)]^{n-1}$$

I represents the current rate of interest, *N* is the year in which the revenue will be made, and *RF* is the optional risk factor by which the rate of interest is multiplied. This is dependent upon such future business risks as increased interest rates and tougher competition.

Lifetime value is the cumulative net present value over the total number of years divided by the number of customers you started with in year 1. That gives you the expected yield from the average new customer over that number of years. Naturally, you can also calculate based upon weeks, months or quarters.

Hughes discusses a number of "laws" governing these factors:

- The retention rate increases over the years. This is because the longer customers buy goods or services from a company, the more loyal they tend to become.
- Spending per customer increases with time. The longer somebody remains a customer, the more likely he is to buy more—or more expensive—products. The "share of wallet" increases.
- Variable costs fall the longer somebody has been a customer because, for example, they are using less customer service support now that they've built up more experience with the company and its products.

This model makes it immediately clear which methods can be used to increase LTV.

- Improve customer retention ("keep").
- Increase the average spend per customer by customer development: cross-selling and up-selling ("build").
- Reduce the direct and marketing costs per customer (by, for example, using more efficient channels of distribution and communication for certain customers).

Lifetime value is key to prospecting effectiveness, but not in the way many marketers would expect because retention and future sales increase the value of customers. In cases where marketers cannot afford to prospect effectively, it is usually because they are doing a poor job of retaining customers. If they could increase the lifetime value of the customers they have, they could afford to spend more to acquire a customer.

Exhibit 6.8. Calculating Retention Rate

Year	2004	2005	2006	2007	2008
Customers	7,300	3,900	2,500	1,700	1,200
Retention rate	53%	64%	68%	71%	

So, the LTV model makes use of all the factors discussed using the "customer value cube"—acquisition, development, and retention—as the following example illustrates.

A manufacturer of napkins and placemats printed with customers' logos and designs discovered that it had a massive rate of customer churn. Information from the database revealed that about 7,300 customers had bought these products in 2004. Then the number of them still buying four years later was looked at. The results (Exhibit 6.8) were shocking.

From these figures it was possible to calculate the annual retention rate, by dividing the number of customers in one year by that in the previous year. These percentages are shown in Exhibit 6.8.

In the first year, the company lost almost half of all the customers it had invested so heavily in recruiting. Each acquisition required an average of between two and three visits by a sales rep at $50 each, so every order incurred some $125 in acquisition costs. The average annual order was 24 boxes, at an average price per box of $40

The variable costs (COGS) were estimated at 70 percent of turnover. This data enabled the company to compile a lifetime value model calculating the worth of the average new customer over a period of five years. For the purposes of this calculation, it was assumed that 4,500 new customers were recruited each year.

Discussion

The average number of new customers (4,500) is shown in year 1. Applying the calculated retention ratios to this figure reveals how many of them remain in years 2–5. This is a real eye-opener: because of the low retention rate, only 737 of the original 4,500 (16 percent!) are left by year 5.

The average spend per customer is 24 boxes at $40 each, or a total of $960 per annum. In this case, we assume that average spend remains constant over the years. The annual turnover from the customers recruited in year 1 can thus be calculated simply by multiplying those remaining by $960. Multiplying net sales by 70 percent arrives at the variable costs (COGS). The acquisition costs apply only in the first year, when the customers are actually recruited, and equal $125 times the number of new customers (4,500). Subtracting the costs from net sales then reveals the profit in a year.

For the sake of simplicity, it is assumed that the rate of interest plus risk is 10

Exhibit 6.9. Calculating Lifetime Value without the Marketing Program

Year	1	2	3	4	5
Customers	4,500	2,385	1,526	1,038	737
Retention rate	53%	64%	68%	71%	
Average spend per customer	960	960	960	960	960
Net Sales	4,320,000	2,289,600	1,465,344	996,434	707,468
Variable costs (COGS)	3,024,000	1,602,720	1,025,741	697,504	495,228
Acquisition costs	562,500				
Net Profit	733,500	686,880	439,603	298,930	212,240
Discount rate	1.00	1.10	1.21	1.33	1.46
NPV profit	733,500	624,436	363,308	224,591	144,963
NPV cumulative profit	733,500	1,357,936	1,721,245	1,945,835	2,090,799
Lifetime value	163	302	382	432	465

percent. The discount rates can be calculated using the formula given earlier and the net present value of the profit in any year then established by dividing the annual profit by the relevant discount rate. The cumulative profit is that in a given year plus that in all previous years.

Finally, the lifetime value in a year is arrived at by dividing that year's cumulative profit by the number of customers recruited in year 1. This calculation reveals that a total of $163 had been earned from the average new customer after one year, $302 after two years, and so on. At the end of five years, a total of $465 had been earned from the average new customer recruited in year 1.

That may look like a pretty good figure, but if all of the original customers had remained loyal, then the amount earned from each would not have been $465 but $1077 (NPV). In other words, customer leakage has cost the company $612 in pure net present value profit per average customer over five years—more than half of the potential value per average customer.

Of course, 100 percent loyalty—or rather retention—is a utopian concept. It is possible, though, to use marketing programs to staunch the loss of customers. This is where the LTV model reveals its real utility. This is because we can compile a second table incorporating the costs and estimated effects of such a marketing program and, thus, see whether it improves the situation.

First of all, the problem areas in the original situation need to be identified. Once customers had been acquired in the first place, the sales force was paying little or no attention to generating repeat orders because they were rewarded only for bringing in new customers. Nor did the marketing department have any program in place to counter the loss of customers. The company realized that there was little further contact with the customers after the first order had been received. Once the initial order was in, no effort was made to build up an ongoing relationship, so it was hardly surprising that customers started "shopping around" when their supplies were exhausted.

To overcome this, the firm devised a relatively straightforward event-driven marketing program to improve retention. When taking an order, the sales force started estimating how long it would take the customer to use up that stock. This period was linked to the delivery date to generate an estimated reorder date. The plan was to call the customer a month before that estimated date to inquire whether he still had sufficient inventory. If so, a new date for the next telephone "check" was set. If not, he could be given the opportunity to reorder then and there. And if the customer hesitated, he could be offered a quantity of free product on top of his new order (an incentive that costs less than giving a discount).

Because the company's internal telemarketing capacity was very limited, it asked a specialist firm to quote for this new activity. Its price was approximately $4 per customer contact. Assuming that an average of 1.5 calls would be needed for each, this produced an annual cost per customer of $6. On the returns side, a cautious estimate was made: an increase of 15 percent in the absolute annual retention rate as a result of the telemarketing program. In other words, 32 percent of customers would be lost after the first year instead of the current figure of 47 percent. For the sake of simplicity, that same figure of 15 percent was used in the subsequent years as well. From this, a new set of calculations was made (Exhibit 6.10).

In the first year, the returns are a little down on the old situation. This is due to the costs of the EDM program. However, the calculations show that the extra effort does pay off in the longer term. By year 2 profit is up 10 percent, and over five years no less than 34 percent more profit has been made from the average customer.

Is this a guarantee? Definitely not. The actual increase in the retention rate could be higher or lower than estimated. The competition could take steps that prevent your program from succeeding. The costs could turn out to be higher than expected. But what the calculations do show is that the program has the potential to be very profitable. Moreover, the data in the above tables can easily be worked into spreadsheets to reveal the results in a range of scenarios. It is then advisable to verify the assumptions—in this case, an average cost $6 per customer and an increase of 15 percent in the retention rate—by first trying out the program on a small sample group.

Of course, the results of such calculations can vary widely according to the type of product, the type of customer, and the margin on the product. Nevertheless, LTV calculations can always help you to forecast whether an EDM program is likely to prove profitable and is therefore worth implementing. Moreover, LTV calculations are very helpful in presenting plans to decision-makers for approval and

Exhibit 6.10. Calculating Lifetime Value with the Marketing Program

Year	1	2	3	4	5
Customers	4,500	2,385	1,526	1,038	737
Retention rate	68%	79%	83%	86%	
Average spend per customer	960	960	960	960	960
Net Sales	4,320,000	2,937,600	2,320,704	1,926,184	1,656,519
Variable costs (COGS)	3,024,000	2,056,320	1,624,493	1,348,329	1,159,563
Acquisition costs	562,500				
EDM program	27,000	18,360	14,504	12,038	10,353
Net Profit	706,500	862,920	681,707	565,817	486,602
Discount rate	1.00	1.10	1.21	1.33	1.46
NPV profit	706,500	784,473	563,394	425,106	332,356
NPV cumulative profit	706,500	1,490,973	2,054,367	2,479,473	2,811,829
Lifetime value	157	331	457	551	625
Old lifetime value	163	302	382	432	465
Increase	96%	110%	120%	128%	134%

budget allocation. A management team is always more receptive to actual figures for additional profit than to pretty pictures by a creative agency alone.

Some more examples of LTV calculations are provided in the premium pet food case in Case Study 5.

An alternative LTV calculation, using annual response rates to marketing efforts instead of retention rates, can be found in Appendix 2 among the cases to practice.

Method 5: Understanding Payback Period

Payback period describes how long it takes to recoup an initial marketing expense. While minimizing payback period is generally the goal, it does not always lead to maximizing lifetime value. The best customers or offers in the short to medium term may or may not be the best customers or offers in the longer term. So use payback period carefully or combine it with lifetime value calculations.

Things become a little more complicated when we are concerned with consumable products subject to repeat purchases. Consider, for example, baby food, diapers or pet food (see also case studies 4 and 5). In this case, a successful approach using an EDM program will normally result in a series of purchases over a given period. The time taken to recover the amount spent on the campaign now comes into play.

Take a diaper manufacturer that uses a response coupon in a magazine for

Exhibit 6.11. Calculating Payback Period

Direct Response Advert	$5,000
Response (addresses)	20,000
Processing cost per response	$1
Total Processing costs response	**$20,000**
Cost per mailing	$3
Total Mailing costs	**$60,000**
Conversion%	25%
Conversion (absolute)	5,000
Processing costs per Saving Card	$0.75
Total processing costs Saving Cards	**$3,750**
Premium cost (incl. Postage)	$5
Total Premium costs	**$25,000**
Total Program costs	$113,750
Net Margin per customer per month	$10
Total Program Net Margin per month	$50,000
Pay Back Period (months)	2.3

Note:
- Total processing costs response = response x processing costs per response
- Cost per mailing = response x cost per mailing
- Conversion (absolute) = conversion% x response
- Total processing costs Saving Cards = conversion (absolute) x processing costs per Saving Card
- Total Premium costs = conversion (absolute) x premium cost
- Total Program costs = total processing costs response + total mailing costs + total processing costs Saving Cards + total premium costs
- Total Program Net Margin per month = conversion (absolute) x net margin per customer per month
- Payback Period (months) = total program costs / total program net margin per month

young mothers to identify potential customers. The advertisement costs $5,000 and generates 20,000 names and addresses. The cost of a postage paid return envelope, data processing, and the database itself amount to $1 per address. All identified parents receive a direct mailing containing a card to which they can paste points cut from the diaper packaging. The mailing costs $3 per piece and the return postage and processing of the cards 75 cents each. One recipient in four starts buying the product and takes part in the saving scheme. For each full card sent in, they are sent a free gift worth $5 including postage and packing. Each participant generates a margin of $10 per month. The payback period calculation is shown in Exhibit 6.11.

In this example, the program recoups the investment in it after a little over two months. A payback period of this order should be relatively easy to achieve with a product like diapers. Moreover, it can be expected that use of the product will continue for several more months. Based upon these results, it is sensible to organize the promotion offer so that participants need to buy the product for a period of at least 2.3 months in order to qualify for the gift. Only after that interval does the company start earning from the customer.

Here again, though, the calculation should be based upon the lift: that is, the number of additional customers acquired as a result of the program. If all 5,000 consumers in the example would have bought this particular brand of diapers anyway, then the entire investment of $113,750 is money wasted.

What counts as an acceptable payback period depends upon a number of factors, including the nature of the product and how loyal the buyers are. If the product is one where users tend to switch brands on a regular basis or consumers are sensitive to in-store price promotions, then a very short payback period is probably desirable.

In a practical sense, payback period usually replaces lifetime value in the real world. That is because marketers are often charged with recouping their expenses within a specific time period, such as 90 days, 6 months, or one year. While lifetime value is generally the better tool over time, payback period is more useful in meeting the information demands placed on most marketers.

Appendix 2 includes a case for practicing this calculation.

Using Payback Period to Calculate Costs per Contact

When a payback period to aim for has been set by management, it can be very helpful when setting up new marketing campaigns, since it helps you to determine the maximum cost per reach at which the Payback Period can be met. Here's an example.

An advertising agency working for a financial services company presented several highly creative ideas during a pitch for a campaign. Everybody present was extremely enthusiastic with the exception of the database marketer that normally made the ROI calculations prior to executing marketing campaigns. He estimated that the proposals presented would cost at least $10 per customer reached and had serious doubts if the campaign would ever meet the maximum payback period of 10 months set by management for the given product.

He went off to do some additional calculations. The target group for the campaign were small business, mostly consisting of sole traders. Prior campaigns had shown very low conversion rates of 0.5%, which were however compensated by the high absolute volume of contracts. The average contract for a customer in this target group had a gross margin of just $50 per month. As such, the 10-month payback period set by management corresponded to a maximum investment per new contract of $500.

With a conversion rate of 0.5% the company needed to reach 200 customers to get one contract. In other words, the maximum allowed cost per reach was $2.50 ($500/$200). This amount needed to cover both the fixed and variable costs for the campaign. It was obvious that it was back to the drawing board for the advertising agency. Later they would admit that they had never taken calculations like this into account but would certainly start doing so from now on.

CASE 4: EDM in Fast-Moving Consumer Goods and Baby Care

As yet, few companies in the fast-moving consumer goods (FMCG) sector make use of EDM. But those that do often achieve excellent additional margins, mostly because of customer retention, cross-selling, and up-selling. So it is only a question of time before other FMCG businesses adopt EDM, even though by no means all fast movers are suitable for it. This case evaluates the pitfalls of event-driven marketing in fast-moving consumer goods and looks at examples from the Baby Care market for some best practices.

Wafer-Thin Margins and Low Involvement

The benefits of direct marketing in general and of database and event-driven marketing in particular are a matter of heated debate in the world of fast-moving consumer goods at the moment. The crux of the problem is that it is difficult to turn a profit from such activities. The difference between the margins on the products, and the cost of a campaign quite often is simply too great.

Say the average mailing has a response rate of 2 percent. That means that you have to send 50 pieces to sell one product. Even the simplest mailing easily costs $1 per unit in fixed and variable costs, so you need to invest $50 to sell one product. Add to that the fact that most FMCG products are worth only a few tens of cents per item in margin for the manufacturer and only a few cents for the supermarket, and you have a recipe for disaster. The 2 percent who actually start using the product are going to have to keep buying it faithfully for a very long time before the investment in their acquisition is recouped. Depending upon the product's rate of consumption, and hence the frequency of repeat purchases, that can become an absurdly long time. Achieving such a long-term customer relationship is often totally unrealistic, especially given the relatively low level of brand loyalty in many FMCG products.

A company like Procter & Gamble pays an average of $1 per contact for the use of direct mail. For the same price, it can reach 40 people through television. So a mailing has to be at least forty times as effective as a TV commercial. Unaddressed door-to-door distribution, with a sample enclosed, costs half the price of a mailing. Admittedly, you cannot directly compare the response and buying criteria of these media, but what we are comparing here are the investments in consumer contact.

There's another factor that has a negative impact upon the practicality of direct marketing for FMCG. For many of these products the consumer's interest is usually very low. They are commodities on which one does not wish to spend an awful lot of time. After all, who is really interested in engaging in a "dialog" with a brand of toilet paper or kitchen salt? This disinterest and often-resulting disloyalty to premium brands also helps to explain the steady growth of private labels, as evidenced by the huge success of discount outlets.

Conversely, the potential effectiveness of DM techniques increases considerably if a product or brand enjoys high interest. The consumer is prepared to invest more time in a message–be it mail, a direct-response commercial, or telemarketing–and so the response rate will be higher, the return on investment (ROI) better and the payback time shorter.

A pet food manufacturer sent a mailing to a large number of consumers from its database. The "conversion mailing" offered a tailored guide to the food best suited for the recipient's dog, plus one kilogram of free product in return for filling out and returning a questionnaire. The response was a stunning 27 percent, which shows that the correct offer and a high-interest topic like pets can produce amazing results. Case Study 5 will look in greater detail at the possibilities of EDM in the pet food market.

One way of increasing the consumers' interest is to talk to them about a concept or category rather than a particular product. The average woman, for instance, is very interested in "beauty care" but relatively uninterested in cotton pads to remove make-up. Grouping together products designed for the same kind of use or for the same occasion is also possible. So talk about "baby products" rather than "diapers." Giants like Procter & Gamble divide up their business units in a similar fashion: "femcare" (products like pantyliners and tampons), skin care, baby care, pet care, and so on.

One ongoing development with a major positive impact on the ability to apply DM techniques to FMCG is the rise of Internet and email marketing. These media make it a lot cheaper to communicate with the target group. One question remains, though: How do you persuade consumers to visit your web site and to register for, say, a newsletter. On the Internet, after all, we are dealing with so-called "reverse initiative." With other media people are constantly being interrupted in what they are doing. They are reading the paper, watching TV, or listening to music on the radio, and there suddenly, totally uninvited, is an advertisement. But the Internet works in a different way. Consumers themselves have to decide to visit a site, view the pages, and register for the e-newsletters. Moreover, a newsletter or email marketing message should have something useful to say. People's inboxes are already clogged with unsolicited emails (spam), so the last thing they want is more irrelevant rubbish. Ultimately, a web site without visitors and a newsletter without readers are even more expensive per "effective" contact than the traditional mass media or DM. email marketing may look affordable, but it still is results that count.

From all the above obstacles, we can distill a set of criteria with which a brand or product should really comply for its event-driven marketing to be profitable:

- A high absolute margin per product . . .
- . . . and/or a short consumption cycle (and hence quick repeat purchases).
- High involvement with the brand, the product category or the context in which the product can be placed.
- A specific and clearly defined target group.
- A message of sufficient interest to the customer.
- Low communication costs if margins are limited.

Point-of-Market Entry in Relation to EDM

Some event-driven marketing programs are based upon so-called "point of market entry." This refers to the moment at which consumers first becomes part of the market for a particular product. Such market entry suddenly makes them potential customers. (Case Studies 4 and 5 both revolve around identifying consumers at that exact point of entry.) When a woman becomes pregnant, she suddenly is interested in all kinds of products for expectant mothers, but also in items for her new baby's room. Childbirth itself is the point of market entry for baby food, diapers, and the like. Comparable points can be identified for pet food and many other product categories. Gillette in the United States, which sends young men samples of its shaving products when they reach the age of eighteen, provides another good example of point-of-entry marketing.

Retailer Versus Manufacturer

A consumer could be approached by either the retailer (supermarket or shopkeeper) or the manufacturer of a product. Although the latter can communicate as a brand, it is often the retailer that—theoretically, at least—has an advantage when it comes to EDM. That is because it has access to one thing that the manufacturer probably does not have: data about the consumer. The retailer has a direct relationship with its customers, and can use means like loyalty cards to collect information about what they buy. This is why a lengthy form normally often has to be filled out in order to obtain such a card. It asks questions designed to establish the timing of predictable events. Other events can be deduced from individual buying patterns. And combining this demographic and transaction data generates a wealth of opportunities for database and event-driven marketing.

For example, in the US, most consumers regularly shop at three or more grocery stores. They may buy some things at the local supermarket, some things at Wal-Mart, and others at Costco. By using a loyalty card to see what consumers are buying—and not buying—from them, grocers can deduce share of wallet and target customers for cross-selling offers. They can focus on additional purchases of things the consumer wasn't buying from them, increase share of wallet, and avoid offers that cannibalize margins on things consumers would buy anyway.

Some manufacturers would kill to get their hands on that sort of data. The absence of any direct financial relationship with the final consumer means that, as a rule, they have no idea which individuals are actually using their products. They have an image of their average ultimate buyer, based upon market research and the product's positioning, but no hard data. A manufacturer can only use secondary methods of gathering information to build up a customer database: coupons, reply cards, web sites and so on. But it is almost impossible for them to collect details of actual purchasing and consumption behavior. And so they have no way of telling whether or not somebody who signs up to an event-driven marketing program is actually buying the product. A pet food manufacturer solved this problem by including reply cards inside the product packaging. For every card returned one could be pretty sure that an actual user of the product sent it.

The result of these conditions is a situation in which manufacturers have little or no usable data while retailers hold huge quantities of detailed information, often so much that they cannot see the forest for the trees. Not that this automatically means that the manufacturer wants to acquire all that data from the retailer. That was part of the original thinking behind the introduction of loyalty cards in the United States, and later in Europe, but in practice most manufacturers did not know what to do with the small amount of information they already had, never mind the vast quantities of transaction data they were now being offered. And the limitations of DM in FMCG, which we have already mentioned, still applied. So, to put it mildly, not all loyalty card schemes have been a resounding success.

So far, even retailers have failed to make full use of this source. By totaling up amounts spent, they can use it to gain an idea of a consumer's value to them, but little is being done with the data at the product level. One possibility open to retailers is to group products into concepts and categories, as described above. They could then communicate effectively with consumers about "pet products" or "baby products" because they stock a wide range of relevant items, whereas an individual manufacturer usually accounts for only a limited part of the entire category. Retailers could also set up joint marketing programs in partnership with a group of producers within a category. An example might be a "baby club" involving suppliers of baby food, milk formula, diapers and baby-care products. Similar groups are imaginable in areas ranging from health food to pet food to exotic food and drink. Consider a club for Francophiles, for instance: Members would receive regular information about wines, cheeses, holidays, language courses "et beaucoup plus encore." This, too, is linkable to events. Just imagine that you could find out who travels to France and exactly when they return. When they get back, they find a free club membership on the doorstep: an opportunity to extend the holiday feeling, perfectly timed.

Even something as simple as product categories may require changes to implement EDM. A manufacturer may categorize products based on how they are made.

A retailer may categorize products based on where they are displayed. A consumer may think of and use products in an entirely different manner than sellers categorize them. Understanding the categories the way the consumer does is crucial to optimizing cross-selling offers.

There are many opportunities for cross-selling—stimulating the purchase of related products that the consumer has not yet tried or may be buying from someone else—within any particular product category. The consumer can also be encouraged to make all purchases within that category from one retailer, instead of sometimes using specialist outlets like a pet shop or chemist's. And that can considerably increase share of wallet: the proportion of the consumer's total spending on a category that goes to a specific retailer. At the end of this case study we discuss an example where Kmart in the United States boosted its sales of prenatal and baby products by 15 percent through the clever use of its database.

An additional benefit of such clustering and partnerships is that costs can be shared, and in fact will largely be borne by the manufacturers involved. That increases ROI and reduces the investment payback period, as discussed earlier in this chapter.

Event-Driven Marketing in Baby Care

Baby Care is one of the sectors where event-driven marketing (EDM) has been used successfully for many years. Using a case from The Netherlands, the rest of this case study examines why EDM is so interesting within this sector, how manufacturers obtain the requisite data through different consumer data providers, and how it has been put to use by such brands as Nutricia and Zwitsal.

Many manufacturers of Baby Care products have opted for the (partial) use of event-driven (direct) marketing instead of (full) mass media communication. They have done so because mothers of babies are relatively easy to trace, but also because of the huge volume of *waste* associated with the use of mass media, given that the majority of people who receive the message do not belong to the target group. It is of course possible to advertise around TV programs about pregnancies and young children in order to ensure better *targeting*, but costs also increase in turn. Furthermore, this mass media approach, as opposed to event-driven marketing, remains an impersonal means of communication, and its timing is not geared to the individual recipient.

Like Pet Food, which is described in detail in Case Study 5, the emotional involvement with a baby and everything that this entails is considerable. In addition, expectant parents suddenly become potential buyers for a huge range of products, varying from diapers and baby food to complete furnishings for baby's bedroom and saving accounts for later (see Exhibit CS4.1).

In the Netherlands (population: 16.5 million), for instance, some 200,000 babies are born every year. Parents spend nearly €750 m on their newborns during

Exhibit CS4.1. Spending on Baby Care Products in the Netherlands

Product category	Pregnancy (amounts in €)	Baby's first year (amounts in €)	% total
Baby's room	260	355	15%
Food		600	15%
Diapers		595	15%
Saving accounts	150	285	11%
Travel items (incl. pram)	150	195	9%
Electronic equipment (incl. baby monitor, hand blender, camera)	80	265	9%
Baby's skin care		230	6%
Mother's skin care	180	35	5%
Baby clothing	45	150	5%
Feeding aids (bottles, etc.)	35	60	2%
Maternity clothing	95		2%
Toys	10	55	2%
Nutritional supplements	40	15	1%
Books, CDs & Videos	15	25	1%
Medicine & Personal Care for baby*		35	1%
Medicine & Personal Care for mother*	20	5	1%
Total	**1,080**	**2,905**	**100%**

* where not covered by health insurance

the pregnancy and the first year[1], which works out to almost €4,000 per baby—an interesting amount, and many want their *share* of this *wallet*. Exhinit CS4.1 contains a breakdown per product category of expenditure by (expectant) parents during the pregnancy and the first year of the baby's life[2].

Incidentally, the table does not take into account the fact that half of all baby clothing, CDs, books, videos and financial schemes are not purchased by parents themselves, but are actually gifts from friends and family. For toys, that comprises two-thirds of the total. Finally, roughly one-fifth of parents seize the opportunity provided by an addition to the family to purchase another car. The amounts in the table make it absolutely clear why many manufacturers and service providers in the listed product categories try to come into contact with this target group at the right moment. They can endeavor to do so on their own or engage the help of companies that will enable them to reach the majority of expectant parents without having to do anything themselves.

This case from the Netherlands deals with two examples of initiatives whereby

---

[1] TNS NIPO 'Op de kleintjes letten'. Study on baby market expenditure commissioned by Wij Special Media.

[2] TNS NIPO 'Op de kleintjes letten'. Study on baby market expenditure commissioned by Wij Special Media.

manufacturers can establish first contact (the free gift package "The Happy Box" from WSM and the "Baby Box" from Felicitas), followed by three brief descriptions of cases in which event-driven marketing has been used successfully by manufacturers of baby products (Zwitsal and Nutricia) and retailers (Kmart). These descriptions emphasize the manner in which data is acquired and the clever timing of contacts with consumers. Where available the actual results of the campaigns have been included.

The Happy Box/The Baby Box (Wij Special Media)

The Happy Box is a product from Dutch media company Wij Special Media (WSM), a joint venture between Prénatal, a major retailer in baby products, and Wegener Direct Marketing, one of the leading direct marketing agencies and consumer data providers in the Netherlands. This package, which expectant parents can collect from the baby specialty store Prénatal during the seventh month of pregnancy, is filled with samples and offers and also includes a free annual subscription to a magazine. Participating FMCG manufacturers include Zwitsal, BiBi teats, Nutricia (baby food) and Pampers (diapers). Upon payment of a small fee, the (expectant) mother can also join the Young Parents Club, entitling them to even more discounts. Moreover, a web site also provides information-hungry parents with an additional wealth of material.

Exhibit CS4.2. The Happy Box and Baby Box by WSM

Exhibit CS4.3. WSM Communication Program

Timing	Communication
From the 3rd month of pregnancy	Free magazine through midwives
7th month of pregnancy	Special 'Birth' issue of free magazine for young parents
7th month of pregnancy	The Happy Box
Baby 1 month old	Validation by phone
Baby 3 months old	The Baby Box
Baby 11 months old	'1st Year' special issue of free magazine for young parents

The Happy Box manages to reach approximately 85% of expectant parents, making WSM the market leader with regard to the compilation of addresses of expectant and new parents. One of the methods used to obtain the names and addresses of the mother-to-be is via a magazine that is distributed for free by, among others, midwives (the use of *influencers* in this manner will reappear in the following Case Study 5). The largest address sources, however, are the Prénatal stores and the aforementioned (free) magazine that is sent to the target group by means of "controlled circulation."

After the birth of the baby, telemarketing is used to find out whether the child came into the world safe and sound and what its name is. This contact opportunity is seized to enrich information about the parents and child further. The Baby Box, which contains even more samples and product information, may then be collected three months after the birth.

Schematically, the communication program of WSM looks like the one in Exhibit CS4.3.

For several FMCG manufacturers, the Happy Box is their first contact with expectant parents. That is why they usually include reply cards with their folders and samples that can be returned, allowing the parents in question to join the manufacturer's own EDM program. The Happy Box is, therefore, a form of *Event Driven Prospecting* for them, as discussed in Chapter 1. These manufacturers also make intensive use of the database compiled by WSM. This applies to brands such as Zwitsal and Nutricia, which will be discussed in greater detail later on.

Felicitas Congratulatory Service

Felicitas is a wholly owned subsidiary of international publishing group Sanoma. It operates a multibrand EDM program for babies. Active in a number of countries, Felicitas is a "congratulatory service" that surprises people with product information and samples when they marry or are expecting a baby. This activity is linked to a number of magazines. In the Netherlands, it supplies two products: a "Pregnancy

Exhibit CS4.4. The Felicitas Media Pack

Pack" and a "Baby Pack." These can be ordered through a range of channels like coupons cut from printed advertisements. These can be used to register yourself or a friend, by post, fax, telephone, or web site. Another important source of registrations is the Felicitas hostesses who visit some 125,000 Dutch households each year between five and two months before their baby is due. About 135,000 households are also visited between two and four months after the birth. Other sources are in-store displays, consumer exhibitions and the Internet.

Registrations begin in the very earliest stages of pregnancy, with a peak in the third month. Of the 180,000 expectant mothers who register each year, more than three-quarters do so at least two months before their baby is due. Those who register are sent a special magazine and an invitation to pick up their Pregnancy Pack at any branch of personal-care chain Etos. Like the similar "Happy Box" from WSM, the Pregnancy Pack contains information and product samples. These are provided by brands offering such products as diapers, homeopathic products, baby food and baby clothing. In all, Felicitas distributes about 165,000 packs a year, reaching about 85 percent of all expectant mothers in the Netherlands. WSM achieves more or less the same reach.

Between two and four months after the birth, the army of three hundred Felicitas hostesses swings into action. They personally deliver a total of 135,000 Baby Packs to new mothers each year. These contain samples and brochures from products like baby food, shampoo, diapers, female care products, insurance, and holiday parks. The Baby Pack achieves a reach of 80 percent. As well as providing contents for the pack, manufacturers can also "hire" the hostesses to explain their products, make sales and generate leads.

Felicitas has understood that accurate data about families with babies is a goldmine. As well as supplying the packs described above, it also rents the data it

Exhibit CS4.5. Zwitsal's Communication Program

Timing	Communication
7 months pregnant	Information in the "Happy Box" of WSM
Baby 2–3 months olds	'Congratulations mailing'
Baby 3 months old	Felicitas Baby Pack
Baby 7 months old	'Bottom Mailing' with information on care for baby bottoms, including samples
Baby 13 months old	'Safety Mailing'

has collected to companies with an interest in the baby-care market. After validation by the hostesses, some 115,000 addresses are left each year. For the once-only use for a mailing of each address in the Netherlands with a new-born baby, you pay fifty cents. And that rises to one dollar if you want to use them for telemarketing activities. A real money generator.

Zwitsal

We have just looked at two organizations that facilitate communications with mothers-to-be. Now it is time to evaluate how FMCG manufacturers incorporate these opportunities into their own marketing programs. Our first example is Sara Lee's Zwitsal brand of baby skin care and hair care products.

Zwitsal has been active in the direct marketing of baby care products since the mid-1990s. In fact, the majority of its marketing budget is devoted to this form of communication. Originally, the Zwitsal EDM program was structured as shown in Exhibit CS4.5.

The so-called "bottom mailing" is timed to coincide with the start of teething (at about seven months), which can also cause babies to suffer sore bottoms. That makes it an event-driven action. As well as the specific mailings mentioned in Exhibit CS4.5, Zwitsal also operates an ongoing savings scheme.

Research shows that some 60 percent of those who received the Baby Pack subsequently buy one or more Zwitsal products. As a result, the brand added some 15,000 new mothers to its clientele each month. And, on average, a parent remained a Zwitsal customer for 18 months. With some 20 to 30 different products in its range, that is more than enough time to recoup the investment.

Some of Zwitsal's data-gathering activities have now been transferred to the Internet. Here, parents can maintain an online growth log and send digital birth announcement cards. Naturally, the site is used to collect relevant data about the parents and child for use in the EDM program.

Meanwhile, the printed direct-mail program has been cut back somewhat since its launch in 1998. Use of the Felicitas Baby Pack has ended, as has the so-called "safety mailing" while the "bottom mailing" has been moved forward to five

Exhibit CS4.6. Zwitsal Shifts EDM to the Internet

months. This shows that after implementation it's important to monitor the costs and results of your EDM program and search for more cost-effective ways of doing things. When these present themselves you will need to adapt your program, resulting in improved return on investment.

Nutricia Growth Guide

Nutricia was keen to generate authority for its Olvarit, Bambix, Nutrix, and Nutrilon baby food brands, with the ultimate aim of becoming the "preferred supplier" in this market category. To achieve that, it developed an event-driven marketing program called "Growth Guide" and a telephone-based Child Nutrition Service. Some 6.000 parents called this free 24-hour helpline every month: a quarter of the entire target group!

For our purposes, however, the more interesting of these projects is the Growth Guide: a binder that started off with a sturdy but empty folder enclosed in the "Happy Box" and over 14 months developed into a valuable work of reference consisting of more than two hundred half-page ad pages. In five phases, parents were informed about recipes, breast- and bottle-feeding, allergies and many other aspects of baby nutrition.

The folder and the first information pack were received from the Felicitas hostess in the seventh-month of pregnancy. This starter kit, entitled "The Last Lap," contained information and tips about the physical problems that could arise during the final months of pregnancy, information about good prenatal nutrition, a layette checklist, and details of childbirth traditions.

For almost the next year and a half, the parents were then led through the

Exhibit CS4.7. The Nutricia Growth Guide

world of infant nutrition. Each of the information packs sent could be added to the folder.

The reasons for waiting until three months after the birth before sending the second pack were that the parents would be too busy to use it any earlier and that that is when most questions about nutrition start to arise. In later phases, the specifically nutrition-related content of the program was deliberately reduced. The mailing to mark the baby's first birthday, for example, was devoted mainly to birthday party tips.

Each new section of the Growth Guide drew a clear distinction between informative articles and product advertising. In fact, products were only discussed in detail in the supplements, not in the main texts. The design, with its soft pastel colors and witty drawings, fitted in well with the world as new parents see it. All in all, the combination meant that the guide was highly appreciated.

Nutricia distributed a million mailings each year in support of this program: 300,000 of them in the Happy Box and Baby Pack, the rest through the free WSM magazine for young parents. A considerable investment, but certainly not a waste of money. Market research showed that appreciation for Nutricia, knowledge of its products and awareness of its brands increased massively from 1997 as a result of the program. The warm and witty design combined with the useful, informative content produced an exceptionally high appreciation rating: 8+ out of 10. Seven out of 10 mothers claimed they had learned something from the Growth Guide. It also raised interest in Nutricia's print advertising. During the life of the program,

Exhibit CS4.8. Nutricia's Growth Guide Communication Program

Timing	Communication
7 months pregnant	Folder and first information pack ('The Last Lap') via the 'Happy Box'
3 months after birth	Hostess hands over a box with product samples, the second information pack ('0–4 months') and a baby spoon in the 'Baby Box'
5 months after birth	Third information pack with the free WSM magazine ('4–6 months'), including a Mickey Mouse toothbrush.
7 months after birth	Fourth information pack with the free WSM magazine ('6–12 months')
12 months after birth	Fifth information pack with the free WSM magazine ('1–2 jaar') including a birthday card.

Exhibit CS4.9. Nutricia moves EDM from print to the Internet

recipients' familiarity with the Olvarit brand doubled from 50 to 100 percent. The overall market for baby food grew by 8 percent. Nutricia's programs doubtless made an important contribution to that.

As well as this EDM program and the Child Nutrition Service, the Nutricia media mix also included print campaigns, a savings program, exhibitions, and PR. So event-driven marketing was used not in isolation but in combination with other forms of communication.

The Growth Guide was successful and popular with its target group. Nevertheless, Nutricia has now discontinued the program in print form and–like Zwitsal–shifted part of its activities to the more cost-effective medium of the Internet.

Baby Care EDM and Retailers

In many countries, event-driven marketing in the baby care sector still remains largely confined to manufacturer programs of the type described above. It is typical of these that they are based on name and address information volunteered by the consumer. There is another way of identifying parents-to-be: by their buying patterns. In their aggregated transaction data, supermarkets and departments that use loyalty cards hold information with vast but as yet often untapped potential. We have already discussed this situation briefly. Perhaps it is some consumers' fear of sharing "privacy-sensitive" data that is holding back retailers from making full use of the information available to them. In the Netherlands, there was huge public uproar when leading supermarket chain Albert Heijn introduced its loyalty card, linked to a data warehouse. That ultimately led to a reprimand from the Dutch Data Protection Authority.

In the United States, consumers tend to be much more willing to share personal information than they are in many parts of Europe. In his excellent book *The Customer Loyalty Solution*,[3] Arthur Hughes describes how retail chain Kmart was able to use a well-thought out strategy to reach a third of all expectant mothers before their baby was born. It did this by identifying them from purchases of prenatal products like maternity wear, with statistical analysis of demographic data and purchasing history used to filter out relatives and friends buying these items as gifts. As a result, the chain became the first to make contact with this group of potential customers and to offer them special promotions.

To check the program's effectiveness, the promotional mailings were sent to a test group. Meanwhile, a control group of known expectant mothers was sent nothing. The results were astonishing: Sales increased by 15 percent despite a fall in direct mailing costs of 35 percent. The response rate from the test group was four times higher than that of the control group, and their average spend was 20 percent higher.

Baby Care Programs and the EDM Quadrant

The programs described in this case study start out as event-driven prospecting programs in the *interactive* section of the EDM Quadrant. The predictability is low since the Nutricia and Zwitsal brands do not yet have any information on expecting mothers and, therefore, have to rely on external data providers like WSM and Felicitas to offer them *explicit indicators* in the form of registrations by mothers wanting to receive the gift boxes. In the case of Kmart however, the retailer's own database provided *implicit indicators* of the event: purchase of certain products in combination with demographics.

Once a brand would add the details of a baby's birthday in their own databases

---

[3] Arthur Middleton Hughes. *The Customer Loyalty Solution* (New York: McGraw-Hill, 2003).

the further EDM programs become examples of the *recurring* section of the EDM Quadrant. The baby's date of birth can then be used as a periodic reference (for instance for a birthday mailing) or as a relative reference (in order to mail communications x months from the date of birth).

Carelessness and Risks

And, finally, one more example of how it should *not* be done. For several years, the author of this case study has received regular mailings from Baby Dump, a discounter for baby furniture and other baby-related articles. Besides the fact that this company's name is ghastly, my youngest son was already five years old at the time, and we had already been on their database for 9 years, way back when my eldest son was born. Should I notify them about the change of address the moment my sons leave home?

Proper database maintenance and the verification of parenthood is crucial in programs like the ones described in this case study. In the Netherlands alone, every year 1,200 children die after the 24th week of pregnancy. Although this may be considered a small percentage (0.6%), that is irrelevant for the parents concerned. And then we have not mentioned the miscarriages that can occur during the 24-week period. Receiving all kinds of offers by mail or via hostesses at the door is the last thing such parents want, and can often be a painful reminder of what happened. Always ensure, therefore, that you have access to properly verified data in these EDM programs. Smart and cost-efficient methods can be used, by the way, to verify data, such as by asking expectant parents to send a birth announcement card in exchange for an incentive. This spares many parents a considerable amount of unnecessary pain. Decency is essential in this respect. Never forget that you are making a "deal" with parents. Of course, you want to earn money, but supply and demand must be harmonized properly. Even small giveaways and free gifts can generate a lot of goodwill.

CASE 5: Event-Driven Marketing for Premium Pet Food

In Case 4, we saw what makes the baby care market so interesting: It has an enormous market value, but, expressed in purely monetary terms, the pet care market in many countries is many times bigger than that of baby care. And consumer involvement is almost as high. Moreover, the lifecycle of the pet care customer is much longer than that of the baby care customer. A baby, after all, soon becomes a toddler, but a dog or cat can easily live 10 to 15 years or more. US pet owners spend an annual average of $1,425 per dog and $990 per cat[1]. Roughly one-third of pet care spending is on food, making it another interesting market to concentrate on.

An Introduction to the World of Premium Pet Food

If the statistics are to be believed, then there is a chance of about one in three that you have a dog and/or cat at home. Yet it is much less likely that you are familiar with the leading brands of premium pet food (PPF). These high-quality products are sold solely through specialist pet shops and some vets, where only a quarter of pet owners buy their food.

Whereas the European supermarket shelves are dominated by brands as Pedigree, Frolic, and Friskies for dogs, and Whiskas, Felix, and Sheba for cats, the picture in pet shops is very different. Brands like Royal Canin, Hills, Proplan, Iams, and Eukanuba are much more prominent there. One of the main reasons for choosing this form of selective distribution for PPF is that the wide range of expensive products—with different varieties for each life phase, size of animal, and health condition—requires professional accompanying advice. Since the average shelf filler at your local supermarket can do no more than point you to the right aisle for pet food, the manufacturers of PPF have decided to put their trust in the expertise of vets and pet shop owners to help the caring consumer with the professional advice they need.

In general, it can be assumed that the quality of these premium brands is better than that of the average supermarket product. Certainly, their properties are tailored to the individual requirements of various kinds of cats and dogs. A puppy's nutritional needs are very different from those of an elderly dog, and those of a hyperactive Chihuahua very different from those of an overweight Great Dane. PPFs are considerably more expensive than everyday brands—and not just because the cost price of the product itself is higher. The premium also helps generate sufficient margins to be able to invest in the individual customer. These margins, combined with the high-involvement nature of anything to do

---

[1] Source: 2007–2008 APPA National Pet Owners Survey

Exhibit CS5.1. The Smile Theory

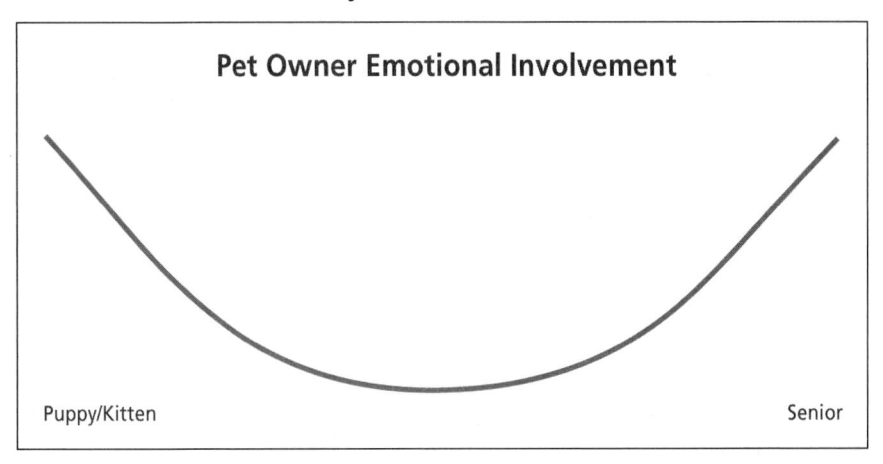

```
              Pet Owner Emotional Involvement
```

[Curve showing involvement high at Puppy/Kitten stage, dipping low in middle, rising again at Senior stage]

Puppy/Kitten   Senior

with pets and the excellent opportunities to exploit events, make PPF an EDM market par excellence.

PPF brands' programs usually take the dog or cat rather than the product as their starting point, using specific events in the animal's life as triggers for communications that often have a scientific edge to them. That makes those messages many times more relevant to the recipient than the equivalents from supermarket products.

The Emotional Involvement Curve and Influencer Marketing

Two concepts are crucial in understanding the approach to EDM used in pet food: "influencer marketing" and the "emotional involvement curve." The latter is based upon the theory that an owner's interest in his pet is greatest when it is young. The animal receives lots of attention, the best food, and plenty of fun toys, and it is taken to the vet on a regular basis. As the pet grows up, that interest wanes somewhat; it becomes part of the family but has to make do with rather less attention. At this point, many owners switch to cheaper brands of food, and the vet is only seen for the occasional check-up. Eventually, however, as the cat or dog grows older and its age starts to show, interest picks up again. The vet's becomes a regular destination once again, and the owner is happy to invest in special diets if he can help extend the animal's life or at least improve the quality of that life. Known as the "smile theory," this concept is illustrated in the Exhibit CS5.1.

In 1998, Willem Smit of Erasmus University in Rotterdam published a comparable model[2] that, with slight modifications, is shown in Exhibit CS5.2, which reveals the phases in the "pet lifecycle" and which products come to the fore in each.

---

[2] Willem Smit, Winkelpret met je pet ("Shopping pleasure with your pet"). In: Tijdschrift voor Marketing, October 1998.

Exhibit CS5.2. The Pet Lifecycle

Purchase	Pet ownership							Farewell
	Feeding and health	Pampering and play	Raising	Outward appearance	Holiday accommodation	Medical treatment		Cremation/ Burial
Choice of animal/ breed	Food, Vaccinations	Pet products	Training	Groomer	Kennels/ cattery	Vets, diets	Pet funeral

What all this means is that the pet owner is most receptive to PPF in the early and late stages of life. Investment in a consumer, however, is easier to recoup when you focus upon puppies and kittens, since there is a much smaller chance that the owner of an older pet will carry on using the product for a very long time, at least for that specific animal. So, most EDM activities by PPF manufacturers focus on people with the youngest possible animals.

The second concept applied in this area is Influencer Marketing. This is based upon the idea that consumers allow themselves to be guided in their purchases by authorities in the field concerned. When it comes to high-involvement products, a consumer will actively seek out information. In the case of cat and dog food, the principle authorities are the breeder from whom they buy the animal, their vet, the specialist pet shop, and friends or acquaintances with pets of their own. The last of these categories is very difficult to pin down, but the others are relatively easy to identify and to recruit as participants in influencer marketing programs. These are designed to create a preference for the product in question on the part of the influencer, so that he will then recommend it to others. This is usually done by allowing the influencer to test the product free of charge, so that he can experience its benefits, and by rewarding him for actually recommending it.

The PPF manufacturers use influencer marketing on all three fronts—pet shops, vets, and breeders—in an effort to press home as early as possible to new puppy and kitten owners that theirs is the product to use. And where they can, they try to coordinate the advice coming from the three sources. In practice, though, that can be extremely difficult since each manufacturer claims part of the influencer "universe." Pedigree Advance is in a strong position with breeders, for example, whereas Hills tends to be preferred by vets.

Some manufacturers also try to collect consumer data for follow up activities through these influencer programs. In the next section we look more closely at one way of doing this, so-called "breeder clubs."

Point-of-Market Entry: Breeders as a Source of Data

As mentioned the PPF should be considered high-end products, targeted at a high-spending niche. This makes breeders an excellent channel to get into contact with

Exhibit CS5.3. Examples of "Puppy Packs"

the target group. After all, consumers willing to spend hundreds of dollars on a pet (that is often pedigreed) will also be more willing to spend the extra dollar on superior food for their precious purchase. In most countries the percentage of pets bought through a breeder represents a minority, but the profile of the customer fits the buyers of PPF much better than the average pet owner. But that's not the only reason why breeders are so interesting. The aspect of timing is as important.

If you are the first brand a potential customer comes across, and that encounter is coupled with a positive recommendation from an authority, then there is a very good chance that the prospect will actually become a customer. In PPF, the use of influencer marketing and the emotional involvement curve are combined in the form of exclusive "clubs" set up by manufacturers for breeders of cats and dogs. Membership offers a range of benefits: cheap or even free pet food, premiums, merchandise, the chance to be the first to try out new products, receive sponsoring at cat and dog shows and free newsletters.

The most important element for the manufacturer, however, is the so-called "trial pack": a box containing product samples, brochures, discount coupons and other items (see Exhibit CS5.3), which the breeders give away to their customers, together with a product recommendation, each time they sell an animal. Members of a breeders club can usually obtain these packs for free by sending the manufacturer a reply card each time a litter is born. In many cases, they also receive a reward in the form of free food for submitting buyers' names and addresses together with details of the puppy or kitten they have sold these people. As we shall see, this data is vital to the further conduct of the EDM program. The first event has already taken place, though. The birth of the litter (event) is identified through the reply card sent in by the breeder (indicator) and results in the trial packs being distributed (action).

This has proven to be a very successful approach. One brand reports that about half of all the consumers who receive its trial pack actually buy the concerned brand over a long period: a conversion rate of 50 percent. But the danger that consumers will switch brand is always present and only increases as their emotional involvement begins to wane. They could even abandon PPF brands altogether in favor of the convenience of picking their pet food off the supermarket shelf together with the rest of their weekly groceries. To combat this, the focus of the EDM program now shifts from the acquisition of new customers to the retention of existing ones.

The Retention Program

The retention phase of the EDM programs operated by PPF manufacturers is designed to ensure that consumers who have chosen a particular brand carry on buying it even after their puppy or kitten has reached adulthood. The trick now is to keep the customers loyal to your brand for many years to come, right into their pet's later years when you can recommend that they switch to your special food for "seniors."

Price and convenience are the most important factors making pet owners switch from a PPF brand to a grocery brand. The goal, therefore, is to reinforce their decision to use the PPF brand and stress the fact that using this superior quality product is well worth the extra time involved to buy it (at a pet shop instead of the supermarket) and the extra dollars the pet owner has to cough up.

EDM programs generally work well here because of the product's relevance. And the more relevant the communications are to their recipient, the greater their impact will be. In the case of pets, though, the content is as important as the timing. Dogs, for example, come in all shapes and sizes—each with its own lifecycle. Exhibt CS5.4 shows how these can be broken down in broad terms.

The exhibit shows that smaller dogs reach adulthood earlier and old age later than bigger ones. For each of the cells in the table, most PPF brands have developed one or more distinct products. The timing and content of EDM communications—recommending a specific product, for example—are thus determined by two factors: the dog's age and its size. This is why breeders are asked to submit the dog's date of birth and its breed when they register their customers' data.

Enter these two facts into the database, together with the owner's name and address, and you have the basic information needed for the various communication sets that make up the EDM program. A specific set of materials, such as a

Exhibit CS5.4. Dog Lifecycles by Breed Size

Size of breed	Puppy phase	Adult phase	Senior phase
Small	0–8 months	8 months–8 years	From 8 years onwards
Medium	0–12 months	1–7 years	From 7 years onwards
Large	0–15 months	15 months–6 years	From 6 years onwards

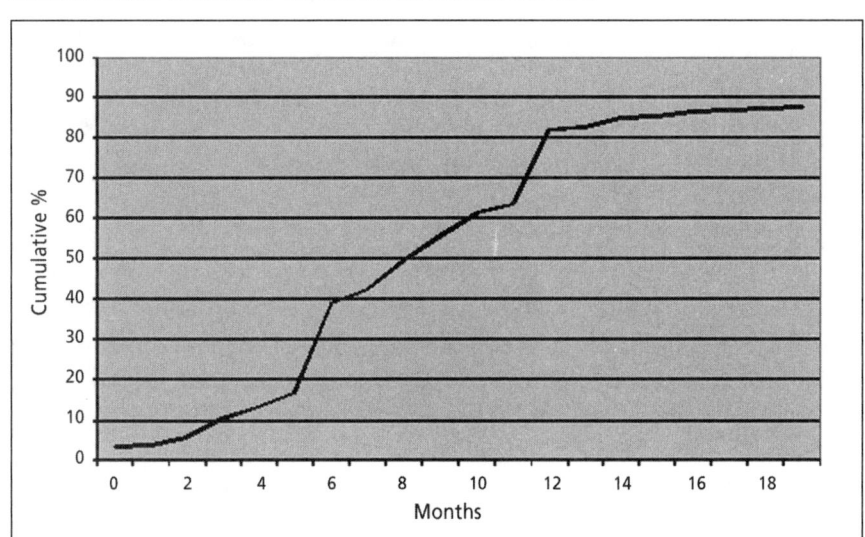

Exhibit CS5.5. Consumer Transition to Adult Pet Food

brochure about caring for older dogs, can be sent together with a variable copy letter at the moment the animal "jumps" from one cell (life phase) to the next.

Using the data in the exhibit, you can send the owner of a little Yorkshire terrier a letter when it reaches the age of eight months. In this letter you recommend a change to your adult food for small dogs and enclose a discount coupon for the first purchase. These coupons can also be used as a source of information, to track whether or not the consumer has indeed started buying the product. In all, the exhibit table can be translated into nine different communication sets, which lead the owners by the hand through each moment of transition in their dog's life, from puppy to adult to senior.

Unfortunately it isn't quite that simple . . . One PPF manufacturer developed just such a program based upon these principles, but it made one mistake. It forgot to think from the customer's point of view, about how the buyer treats the products. Its brand managers thought that the consumers would read and follow the instructions on the bag and automatically change over to the adult food at the recommended age. This, of course, turned out to be a classic example of "Marketing Myopia" we discussed earlier in this book. Most pet owners don't actually read all the details on the packaging, instead basing their choices on their own perception. As soon as their animal seemed to stop growing, they would start feeding it adult food—usually another brand. As a result, about half the customers acquired through influencer marketing were lost before the brand had even communicated with them.

The database marketer responsible for organizing this manufacturer's retention program decided to survey dog owners to find out when they actually change

Exhibit CS5.6. Retention Program Timetable

	Registration	5 months	8 months	12 months	15 months
Small	Welcome mailing	Growth mailing 1	Transition mailing		
Medium	Welcome mailing	Growth mailing 1	Growth mailing 2	Transition mailing	
Large	Welcome mailing	Growth mailing 1	Growth mailing 2	Growth mailing 3	Transition mailing

over from puppy food to the adult variety. That survey confirmed the misconception. By the time the first mailing was sent out, some 80 percent of consumers had already made the switch (see Exhibit CS5.5). In most cases, then, the advice that this "transition mailing" provided about adult food had missed the boat. What was needed were additional communications at an earlier stage, explaining to recipients that their dog was still growing and so should be kept on puppy food for the time being, until they received advice to switch products.

During the puppy phase, a series of communication moments now culminate with the transition mailing on the changeover to adult food (Exhibit CS 5.6). A second transition takes place when the dog enters the senior phase. During the longer adult phase between these two transitions, contact with the customer can be maintained at a range of communication moments, some event-driven (e.g., when health problems are identified through data gathered on reply cards or through call center contact) and some promotion-driven (like the launch of a relevant new product).

This resulted in a very comprehensive program including at least three mailings during the puppy phase (see Exhibit CS5.6). Both the letters sent and the brochures enclosed varied according to the dog's size and age, in order to correspond as closely as possible with the owner's situation. Given the fact that EDM programs are cyclical, not periodic, in nature, a minimum of nine selections had to be made from the database of pet owners each month, for the nine different mailings. And on top of that there were also the mailings to breeders and to the owners of dogs in the adult and senior phases. As you will understand, all this resulted in a wide variety of materials and procedures which had to be carefully coordinated and managed—in some cases, with the assistance of outside professional service providers.

Summary: Events, Triggers and Actions

The point-of-entry and retention programs are summarized in Exhibit CS5.7.

As well as the event-driven communications, more straightforward DM tactics are also used to stay in touch with the customer. These can include free sponsored magazines, mailings announcing new products, direct response campaigns, savings

Exhibit CS5.7. Events, Triggers, and Actions

Event	Indicator/Trigger	Action
Birth of the litter.	Breeder requests trial packs through reply cards.	Packs are assembled and sent to breeder.
Breeder sells puppies/kittens.	Breeder hands out the trial packs and sends in registration form with pet and buyer details.	Consumer is recorded in the database. Breeder is rewarded. Introductory mailing to the consumer.
Inclination to change over to adult food.	Age = six months (Repeat possible with larger breeds).	Informative mailing, possibly including coupon or premium.
Pet reaches adulthood.	Age = 10, 12 or 18 months (according to breed).	Transition mailing, including coupon for trial of adult food.
Various events during adulthood (eg., pet's birthday, illness, skin/coat problems).	Various triggers (reply cards, contact with customer service, savings schemes, etc.).	Various actions, according to event and trigger.
Pet reaches senior phase.	Age = 6, 7 or 8 years (according to breed).	Transition mailing, including coupon for trial of senior food.

plans, and so on. Even though such activities are not triggered by specific events, they should still be used to check and enrich the information held in the database. That can lead to interesting new events being identified. For instance, if one of the questions on a reply card asks the pet owner if their pet has weight or skin and coat problems an offer for a special care product can be mailed.

Applying Lifetime Value Calculations

In Chapter 6 we saw how lifetime value calculations can be used to establish whether EDM is likely to be profitable or not. It will also help to sell the program to management, which was done with the retention program described previously.

First, the lifetime value of a customer whose dog lives 10 years was worked out. That was based upon known data such as gross margin per customer and retention rate. For the sake of simplicity, Exhibit CS5.8 below uses a notional thousand customers.

Exhibit CS5.8 shows how many customers remain in each successive year based upon the retention rate in the previous one. This assumes increasing loyalty the longer customers are retained; hence the rise in percentage. The calculation reveals that the average acquired customer generates a total profit of approximately $150 during their dog's lifetime.

A second calculation was then made, incorporating the following assumptions regarding the proposed retention program:

- The initial retention rate rises from 50 to 75 percent. Market research had shown that this was feasible. The maximum retention rate is 95 percent. Total loyalty is impossible to achieve, since some customers will always be lost.

- Regular communications increase the share of wallet, and hence the margin per customer (more of the brand's food is bought). This raises the gross margin to $80.

- The cost of the program is estimated at $10 per customer per annum during the puppy phase, falling to $6 annually thereafter.

- The new total margin is thus $80 multiplied by the number of customers in a year, minus the cost per customer ($10 or $6) times the number of customers in a year (the program costs).

Exhibit CS 5.9 shows the effect of these assumptions on the customer lifetime value. As a result of the investment in the program, earnings per customer fall by $3 in the first year. But the substantial increase in retention rate has already made up for that in the second year, and an additional $128 is earned from each customer over the full 10 years. That represents a near doubling of customer lifetime value.

The question, of course, is whether the assumptions are correct. In practice, there will undoubtedly be some factors that have been estimated too optimistically or pessimistically. For this reason, it is important to keep on measuring the effects of an EDM program carefully throughout its life. If necessary, it can then be "tweaked" by adjusting the various components of customer value. Regardless of that, however, this calculation shows just how profitable EDM can be. Follow this

Exhibit CS5.8. Lifetime Value without Retention Program

	Year									
	1	2	3	4	5	6	7	8	9	10
Customers	1,000	500	275	165	107	75	56	45	38	34
Retention rate	50%	55%	60%	65%	70%	75%	80%	85%	90%	90%
Margin per customer	73	73	73	73	73	73	73	73	73	73
Total margin	73,038	36,519	20,085	12,051	7,833	5,483	4,112	3,290	2,796	2,517
Discount rate	1.00	1.10	1.21	1.33	1.46	1.61	1.77	1.95	2.14	2.36
NPV profit	73,038	33,199	16,600	9,054	5,350	3,405	2,321	1,688	1,305	1,067
Cumulative NPV profit	73,038	106,237	122,837	131,891	137,241	140,646	142,967	144,656	145,960	147,028
Lifetime value	73	106	123	132	137	141	143	145	146	147

Exhibit CS5.9. Lifetime Value with Retention Program

	Year									
	1	2	3	4	5	6	7	8	9	10
Customers	1,000	750	600	510	459	413	372	335	301	271
Retention rate	75%	80%	85%	90%	90%	90%	90%	90%	90%	90%
Margin per customer	80	80	80	80	80	80	80	80	80	80
Costs per customer	10	6	6	6	6	6	6	6	6	6
Program costs	10,000	4,500	3,600	3,060	2,754	2,479	2,231	2,008	1,807	1,626
Total margin	70,000	55,500	44,400	37,740	33,966	30,569	27,512	24,761	22,285	20,057
Discount rate	1.00	1.10	1.21	1.33	1.46	1.61	1.77	1.95	2.14	2.36
NPV profit	70,000	50,455	36,694	28,355	23,199	18,981	15,530	12,706	10,396	8,506
Cumulative NPV profit	70,000	120,455	157,149	185,503	208,703	227,684	243,214	255,920	266,316	274,822
Lifetime Value	70	120	157	186	209	228	243	256	266	275
Old Lifetime Value	73	106	123	132	137	141	143	145	146	147
Lift	-3	14	34	54	72	87	100	111	120	128

case, then, and there is a good chance that you will be able to sell your program to management, as easily as this one was.

Besides monitoring the ROI of your program it's also important to constantly look for new ways to get into contact with pet owners. For instance, look for communication methods to decrease the dependence on specific channels (e.g., breeders) and the costs involved. A good example is the use of the Internet by PPF brand. Many of them now offer trial packs through their web sites, asking the pet owner for additional information in the process. This additional data can exceed the information gathered through other channels and will help to optimize the brand's CRM activities and further differentiate their communication strategies.

7

CRM, Databases, and Marketing Information

> It is a capital mistake to theorize before one has data. Insensibly one begins to twist facts to suit theories, instead of theories to suit facts.
> —*Sherlock Holmes*

Data and databases have reached to the heart of our relationships with customers, yet many businesses fail to take advantage of what can be done with them—and understandably so. Certainly many CRM systems have failed to produce any benefit despite enormous costs for equipment and software to manage customer relationships that often produced no positive, tangible advantage at all.

In order to understand why so many efforts fail rather than succeed, and to avoid failure and ensure success for ourselves, it is important to first understand what marketing databases are, what they are used for, and how we can use them.

To begin with, there are three kinds of information systems. They are:

- Transaction Processing.
- Management Information.
- Decision Support.

A transaction-processing system runs the business of the business. A common example is the cash registers in a grocery store. Have you ever been in a grocery store when the power went out, or, for whatever reason, the registers went down? For all practical means and purposes, the store was closed. This is why the transaction processing system is described as a mission-critical system. If the system is down, the business cannot conduct its mission, which in the case of a grocery store is to sell groceries.

A transaction-processing system is "real time," which means as products are sold or entered into inventory, it is reflected immediately in the system. It tends to make lots of little changes and have many operators. In our grocery example, there could be many cashiers making a lot of little data inputs, constantly keying in or scanning things such as one package of cereal, one head of lettuce, and so on.

Because transaction-processing systems are mission critical and because they are designed for a lot of operators to make a lot of small changes, they are not well suited for analysis. Part of this is by design, and part is the nature of any database system. No two operators can change the same piece of data at the same time. So when marketers "grab" a piece of data, no one else can access it and change it. If a marketer is looking at, say, head lettuce data, and someone is trying to buy a head of lettuce, the system will stop. A few shouts and angry phone calls later, the marketer learns not to tie up the transaction-processing system.

A management information system manages the business of the business. A common example is the accounting system almost every business might have. It helps track payroll, accounts receivable, account payable, and so on. If the system goes down, the business can continue to function for a while. Hence it is not mission critical.

A management information system is period and report driven, and reports often must conform to certain standards, as with accounting reports. Reports are designed around days, weeks, months, and accounting periods. Most reports are predesigned and then updated and recreated over and over. This would include balance sheets, profit and loss statements, inventory reports, and so on. The system is designed to create a report set that is needed to manage the business. The system may have several users, but usually fewer than the transaction-processing system. A management information system usually contains only specific sets of information, such as accounting and payroll, and does not contain information from sources outside of the company or a department.

Because a management information system is period and report driven, and reports must conform to certain standards, the system is designed to store, manage, and report data in specific ways. It is often possible to create unique reports, but by and large the system is designed to create the same reports over again each period. Since the system usually does not contain information from outside the company, it is not useful for analysis comparing different companies, divisions, or markets.

A decision support system is the broader term marketing databases fall under. A decision support system is not mission critical, nor does it produce a predefined set of periodic reports. A decision support system is designed for data exploration, for asking questions that were not or cannot be pre-planned, regardless of whether the data is from one system or disparate systems.

Decision support systems usually contain data from different data sources, that are run by different hardware and software and may have different native formats. No matter, the meaning of the data is determined and data is gathered, converted, cleaned, matched, and loaded into the decision support system. This makes the system useful for analyzing data that came from different sources inside and outside the organization.

A decision support system avoids the problems of analyzing data in a transaction processing system by storing data off-line, where the actions of the analyst will not adversely impact how the transaction-processing system operates. It avoids the problems of the management information system by combining data from disparate systems in one place with a set of tools that make creating unique reports practical. A marketing database is normally designed as a decision support system.

Data Warehouses

A decision support system is a data warehouse that combines data from several or many sources into one place for strategic decision-making purposes. There is a problem, however, with the term data warehouse that often leads to misunderstanding.

The purpose of a data warehouse is not to "archive" data but to gather different pieces of data, large and small, from different places, and ship them back out to the right people at the right time. Just like a freight terminal, data warehouses are necessary for the coordinated movement of information throughout an organization, which brings us back to one of the main reasons why so many marketing databases fail to produce any benefit. Organizations set out to build a system to store data, rather than ship and receive it. More money, faster computers, bigger hard drives, and better networks cannot overcome designing a system based on the wrong premise.

Because some managers have viewed marketing databases and data warehouses as technical challenges that could be overcome by large systems and large budgets, failures have become more spectacular. Recently a company that sells communication equipment spent several tens of millions of dollars on a marketing database with no tangible results. Their parent company was so displeased they fired the president—and every single vice president—and installed new management.

The desired result of having a marketing database is to have a better understanding of customers, their behaviors, and their relationships with your organization. Approaching it from a standpoint of employing massive technical expertise is a road to failure. The way to succeed is to understand first what you are really trying to do and then deciding on the resources necessary to do the job.

Logic, Matching, and Understanding

Most challenges in database marketing are not technical challenges; most challenges are logical problems. Do we understand what we are asking for? Do we understand who the customer is? And so on.

Merge/purge, or finding, matching, tagging, or removing duplicate customers is at the heart of all database marketing. How can this be so? Here are some examples.

The GSA (General Services Agency—www.gsa.gov) supplies various government offices, military bases, and federal agencies everything from office supplies to computers to real estate. The GSA has several divisions, and each competes and sells much like a business. Any government employee could buy from any GSA office or branch, regardless of their own location.

One GSA division was experiencing rapid customer turnover. They employed database marketing methods and tracked each customer at an individual level. Because many of their customers were supply sergeants, and supply sergeants tend to get transferred from base to base, this GSA had a lot of keeping up to do.

If a sergeant moved from one base to another, his record was updated. This kept duplicates from popping up where the same sergeant had served at two, three, or four bases. Presumably, this was a good idea.

But here is what they did not do. They did not consider the base, office, or agency as the customer. So an army base could be a "regular customer," but as supply sergeants transfer place to place, not to mention join and leave the military, it did not look that way.

So in order to better understand who their customers really are, they started matching on the individual level, and the location (base or office) level, and the agency level. This completely changed the picture of who are their customers. Now they can target locations where they sell to only one ore two people and seek more buying contacts. Their customer turnover rate looks completely different when "customer" is viewed in a different manner.

The same type of problem occurs in a variety of industries. If we sell components to manufacturers, we may need to know the specifying engineer, the product manager, and the purchasing agent in order to make a sale. Matching them as part of the same group, and keeping them apart as different types of decision makers is crucial. How to do this must first be determine, and described, by management, then it can programmed by IT.

How we do merge/purge, matching, tagging, or removing duplicate customers is based on our understanding of who our customer is. It is at the heart of all database marketing.

Harmonizing Supply and Demand

There are many definitions of marketing, but in simple terms it can be described as "harmonizing supply and demand." To a greater or lesser extent, this is something every business does.

For an organization to harmonize supply and demand effectively, reliable supporting information is needed. The data warehouse can help us to gather raw data, to interpret it and to convert it into usable information. This enables decisions to be taken on a very large base of information quickly, cheaply, and accurately enough to be useful.

Quickly, cheaply, and accurately enough to be useful is the challenge. A number of factors continue to come together to help marketers overcome these challenges. They include:

1. Market focus has increased the importance of customer data, driven by a desire for more information. This is enough to overcome internal boundaries, by forcing managers in different areas and with different systems to share data.

2. Economies of scale as large data sets allow for lower costs on a per customer basis (despite higher overall costs) as well as economies of scale for software manufacturers that create and sell more common products and systems.

3. Rapid developments in computer technology. Both hardware and software have increased in functionality yet fallen drastically in price. This allows organizations to:

    - Meet their existing information needs more quickly, cheaply, and effectively.
    - Adapt the utility of their existing information in response to changing cost-benefit patterns.
    - Combine disparate data more easily, to create new information.

4. The social context. As more organizations succeed with marketing databases, there are more vendors, friends, and experiences to draw on and emulate.

5. The legal context. Accounting and reporting regulations are being tightened all the time. A thorough and accurate picture of customer relationships, touch points, and what is (and is not) tracked or stored can be a legal necessity.

6. Illustrating change to management. Marketing databases don't just show what happened; they show what changed. This helps management react to new environments.

Many marketing database systems have come onto the market in recent years, yet the mass of evidence available from seminars, conferences, and everyday practice indicates that marketing people still tend to use the computer much less consistently than do their colleagues in other disciplines. Moreover, the systems currently available rarely meet all the many specifications expected of them. Clearly, supply and demand are yet to match.

Information Versus Data

> Information? That is data you can do something with.
> Data? That is information you can do nothing with.

The goal is to turn direct and event-driven marketing into self-learning processes. A self-learning process is reinforced as the amount of experience (gained from the database) increases.

Experience-based feedback into databases has been embraced enthusiastically in the world of IT, producing a raft of hardware, software, and fine promises. Data warehouses, neural networking, and the identification of "hidden" patterns have become much-loved topics, but some caution is advisable here. This is an area that has not entirely escaped fads that, with hindsight, deliver much less than had originally been expected. And comparatively simple tools like statistics packages can often achieve almost as much as the most advanced ones.

What is important is that, however honed the tool, it must suit the functions you need to manage. Databases can be used to streamline normal commercial activities and to structure them better to provide added-value use. *Added-value use* means working with the information that displays the highest degree of correlation with future buying patterns or other relevant behavior. It is in this area that marketing databases can prove really profitable.

Put simply, information is a collection of data that is of interest to you. In itself, data is not information.

> Information is knowledge you can do something with in its present form. Data is information you can do nothing with in its present form. How we receive, modify, combine, compare, add meaning, and ship to the right user determines how well we can transform data into information that imparts useful knowledge.

The word *information* comes from the Latin "in forma," meaning "in [the right] form". Information consists of structured data from which we can extract something of use to us. In the context of marketing and sales information systems, we can define marketing information as a combination of marketing and sales data grouped and structured in a way relevant to the user's needs, that user being you or your colleagues within the organization.

Information can be either rational or emotional. They are not separate forms, but complementary ones. Although the typical analyst has trouble looking at data and information in anything other than a rational way, they most definitively have an emotional component. The rational information about a customer consists of such things as name, address, age, lifestyle, buying patterns, and payment history. You also want access to rational information about your own product, such as rate of stock turnover or average order size per customer. The emotional information, on the other hand, centers on brand value. The fact that Coca-Cola has a particular market share, Y, and a certain number of users, X, is rational information. But there are many different reasons why those people are prepared to spend several euros on a drink that costs only five cents to produce: to "fit in," to buy into the image projected in the advertising because Coke is "a way of life." That is emotional information. There are probably few rational reasons why somebody buys a Harley-Davidson motorcycle, but plenty for buying an Opel Astra van. Emotional information penetrates straight to the associative level; it influences almost every purchasing decision, and is filtered far less stringently than rational (cognitive) information. But both types are important.

The information required is sometimes gathered from internal sources, but external ones are often used as well. Either way, it is important to know what information is needed for what purpose or, to put it another way, what data actually generates useful information. This requires an insight into the relationships between all the data available to you. You can only distill information from that variety of data if you know and understand what pattern it forms. For this reason, information is subjective in nature.

Effective marketing is the product of systematic working: asking the right questions and gathering the right information. This reveals market opportunities and reduces the risks attached to your decision. Access to information may not eliminate the chance of failure, but it will certainly shrink it! Computerizing the marketing function generates more and, above all, better information.

But when changing how you receive business information, you may have to learn new ways of recognizing the patterns it contains. The new or improved data coming in will not always provide you immediately with recognizable and usable information.

The key question in all this remains: How far should you go in gathering information to cut out risk? An organization that wants to eliminate risk completely will incur so many costs in gathering all the information it needs to do so that it will endanger its very profitability. Because we do not know all the questions, it is impossible to find all the answers. And even when we do know the questions, answering them is sometimes so expensive that it's not worth doing.

Useless Information

Managers are being overwhelmed with irrelevant and useless "information" better described as data. And the rise of the computer is largely responsible for that. With or without the aid of the technology, it is often totally impossible to distill the right information from the flood of data.

Between 80 and 90 percent of managers lack technical knowledge, and computer knowledge in particular. They allow the data to overwhelm them and fail to turn it into information—or do so incorrectly. The result: demand for information grows without the new data making any contribution to managerial improvement.

At least 75 percent of the data produced remains unused. If we apply this statistic to a company of average size, it means that tens of thousands of dollars are being spent to absolutely no effect. Extrapolated to the national level, we are talking about many millions of euros being thrown away.

When determining what sort of information should be delivered to different managers, the key challenge is deciding what not to give them. In order to decide what not to do, we must be clear on what our priorities, and their priorities, really are. As they say, if you have more than three priorities, you don't have any.

So to avoid spewing useless data at managers and risk their either failing to weed through it and find what they need or simply ignoring it altogether, we must find what are their:

1. Key Responsibilities?
2. Key Goals?
3. Key Threats and Opportunities?

If we focus our reports on what changed (not just what happened) as it relates to their key responsibilities, goals, threats, and opportunities, any bit of information that meets these criteria will be useful and quickly become indispensable. Anything that does not will be disregarded.

Database Marketing and Data Mining

EDM increases the demand for and discipline placed on marketing databases. Increasingly, marketing activities are being steered by the understanding of customer information extracted from a database. That data is analyzed and coordinated in such a way that marketing better understands the habits and preferences of the customer or prospect. This is what we call database marketing. Database marketing is a technique by which we try to make the right proposition to the right customer through the right channels by use of a marketing database. Database marketing can support all kinds of selling activities and is not limited to just direct marketing and personal selling activities.

Data mining is a technique within database marketing. Data mining means looking for relationships and patterns within and across large databases without defining in advance what they might be. These searches are carried out in order to support management decisions. Typical examples of the functionality provided by data mining software include tracing anomalies, predictive modeling, and database segmentation.

The objectives behind any data mining exercise need to be defined clearly because the technique forms the basis for the use of information held in a data warehouse. The organization has to decide which analyses are applied to the operational data.

For example, the results of any substantive change in understanding for marketing managers are a substantive change in behavior for the marketing department. Here's another way to look at it. If we uncover a new understanding of a customer's behavior, we must first change our own behavior before we can take advantage of how our new understanding might change that customer's behavior to our advantage.

As a result, data mining must be carried out with a clear eye towards what changes we will make based on the information discovered. If it is a big change, the data better be accurate and trustworthy. If it involves understanding what customers are likely to do, we should be using a predictive analytic technique. If it involves understanding what customers are like or what they think, we should use a descriptive analytic technique.

In order to be most effective, data mining to support EDM should be conducted by someone that understands the business, the goals, and the resources marketing employs.

Analyzing Data

Data analysis generally follows the same basic step-by-step progression:

1. Define problem.
2. Determine data needed.
3. Single factor analysis.
4. Cross-Tabulation analysis.
5. Multivariate analysis.

First, we must define the problem. Are we experiencing a loss in sales and want to know what is behind it? Do we want to find new, profitable customers? Do we want to improve how we sell new products to existing customers? Do we want the average customer to spend more with each transaction? Whatever the problem, challenge, or goal, we must state it clearly before beginning the analysis.

With the challenge defined, we can look across the data warehouse to determine which pieces of data are relevant. Then we can define exactly what we need to collect, from where, and over what time periods. After it is defined, we can gather and select the data and put it together to be analyzed.

The single factor analysis is the simplest, but often the most crucial. In the single factor analysis, we count or summarize each variable in the data individually: sales amount, customer counts, product counts, and so on. This becomes our "sanity check," where we can determine whether or not we have the right data and whether or not the data is complete. Many an analyst has made himself look foolish by analyzing only part of an organization's sales data without realizing they were missing information. Checking to make sure the data is correct and complete at the single factor stage of the analysis will prevent many embarrassments and much wasted time.

The cross-tabulation analysis is where we compare each "predictor" variable to what it is we are trying to describe or predict. For example, let's say we are trying to predict how much a customer spends, based on age, income, number of recent purchases, and amount of recent purchases. We would compare each variable, by itself, to spending. This often leads to insights that may be quite useful by themselves. It also may lead to insights that allow a clever analyst to make better use of more advances techniques.

Multivariate analysis is where we analyze many variables at the same time. Complex patterns with interdependent variables that are too complex to easily realize can be uncovered using the right statistical techniques. But what the right techniques are can depend on how well the analyst defined the problem, selected the data, sanity checked the data, and understood simply cross-tab relationships.

In an ideal world, an analysis simply progresses from step one to step five and is concluded. In reality, the problem is often misstated, and that realization isn't discovered until well into the analysis, when things don't seem to make sense. Then there is often some data that nobody realized would be useful at the start which becomes obviously needed somewhere along the way. The right data, with the right counts and amounts, rarely gets picked up the first time, and a repeat data request with revised time periods, variables, or some other major component is needed. Cross-tabulation reports often make for completely different relationships than expected, which leads the analysis in a new direction. Multivariate analysis often produces a completely different result than expected or no result at all. Sometimes the relationships marketers expect just are not there.

Regardless of the number of times we get to step 3 and start again, followed by the times we get to step 4 and start again, the basic progression remains the same. Each step has a purpose, is important, and must be taken to ensure a useful result.

Analysis: From Theory to Practice

The ultimate purpose of database marketing analysis is to lead marketers into those marketing activities that are most closely related to increasing customer lifetime value. As marketers, we do not control customers' behaviors, attitudes, or ideas. What we control is our reaction to customers' behaviors, attitudes, and ideas, so we must focus on what we must do, in order to get the customer to do what we want them to do. In order to fit into direct marketing discipline, we must describe different marketing activities and the likely or potential outcomes of those activities in such a way that it can be fit into business plans and objectives. The art of analysis lies in finding those variables that relate most strongly to the rate of response, expected sale amount, rate of conversion, attrition or other factor you are seeking to explain.

The most logical variables are the ones with "face validity," which means that they appear to be the ones that should have the most impact. The variables that actually have the greatest statistical significance have "statistical validity." Most of the time, though not always, the variables with face validity are also the most statistically significant variables. When we find a significant variable that makes no sense to us, we must consider two things:

- The data is flawed and the relationship is specious.
- Our understanding of the relationship is flawed.

For example, a manufacturer of heavy truck engines wanted to target buyers of its largest diesel engine. They set about determining which trucks were used to haul the heaviest loads. When that was done, they did a cross-tabulation to see how many more of the larger engines this market bought versus the rest of the market. What they found was that truckers hauling heavy loads were no more likely to buy the bigger engine. At first, they were incredulous and did not believe it. It certainly had face validity that heavier trucks needed bigger engines, but it didn't have statistical validity.

Upon further investigation, they realized that their understanding was flawed. As it turns out, heavy trucks are limited by load weight, so the heavier the load, the more important it is that the truck itself weighs less. It makes economic sense for a truck owner hauling heavy loads to buy the smaller and thus lighter engine in order to squeeze in more cargo. This conclusion offset the need for the more powerful engine. Now the manufacturer has a better understanding, and is better able to target, or not target, buyers for a specific size of engine.

The amount of investment in uncovering knowledge is a matter of weighing costs against benefits. With limited investment and effort, it is quite easy to carry out limited analysis. The additional costs of more data—more hardware, more software, and more time—soon outweigh the benefits. In addition, there is only so much information management can digest, act upon, and ultimately use. When marketing management already have their hands full, more analyses have little or no value.

Database Analysis Techniques

Whether just starting or already experienced with database marketing, it is not always easy or even necessary for organizations to choose between the ranges of analytical techniques available prior to starting an analysis. When should what techniques be applied? Trial and error is often the best way to make the right choice. The simplest approach is to apply several techniques to the data and then select the best model based on the outcomes. This way of working means testing the resulting models—if possible, by actually including different test groups in a mailing and measuring the response rates. Techniques' quality can be compared by measuring the ratio of correctly predicted respondents using a particular technique to respondents in a random sample.

Analytical techniques can help answer all sorts of marketing questions. The most important of these pertain to *predictive modeling* that scores the likelihood or degree of an outcome and profile analysis that describes what customers or prospects are like and how segments differ. *Scoring* is about the chance of achieving something: a response, a sale, or a choice of media or channel. Scoring can help to market to customers to the best degree. *Profiling* concerns the identification of customer groups based upon internal homogeneity and mutual heterogeneity. Customers with different profiles may be equally likely to buy but motivated by completely different things. Profiling can help us market to each customer in the best manner.

Various analytical techniques can be used for scoring and profiling. The large number available can be subdivided into visualization techniques, conventional statistical techniques, cluster models, decision trees, and neural networks.

- **Visualization techniques** are particularly useful for discovering patterns, subgroups, or significant variables in the first exploratory phase of the data analysis process. The visualization can be achieved using such tools as histograms, two- or three-dimensional spread diagrams, or pie charts. These techniques are suitable for everything from simple to quite complex scoring and profiling analysis, and the results are easy to interpret. They can also be applied to large data sets. However, these techniques do not stand up well when there are missing values. On the other hand, anomalies are easy to identify.

- **Conventional statistical techniques** are still widely used to answer marketing questions. Traditional statistics describe explanatory models that help us understand why a particular pattern appears in the data. For example, we can investigate the effect of the contact history or the number of products and services on spending patterns. Examples of these techniques include matrices, regression analysis, cluster analysis, and factor analysis. Interpretability is a major advantage of these techniques, but the simplicity of the models often means that they do not accurately reflect the complexity of the data, which means that sometimes certain segments are not recognized. Depending upon which technique is chosen, conventional statistics can be highly suited to scoring and profiling in large data sets. Most are very fast in their calculations. Missing values, anomalies, and contradictory information (rule breaches, for example) can affect the model, with the potential to cause problems; missing values and anomalies need to be recoded into a separate category or deleted.

- **Cluster models** help to group like with like and are the most effective way to describe different groups of customers, survey responders, and prospects. Unlike other techniques, a cluster model has no "predicted" variable. It simply creates groups of the most similar records. This can help us find customer sets that are equally likely to buy, but quite different in circumstances or motivation.

- **Decision trees** help us to differentiate more or less homogeneous customer groups within the database. They are also used as a starting point for further analysis, with an initial selection being made of the variables to be carried forward as input for the rest of the process. The most common decision tree method is known as "chi-square automatic interaction detection" (CHAID). Decision trees are easy to interpret, user-friendly, and suitable for both scoring and profiling. They are also highly suited to large data sets, fast in their calculations, and somewhat more robust than conventional statistical techniques. Above all, though, they are very practical because they can be used by nonstatisticians—in fact, by just about anybody.

- **Neural networks** are structures, made up of multiple layers, trained to solve a problem by learning from examples. Their advantages include the ability to model nonlinear interactions between variables and their robustness with respect to missing data. That makes them suitable for scoring and profiling analysis. One important shortcoming of neural networks, though, is their "black box" character: in most cases, the model is noninterpretable. Also, a network takes a long time to train —especially with large data sets and many variables—and a lot of data pre-processing is required. Finally, there is a risk of "overtraining," which reduces the model's power to generalize. Hybrid forms—combinations of statistical and modern techniques—can overcome that problem, however.

Banks, insurance companies, telecommunications providers, and even retailers with large customer databases have much to gain from analyzing customers thoroughly by means of simple cross-tabs analysis and cross-selling, up-selling, and scoring models.

But you do not always need to squeeze every last drop out of database analysis. Understanding customer behavior will always be an inexact science. Database analysis may be essential, but uncover and understand the simple relationships first before employing more complex tools.

The average B-to-B company with a customer database of only a few thousand people, as well as smaller B-to-C firms, can make do with cross-tab, visualization, and traditional statistical techniques. These alone are enough to reveal interesting patterns and trends in the database information. Decision trees can also support this phase. For these businesses, in fact, it may not really matter which analytical technique is chosen: even with a simple matrix, you can quickly enhance your understanding of the customer database.

Once analytical techniques have delivered their first satisfactory results and the organization wants to further improve its use of the database, more optimization can be pursued.

Formulating Analytical Objectives

Good analysis motivates you to "put your house in order." And that in itself is a big step forward. It is vital to identify and describe all the important information flows. Depending upon the level and structure of your IT, relevant information could be found in many different places and in all sorts of forms. We've described the basic steps in any analysis. Now let's look more deeply at selecting the data we need to begin the analysis. We will need to describe the following:

- What data is needed (what type, and going back how far?).
- Who holds that data.
- Where it is stored (on paper, in computers, in people's heads?).
- What form it is in (what do the components look like?).
- How it is structured (data model).
- What definitions apply to it.
- How the data can be linked.
- What processing it may have to undergo.
- How complete it is.

When defining analytical objectives for the purposes of event-driven marketing—that is, with a customer focus—you start from the questions asked most frequently about customers. Taking a marketing management example, relevant questions might include the following:

- How do we measure a customer's value to the organization?
- When are customers upgrading or leaving?
- How satisfied is the customer with the organization?
- What products has a customer bought from us?
- What is the profile of a customer who owns a particular product?
- To what customer groups can we cross-sell our products?
- Which customers should we approach with a particular marketing proposition?
- How should we approach individual customers?

The above questions can be translated into firm analytical objectives. To start with, you must ask yourself what questions have to be answered on a regular basis and which ones only from time to time. The system must be provided with all the data needed to achieve the analytical objectives. In other words, data that can be shaped into concrete information upon which you can act.

The formulation of analytical objectives will give rise to new questions. Establishing a customer's value to the organization means asking yourself what is meant by "value." Is that the turnover customers generate, the fact that they own certain products or their potential for growth? If the benchmark is turnover, then what exactly is meant by that? Overall turnover is derived from a set of components, and you need to state how each contributes towards it. Although it can often be quantified with a fair degree of exactitude, turnover is not always the best indicator of a customer's value to a business. In some sectors you will find products with both "sustainable" and a "nonsustainable" turnover. The latter may be high, but it can disappear in an instant, making those customers responsible for the lower sustainable turnover more valuable to the organization.

To close this chapter, we discuss two forms of analysis that are of particular worth from the perspective of EDM and customer value: revenue analysis and migration analysis. These can answer two key questions.

Key Question 1. Are you making money from a customer or not?

As well as turnover, *revenue analysis* also calculates the cost per customer relationship. This allows you to work out how much profit or loss you are making on each customer. As with turnover analysis, customers can be segmented according to the level of their returns they account for. From the revenue analysis, you can establish how good your cost-benefit ratio is. This makes it more of a checking tool than a planning one. To determine the budget allocation per customer, you should be using turnover analysis. Marketers largely base their budgets on the level of turnover from each customer or customer group. The other major factor, of course, is the nature of the activities being planned. Unless unprofitable customers have some strategic value, they should be dropped.

Key Question 2. Can you track how customer purchasing patterns evolve?

You want to understand what criteria determine your customer retention and, if possible, help upgrade customer relationships. *Migration analysis* can clarify changes in the customer database or examine customers' satisfaction or their product ownership. Database changes, such as movement between turnover segments, can be used to plan activities targeting specific recorded customers. When the movement is negative, those activities can be used to prevent the customer from being lost. When positive, marketing efforts can be designed to stimulate further upgrading. A *product analysis* reveals relationships between different items and the extent of growth or shrinkage over set periods.

Identifying changes in the customer database can be very useful for an organization wanting to encourage positive movement and stop the negative, which can be an indicator of leakage. Migration analysis can be used to monitor the following elements:

- Movements in customers' contribution to turnover or profit.
- Customer retention and leakage (churn).
- Customer upgrading through cross-selling or activities to increase order sizes.

The analysis of changes provides a strong foundation for the design of activities targeting the individual customer: event-driven marketing. It can even be used to devise specific marketing actions and in setting the budgets for different target segments. When this is done carefully, it allows the customer's future value to be forecast. Data warehouse scores can then be calculated, with that future value as their benchmark, and used to establish how far a customer's performance is in line with expectations.

CASE 6: Developing an Event-Driven Marketing Program

While most of the previous case studies focused on the communicative elements of EDM programs and their results, this chapter goes more into the details of development. Using the example of the End of Lease program of an international financial services provider, we will go through the steps of setting the goals, developing the strategy, and implementing EDM.

An international provider of financial services wanted to increase the retention rate of its customers. Products could be divided into two groups: operational lease and financial lease. In the case of *operational lease* the leased object, which could be anything from a car or an excavator to a printing press, remains the property of the leasing company. Unlike financial leases, operational leases normally come with additional services like maintenance, insurance, etc. Cars and copiers are good examples of objects that are often financed with an operational lease. At the end of the contract's term there would be several options for a customer: return the "asset," extend the leasing term, or buy the asset at its remaining economic value. As such, an operational lease always came with mandatory customer contact at the end of the contract. This provided opportunities to extend the relationship with the customer.

The situation was quite different with so-called *financial lease* contracts. With a financial lease, a form of buying installments, the asset becomes full property of the customer at the end of the term. A financial lease is, therefore, an alternative for financing by loans and almost anything can be financed by this form of lease. Since monthly payments were done by automated encashment, there was no real (administrative) necessity to contact the customer at the end of the contract. He would simply pay his last term, and that would be it. If this customer was serviced by an account manager, there would normally be contact at the end of a contract, but 80% of the company's customers were "small ticket" clients, meaning that they had relative low-value contracts that did not justify the costs of a personal account manager. The local branch offices of the bank of which the leasing company was a subsidiary closed the majority of these contracts. As such, there was no noteworthy direct customer contact between the leasing company and most of its customers. The eminent danger of customers slipping away into obscurity at the end of their contact was therefore substantial.

With an operational lease there's often the mentioned "asset" that is returned to the leasing company. This normally results in an immediate necessity for the customer to invest in a new, up-to-date version of the same asset, especially if it's crucial to the core business of the customer. Imagine a printing company. It would not be printing anything without presses. So if a press is returned it normally needs to be replaced by a new one.

Therefore, customer retention was a relative easy task.

Again, with financial leasing the situation is different. The customer becomes the owner of the asset, and there often is no direct need for a replacement. What's more, a financial lease is normally just a way to finance an investment, whereas an operational lease often comes with additional services like insurance, maintenance, etc.

The positive aspect in all of this is that with each new investment, regardless of the type of asset, a customer might consider a financial lease to finance it. Today it might be the company car, tomorrow a computer network, and next month a full inventory of office furniture. The timing of these investments was therefore quite unrelated to the end date of the current contract.

Determining the Retention Rate

The main goal of the new marketing program was to increase the retention of the number of customers with financial leases. To make this more tangible, the first step taken was analysis of the current level of retention. The following definition of retention was used: the percentage of customers of whom the last contract ends that return with a new contract within 12 months. These 12 months allowed a customer to actually develop a need for a new investment (many operation lease business units used 3 months instead). Focusing on the last ending contract—a specific customer could have more than one contract—ensured that the program placed the necessary focus on those customers that were in danger of churning.

Since the operational data warehouse of the company only stored 6 months of history on completed contracts, the Decision Analytics department had the IT department recover older data from the digital archives. Although there are more accurate ways to determine retention, the fact that a usable file with complete historical data was only available for June 2006 resulted in the following approach to calculate the current retention rate:

- First, a snapshot was made of all customers with a last active contract in June 2006 that would end between June 2006 and December 2007. This long period ensured that the analyst would have sufficient customers for later use in profiling and modeling.

- A check was done among all customers in May 2008 to determine how many of the customers from June 2006 were no longer present. For those customers that were missing it was determined for how many of them the contract had ended longer than 12 months ago. These customers were considered to have churned.

- The retention could then be calculated as follows: Retention = 100%— (Number of churned customers / number of original customers)

This calculation results in a figure of the maximum possible retention at the time. After all, it could not be determined whether or not those customers that were no longer present in May 2008 but whose contracts had only recently ended would return or not. According to these calculations the retention rate was about 45%.

Building a Predictive Model

The next step was to determine which factors predicted retention. To do so, the churned and retained customers from the data set were separated. Together with the company's database marketer, the decision analyst defined assumptions, selection criteria, chose potentially predictive variables, and evaluated the model.

About 100 available variables in the data mart were analyzed to determine whether or not they were predicted retention. Various groupings were applied to define buckets for categorical variables (nonnumerical variables like business sector); all generally used transformations were calculated for continuous variables (numerical variables like turnover or contract value). All variables were checked for correlation with each other, which was taken into account when combining them in the final predictive model. The useful variables were brought down to 30, which had significant correlation with retention. These 30 were chosen to be tested in the multivariate analysis.

Here are some of the trends that were found. Legal form LTD showed in general higher retention than other legal forms. Customers having real estate property, insurance, and loans showed in general higher retention. This was also true for customers with lower credit risks ratings. The higher the number of active contracts, the higher the probability of retention. In general, higher finance exposure within the banking group and a bigger size of a company converted to a higher retention probability. Clients in cities with large population were less likely to be retained than those from small towns. This was also true for bank types: Small banks retained customers better than big banks. Industry sector played an important role in customer retention as well as the type of leased assets.

Seven of the most statistically significant relationships were chosen for the final retention model. The weights for these variables were recalculated in the development data set (Exhibit CS6.1).

For each of the variables in the model the probability of retention was converted to a score. A higher score means a higher probability of retention (Exhibit CS6.2).

In other words, if a customer was leasing construction equipment, there was a high chance of retention while there was a low chance of retention for customers that were leasing office equipment.

For each of the values of the 7 variables in the model the customer received a specific score, depending on the value on the concerned field in the customer's database record. For instance, if a customer was active in the IT sector it received

Exhibit CS6.1 Weight per Predictable Variable

	Predictive variables	Abstract weights in the model
1	Customer Value Segment	33%
2	Asset type	23%
3	Number of active contracts	18%
4	Industry Sector	13%
5	Months since first active contract	5%
6	Lease Penetration at local bank	7%
7	Zip code Urbanization grouping	2%

Exhibit CS6.2 Example of Weight per Value of Variable

	Weight
	27%
Asset type	**Score**
Construction & Excavation	236
Agriculture & Horticulture	236
Medical	236
Metalworking & Woodworking	236
Food Manufacturing	236
Miscellaneous	147
Environment	147
Transport	147
ICT	125
Audio & Video	87
Graphical	87
Office Equipment	0

125 points, while customers in the construction business received 236 points (Exhibit CS6.2). Summing these 7 scores resulted in a total score between 0 and 1019. The higher the score the more the customer matched the profile of a retained customer. In other words: the higher the chance of retention under the circumstances without a retention program. The resulting score was converted to a percentage corresponding to the expected retention for the specific customer.

The statistical power (measured by power statistic, or PI) of the model was determined to be about 45%. The best model, which manages to recognize all cases of retention/churn would have a power statistic of 100%, while the random model would have a power statistic of 0%. The performance in the interval from 20% to

40% is considered as sufficiently good, less than 20% is low and more than 40% is very high. In other words, the model's performance proved to be very high, meaning that there was a high probability of the model giving a correct prediction of retention. This basically meant that it could safely be applied for business purposes.

Applying the Risk/Revenue Matrix: All Customers Are Not Created Equal

While the statisticians had been working on the predictive model, the company's database marketer had developed a way to determine the annual profitability of current customers by calculating and summing the annual gross margin per contract. This value represented the current value of the customer to the company.

As with the telecom provider in Case 2, it was decided to use the risk/revenue matrix for the retention program. The annual profitability analysis showed that customers were not equally valuable to the company, while the predictive model showed that not every customer was as likely to be retained. These two dimensions were combined in a matrix that determined the priority per customer as shown in Exhibit CS6.3.

The ranges for each dimension were determined by assigning one-third of customers to each category. For instance, the predictive model showed that one-third of the customers had a retention probability below 30% and one-third has a probability above 40%, resulting in the ranges shown in Exhibit CS6.4.

The same exercise was done to determine the profitability ranges.

Highly profitable customers with a low probability of retention were given highest priority, while customers with either a low profitability or a high chance of retention were given low priority. All remaining customers, having medium profitability and/or medium probability of retention, were given medium priority.

Exhibit CS 6.3 Risk/Revenue Matrix

Priority matrix		Profitability		
		High	Medium	Low
Probability of retention	Low	A	B	C
	Medium	B	B	C
	High	C	C	C

Exhibit CS 6.4 Retention Probability Segments

High retention probability	40%–100%
Medium retention probability	31%–39%
Low retention probability	0%–29%

Exhibit CS6.5 Customers Assigned to the Risk/Revenue Matrix

SegmentProfitability	Data	SegmentRetention 1. LowRetention 0-30	2. MediumRetention 30 - 40	3. HighRetention >40	Grand Total
1. HighProfit >750	Customers	208	285	714	1207
	Average Retention%	26	37	55	45
	Average Gross Margin	1,208	1,117	1,582	1,408
2. MediumProfit 450 - 750	Customers	486	442	306	1234
	Average Retention%	27	37	49	36
	Average Gross Margin	572	581	594	581
3. LowProfit <450	Customers	586	425	253	1264
	Average Retention%	27	36	49	34
	Average Gross Margin	327	334	306	325
Total Customers		1280	1152	1273	3705
Total Average Retention%		27	37	52	39
Total Average Gross Margin		563	623	1,091	763

Exhibit CS6.6 Data per Priority Segment

Priority A	Customers	208
	Average Retention	26%
	Average Gross Margin	1207
Priority B	Customers	1,213
	Average Retention	33%
	Average Gross Margin	703
Priority C	Customers	2,284
	Average Retention	43%
	Average Gross Margin	754
All Priorities	Total Customers	3,705
	Total Average Retention	38%
	Total Average Gross Margin	762

Combining all the calculations resulted in the following division of customers shown in Exhibit CS6.5.

Note that the overall predicted retention of 39% in Exhibit 6.5 is lower than the retention measured across all customers. This is caused by the fact that this calculation was made for customers with one remaining contract, the group the retention program would focus on. Customers with more contracts were by definition more loyal and increased the company's overall retention rate.

Now that the customers per cell were determined, the average annual gross margin per priority segment could be determined as well. This was an important figure since it would determine the investment per priority (A, B, and C). This is where the beauty of the risk/revenue matrix really comes in. Since different customers have different priorities, the budget invested to retain them should be allocated accordingly.

The goals of the program were determined for each priority segment. For segment A and B these were quite ambitious. The program would be one of the first times the company would engage in real customer contact trying to improve retention, so these goals were assumed to be feasible.

By multiplying the number of additional customers retained per segment with their average annual gross margin (Exhibit CS6.6), the expected extra annual gross margin of the program could be determined. A payback period (see Chapter 6) of no more than 10 months was used as a standard for marketing programs. Using this objective, the maximum budget for the program could be determined.

Creative Concept Development

With the predictive model, the risk/revenue matrix, and the financial parameters done, the next step was to develop the exact proposition and creative messages for the program. Holy Cow! Direct Communications, a specialized direct marketing agency, were hired to develop a compelling offer for the customers. Various calculations and brainstorm sessions resulted in the following requirements per priority segment:

- Priority A: direct mailing with offer for an incentive of max $100 when the customer closed a new contract within 12 months. Reminder mailing 9 months after the initial offer.

- Priority B: direct mailing with offer for an incentive of max $100 when the customer closed a new contract within 12 months. Reminder mailing 9 months after the initial offer.

- Priority C: informative direct mailing without incentive or reminder mailing.

The mentioned values of incentives were determined by using the estimated mailing costs and the 10-month payback period, as calculated in the table in Exhibit CS6.8.

A few words of explanation about Exhibit CS6.8: The customers are the number of customers with a last ending contract to be approached by direct mail (Exhibit CS6.6). The mailing costs include an initial mailing and reminder mailing for priority group A and B and only an initial mailing for group C. The mailing costs are relatively high because the decision was made to use deep personalization in the mailing, which could only be done by digital printing. The total mailing costs are the mailing costs per customer times the number of customers.

The retention rate is the goal per group that was set for the program (Exhibit CS6.7). Since incentives were only granted with an actual new contract, the incentive costs are the number of customers approached times the retention rate times the cost per incentive. As mentioned, no incentives were given to group C.

Exhibit CS 6.7 Goals and Additional Gross Margin per Priority Segment

	Retention	Goal	Retention Increase	Additional Customers	Additional Gross Margin
A	26%	35%	9%	19	23,402
B	33%	42%	9%	112	78,837
C	43%	45%	2%	52	38,864
				183	141,103

Exhibit CS6.8 Program Costs and Payback Period

	A	B	C	Total
Customers	208	1,213	2,284	3,705
Mailing Costs per Customer	14	14	7	
Total Mailing Costs	2,912	16,982	14,846	34,740
Retention Rate	35%	42%	45%	
Incentive Costs per Customer	200	100		
Total Incentive Costs	14,560	50,946	0	65,506
Total Costs	17,472	67,928	14,846	100,246
Additional Annual Gross Margin	23,402	78,837	38,864	165,752
Payback Period	9.0	10.3	4.6	7.3

The total costs are the sum of the mailing costs and incentive costs. The additional margin per group was determined previously (Exhinit CS6.7). The payback period is the total costs divided by the additional annual gross margin times 12 months. As you can see, the payback of the full program remained within the 10-month objective. The slightly higher payback time for group B was acceptable because of this.

Based on all of the above Holy Cow! Direct Communications developed a concept for all three priority groups. Each mailing variant came with a personalized letter from the local bank branch informing the customer of their ending lease contract. The back of the letter displayed the details of this contract. The incentive that was chosen was a free navigation system. Group A was offered a more sophisticated version if they closed a new contract within 12 months. Group B was offered a cheaper, simpler navigation system, while no incentive was offered to group C. Besides this incentive groups A and B were also offered personal advice by their local bank branch, which could be requested by either returning an enclosed reply card, calling their bank, or going online and filling out a form. For both groups different landing pages were developed, each showing the offered navigation system.

Part of the objective of the retention program was to make the customers more familiar with the leasing specialist behind their local bank branch. In order to do so each mailing variant also included a personalized leaflet with information about the advantages of leasing in general and the services of the leasing company in particular. Like the letters, the content of these leaflets was also differentiated based on the priority group of the customer. For groups A and B it showed the offered incentive on the cover while a more generic picture was used on the leaflet for group C. As an extra gimmick, the navigation systems showed the actual location of the customers office on its screen. The actual navigation systems themselves would show the company's logo upon startup, constantly reminding the customers about the company that had offered them this gift.

The reminder mailings that were developed for groups A and B were basically the same mailings as the initial version. The main difference was that it reminded

168 ⇨ Follow That Customer!

Exhibit CS6.9. Leaflet for Priority Group A

+ TomTom GO navigation system

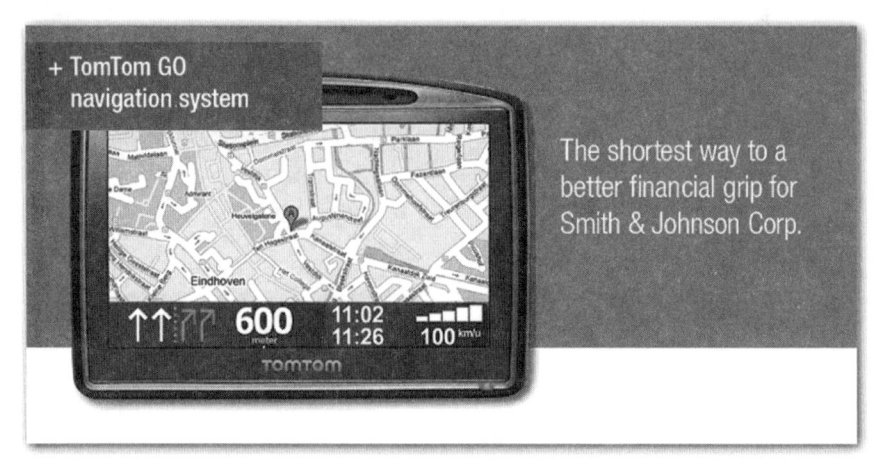

The shortest way to a better financial grip for Smith & Johnson Corp.

Exhibit CS6.10. Leaflet for Priority Group B

+ TomTom ONE navigation system

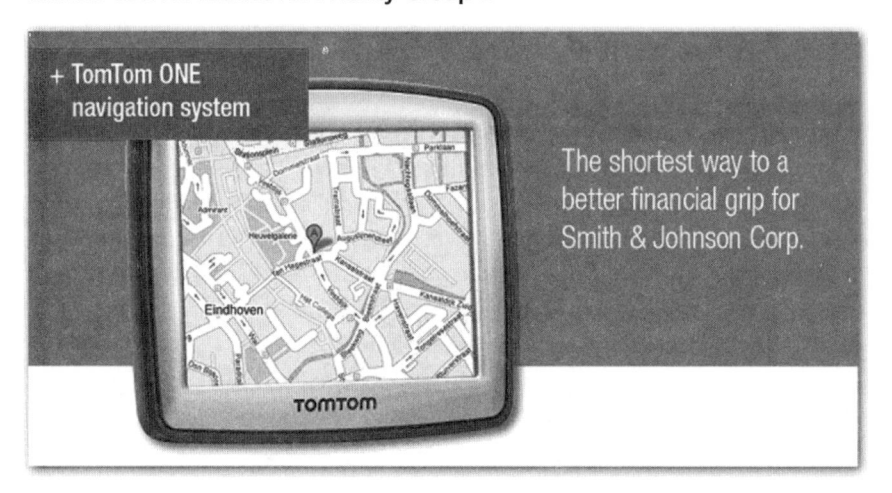

The shortest way to a better financial grip for Smith & Johnson Corp.

Exhibit CS6.11 Leaflet for Priority Group C

LEASING

The shortest way to a better financial grip for Smith & Johnson Corp.

the customer of the offer that was made 9 months ago and informed them that this offer was valid for only 3 more months, urging them to react fast.

The actual incentives mailed to the customers were accompanied by another personalized letter that thanked them for their business. Unlike the initial and reminder mailings, these were not printed on the bank's letterhead but that of the leasing company. The identity of the company was once again stressed. As such, the whole retention program made the leasing company a lot more visible as the expert behind their local bank and built brand awareness.

Selling the Program

Now that the retention program was developed, the agency had to sell the local bank branches, each of which had the authority to decide if they wanted to use the program or not. This was standard policy since customer ownership was supposed to lie with the bank, with any affiliate not being allowed to contact customers without the concerned bank's consent. In other words, in order to maintain their customer base the leasing company had to first convince the various banks to apply the program, just like Traveler had to sell their program to their agents in Case 2.

Several tactics were applied to convince the banks to use the program:

- For the first year, the leasing company would pay all the costs until the program was proven to be successful.
- The bank's head office supported the program and advised all its local branches to participate.
- Extensive information about the program's elements and processes were posted on the bank's Intranet.
- A package with samples of all mailings and variants plus an explanation of the program's mechanics was delivered to each bank's director.
- The leasing company's relationship managers that frequently visit their banks further explained and promoted the program.

All of these efforts, plus the fact that the whole program was centrally managed and coordinated and therefore needed little support from the local bank, paid off very nicely. No less than 80% of all banks decided to join the program, the highest participation rate for any of the banking group's EDM programs so far.

Implementation

Now that all the requirements for the program had been met, it was time to actually implement it. First of all, a monthly database selection of customers that were four months or less from expiration was set up. A set of database queries was programmed in order to determine the profitability and probability of retention of these customers. With this data the priority group could be assigned to each customer, according to the risk/revenue matrix. The selection was then loaded into the bank's campaign management tool, giving local banks the opportunity to screen the selection. Any customer that was no longer deemed creditworthy by the concerned bank could thereby be removed.

Unfortunately the back office systems that were used to make the selection did not contain the contact person at the customer's office. Therefore, the services of an external data supplier were used to enhance the selection with the name of the customer's financial manager or director. Together with the details of the contract the data set was then ready to be supplied to the mailing house.

The mailing house had meanwhile set up a process to personalize and digitally print the correct variety out of 5 letters and 3 leaflets for each customer. Together with reply cards and reply envelopes (where applicable), these were assembled and posted monthly, arriving at the customer's office three months before the end of the contract.

Requests for personal advice by groups A and B that were received through the mail or the Internet were fed into the bank's CRM system, arriving promptly at the local bank, which would contact the concerned customers.

On a monthly basis the leasing company would compare its new contracts with the customers of groups A and B that had received an offer during the past 12 months. When a match was found, a personalized fulfillment letter was printed and, together with the correct version of the navigation system, sent to the customer by registered mail. For the nonmatches if 8 months had passed since the offer, the customer was included in the monthly selection for the reminder mailing.

Closing Thoughts

The EDM program developed by the leasing company is a good example of activities based on *singular* events as described in the EDM Quadrant in Chapter 3. The predictability is very high since one knows exactly when a contract is ending. For each contract the event of contract ending occurs only once, setting singular events apart from recurring events, which also have high predictability. As mentioned in Chapter 3, singular events are often the ones that are most easily available. Setting up EDM programs based on these events most certainly isn't rocket science. Still, by combining it with more advanced disciplines like data mining and digital publishing even activities based on such simple things as singular events can be turned into state-of-the-art marketing programs.

In this case, all of the important elements previously discussed in this book that make a successful program have been included:

- Setting clear objectives.
- Developing a compelling proposition.
- Company and agent branding (Case 2).

Case 6: Developing an Event-Driven Marketing Program — 171

- Advanced personalization for small volumes by digital printing.
- Product-phase event-driven marketing (Chapter 3 and Case 3).
- Process management (Chapter 4).
- Increasing retention (Chapter 5 and Case 5).
- Calculating Return on Investment and Payback Period (Chapter 6).
- Information systems, data analysis and predictive modeling (Chapter 7).

As we've seen in the other cases in this book, not every EDM program has to be as elaborate and advanced as this one. However, if it is as complex, it will not only take considerable time to develop (this concerned program took a total of 9 months from the project's start to actual implementation), but it also involves a large number of participants and business disciplines:

- (Database) marketing and sales.
- Predictive modelers and data analysts.
- CRM and campaign management.
- Creative advertising agencies and communication experts.
- External data suppliers.
- Stakeholders like local agents/branches and headquarters.
- Mailing houses.
- Postal services.
- Web site management.

Such a large number of different disciplines of course requires tight project management by an "EDM champion" within your company. However, with the right skills, cooperation, and drive, winning programs can most certainly be developed.

The writers of this book are planning to share more case material in the future. Please visit www.eventdrivenmarketing.net and sign up for our mailing list and we'll keep you informed. Readers that have developed their own EDM programs are of course welcome to send us their learnings and experiences.

8

EDM and Legislation in the European Union

It's incomprehensible that, when planning both marketing and EDM activities, checks to verify if things are actually legally allowed are done at such a late stage in the process—or not at all! Certain marketing campaigns might actually be forbidden. Too often, planned marketing campaigns have to be cancelled because of realizations in one of those last-minute checks. Your customers are not playthings. There are laws, regulations, and practical obstacles, also with EDM. Map these out before you take your first step.

With Event-Driven Marketing we're dealing with a substantial amount of personal data that is collected, processed, and used for commercial communication and analysis. This also means that we need to take into account certain strict legal regulations regarding privacy. In this chapter we will elaborate on the impact of the usage and protection of personal data when executing EDM programs. We will also look at good taste and decency, since boundaries are set by more than just laws. We will also introduce the term *Event-Forbidden Marketing* (EFM), in case EDM is simply not allowed.

In this chapter we will look at the EU regulations while the next chapter deals with those in the US.

Introduction: Local Regulations

This chapter looks at the European legal aspects of Event-Driven Marketing (EDM). Keep in mind that within the member states of the European Union (EU), differences can occur. But in general for EDM, four categories of laws and regulations need to be considered. These four categories are:
- Rules on the processing of personal data (data protection).
- Rules on content formats: misleading advertising, games of chance.

Exhibit 8.1. The Legal Big Picture

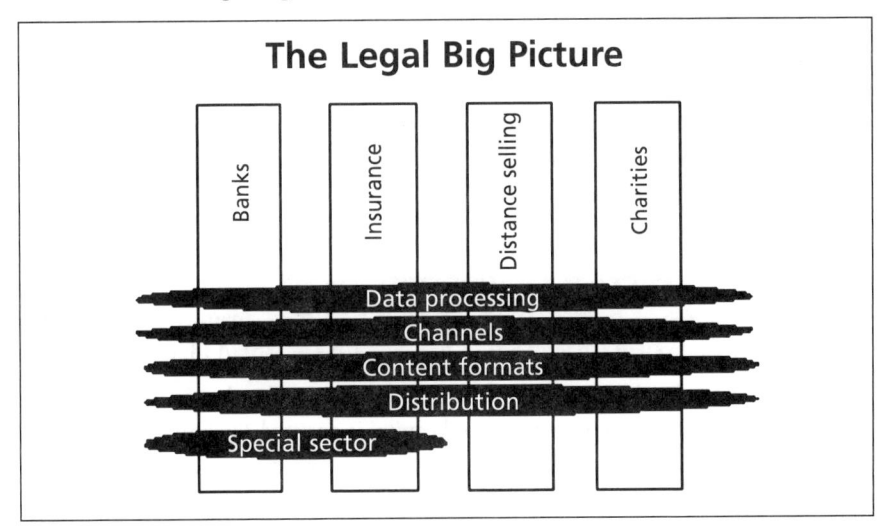

The Legal Big Picture

Banks | Insurance | Distance selling | Charities

- Data processing
- Channels
- Content formats
- Distribution
- Special sector

- Rules on the use of channels: opt-in requirements.
- Rules on distribution: packaging requirements, unaddressed advertising material.

These general rules are applicable to EDM in the broadest sense of meaning, but there are also specific regulations applicable to particular sectors that can affect EDM. Exhibit 8.1 illustrates the legal "big picture."

Laws and regulations vary from country to country, which does not make it any easier for EDM. However, differences in laws and regulations are slowly diminishing.

Universal Principles: Transparency and Confidence

But what is the trend within laws and regulations? The overall regulatory trend—and this is by no means confined solely to the EU—is towards greater transparency in order to increase consumer confidence, because consumer confidence is crucial in today's society. The laws and regulations, as the rest of this chapter will show, state information obligations for companies and organizations—information on, for example, the availability of the terms and conditions, details on the right of withdrawal from distance selling ("cooling off" periods) and the composition of a product. After all, the more transparent a company is about its products and services, the more confidence the consumer will have in the company.

Although it is neither possible nor desirable to achieve total transparency in EDM (this would negate the "surprise" effect of EDM), EDM and transparency are not mutually exclusive. Transparency can enhance confidence in companies practicing EDM by, for instance, providing the consumer with adequate information when personal data is processed.

Events as such cannot be captured into regulatory terms, except in that events arise out of the data subject's direct relationship with the "Controller" or a third party for commercial or charitable purposes. The meaning of the definition of the internal market for events is therefore not different than for personal data. The one who determines the strategic aspect of EDM is the Controller: "the (natural or legal) person that determines the purposes and means of the processing of personal data" (Article 2, Data Protection Directive).

Data Protection-related Directives

The most valuable resource for EDM and all other forms of commercial communication is personal data recorded in a database. Using electronic communication to approach a customer is of great interest. Just imagine an event-driven campaign for which it was allowed to process personal data (events), but not to use the email channel to approach the customer. This is no longer an imaginary situation in the EU; it is increasingly becoming reality.

An outline of the rules that shape the legal framework governing data processing by means of generating commercial communication follows.

Legal Information Requirements Under the Data Protection Directive

At local, national level (i.e., individual EU country) individual obligation by the Controller to inform the data subject is one of the factors to determine whether personal data are being processed fairly and carefully. If personal data are being collected directly from the data subject, the Controller is to provide them with (Article 10, Data Protection Directive):

- The identity of the Controller;
- The purposes for which personal data are being collected;
- As applicable, any further information to ensure fair and careful data processing towards the data subject, such as to block data against use for commercial and/or charitable purposes.

In the case of EDM, the main issues surrounding this obligation to inform concern the latter point. Specifically, under what circumstances does what kind of information need to be provided so that data subjects are aware of this information and the data being processed fairly and carefully. See here a (potential) conflict of interest: the organization does not want to reveal too many details about any planned event, but data subjects have to be informed at the time of registration if personal data about them is processed, or no later than at the moment of first disclosure to a third party (Article 11, Data Protection Directive). Article 11 of the Data Protection Directive covers situations on the basis of an analysis of personal data or an (external) event which may be relevant to EDM, but not noticed by the data subject.[6]

Sometimes, of course, a Controller would prefer to keep quiet about an event. But that is not always possible. In a recent case, a well-known American service provider felt obliged to invalidate all user passwords for its website after an error occurred in its own search engine. This is indisputably a case of an incident that could not and should not be kept quiet, if only because every data subject had to request a new password in order to start using the service again. Moreover, US law requires data subjects to be notified in the event of any potential loss or theft of their data.[7]

Absolute Right to Object

Direct Marketing (DM) and—from a regulatory point of view—EDM are subject to exactly the same rules: Personal data are processed or events are recorded in order to initiate or maintain a direct relationship between the Controller or a third party and the data subject for commercial or charitable purposes.[8] When conducting an event-driven campaign based upon the processing of events for DM purposes, the Controller must at a minimum inform the data subject that he or she has a relatively wide-ranging right: the right to object, on request and free of charge (Article 14, Data Protection Directive).

This right to object is *absolute*. The meaning of this absolute right is that the personal data are blocked from processing for EDM purposes. In practice, this means that personal data are to be "flagged." The rationale behind this rule is to allow data subjects to prevent any unsolicited information being offered to them based upon a personal profile. For such a block to be effective, the right to object has to cover much more than just the sending of commercial communications, both online and offline. It therefore covers all acts of processing required in practice as part of EDM, including target-group profiling and segmentation in marketing databases with a view to approaching individual customers, regardless of channel, timing, or offer.

If personal data are blocked on the basis of the absolute right to object, it is also not allowed to make personal data available to any third party within the context of an EDM campaign. And this rule is not restricted to only the disclosing of personal data; it also applies to the use of data on behalf of a third party, such as

---

[6] Article 10 of the Data Protection Directive covers situations in which personal information is obtained directly from data subjects. In such cases, data subjects must be informed as to whether or not they are obliged to answer queries put by the controller.
[7] *Webwereld Nieuwsbrief,* 4 August 2005.
[8] This definition of direct marketing is based upon Article 41 of the Dutch Personal Data Protection Act.

inserting a coupon. For instance, to insert a coupon with a magazine of another Controller occurs. Is that allowed?

In this case, a clear distinction has to be drawn between general inserts and segmented inserts. For segmented inserts, the customer database is used to select recipients of the insert. Because personal data are considered to be processed in this case, the processing is subject to the right to object: if data subjects have blocked the processing of their personal data for EDM purposes, segmented inserting is not allowed for the customers who objected. General inserting is allowed though, because with general inserting there is no specific processing of personal data on the insert.

As this example shows, the right to object can have far-reaching effects on a company's data management. As a rule, Article 14 of the Data Protection Directive entitles data subjects to object to any use of personal data for commercial communication, not just commercial approaches.[9]

Transborder Flow of Personal Data within the European Union

The transfer of personal data across internal EU borders is regarded as a regular data-processing activity, and is permitted in so far as the processing is necessary for the free flow of personal data. For free flow of personal data, personal data are to be processed on the legal basis, specified in Article 7 of the Data Protection Directive. These include the processing of personal data that is necessary:

1. "for the purposes of the legitimate interests pursued by the Controller or by the third party or parties to whom the data [is] disclosed"; and,

2. "for the performance of a contract to which the data subject is party or in order to take steps at the request of the data subject prior to entering into a contract."

Despite what some other publications claim, the unambiguous consent of the data subject is required only in exceptional circumstances. The legal basis for data processing can often be found back to the way the data subject is informed.

---

[9] Article 14 of the Data Protection Directive also recognizes another right to object, "on compelling legitimate grounds relating to his [the data subject's] particular situation . . . save where otherwise provided by national legislation." This, however, is not generally an issue in the case of direct marketing. An EDM campaign would have to make very serious infringements on a data subject's personal life (decisional privacy) for his invocation of this right to object to stand up. The data subject would have to cite substantial and well-justified grounds for his objection. One case in which he might be able to do this, though, is if an ethnically-driven campaign was based upon certain categories of data being processed in an illegitimate way. A judicial ruling will usually determine whether such an objection is justified.

Exhibit 8.2. Applicability of European Legislation

	Situation				Law applicable	
Cases	Direct marketer established in	Data controller established in	Data processor established in	Data from[10]	To the respective processing	To security measures
1	BE	BE	BE	EU EEA US	BE	BE
2	BE NL UK	BE	NL UK	EU EEA US	BE	NL UK
3	BE	BE NL UK	FR	EU EEA US	BE NL UK	FR
4	BE	BE NL UK	SP PT LUX	EU EEA US	BE NL UK	SP PT LUX

Establishment of the Controller

A data subject has to be informed according to the law where the Controller is established. National laws are virtually uniform in this respect, which makes it possible to provide such information unambiguously. *Unambiguously* means the data subject needs to be informed sufficiently as to what purpose or purposes the EDM-related activities are being developed; for example, contract fulfillment, service provision, market research, and market operating in the course of direct marketing.

Providing the information in an unambiguous way has the added advantage that the Controller does not need to check whether all the communications on the aspect of information lines of establishments elsewhere in the European Union are mutually consistent. If the obligation to inform is complied with sufficiently, the Controller is free to disclose data about the data subject with its own branches and carefully selected partners within the EU.

Establishments which process personal data on behalf of the Controller—known as "Processors"—are required to comply with the local technical and organizational security measures with regard to the processing the Processor carries out. It is not necessary to specify details of the security measures in communications to the consumer; at most, a statement is needed if an incident gives cause for such a statement.

Determining the applicability of the European national legislation is important for the free flow of services. Exhibit 8.2[11] indicates that the European rules defining applicable law with regard to the data processing (the Controller's establishment) and the security measures (the Processor's establishment) constitute a legal discipline in their own.

---

[10] EEA = European Economic Area. The European Economic Area (EEA) was established on 1 January 1994, following an agreement between member states of the European Free Trade Association (EFTA), the European Community (EC), and all member states of the European Union (EU). It allows these EFTA countries to participate in the European single market without joining the EU.

Transfer of Personal Data to Countries Outside the European Union

Transborder personal data flows outside the European Union, also referred to as "transfer to third countries," are permitted only if the country in question ensures an adequate level of protection (Article 25, Data Protection Directive). It is the European Commission that decides whether there is an adequate level of data protection. The current authorized countries are the United States ("Safe Harbor" framework, with compulsory registration on a public list of organizations which are permitted to receive data from the EU)[12], Canada,[13] Argentina,[14] Switzerland,[15] the Isle of Man,[16] and Guernsey[17].

This basic rule is subject to two so-called derogations (Article 26, Data Protection Directive) that are significant with regard to data transfer for the purposes of EDM:

1. Unambiguous consent to a proposed transfer by the data subject; and,
2. The performance of a contract to which the data subject is a party or the implementation of precontractual measures taken in response to a data subject's request.

This means, for example, that an event-driven marketer in the United States, which is not a Safe Harbor participant and wishes to act properly in accordance with the local European regulations, requires the unambiguous consent of the data subject before transferring personal data, or must be acting in fulfillment of a contract with the data subject that requires transfer, where under contractual measures arising out of a request of the data subject. In practice, however, a contract-driven data transfer is not that common and is very narrowly interpreted and enforced as such by the European authorities. If closing a contract prompts a marketer to an event-driven action, then the unambiguous consent of the data subject is still needed before personal data are transferred to the United States. Such operational obstacles can be overcome through contractual arrangements whereby another Controller or an appointed representative in the European Union provides sufficient guarantees for an adequate level of protection and complies with the local European law.

---

[11] *FEDMA European Code of Practice for the Use of Personal Data in Direct Marketing* (2003), Article 1.1: "Direct marketers established in EU/EEA territory".
[12] Commission decision of 26 July 2000.
[13] Commission decision of 20 December 2001.
[14] Commission decision of 30 June 2003.
[15] Commission decision of 26 July 2000.
[16] Commission decision of 28 April 2004.
[17] Commission decision of 21 November 2003.

Legal Information Requirements under the E-communications & Privacy Directive

The legislation regulating the use of electronic messages is increasingly important in EDM campaigning. After all, you have to be able to actually use the (electronic) data collected to contact the customer by email (email marketing), SMS or MMS (mobile marketing) or telephone (outbound telephony). The E-communications & Privacy Directive contains rules for the use of electronic contact data for the purposes of commercial communication (Article 13). This Directive particularizes and complements the regulations contained in the Data Protection Directive, so much of its conceptual framework of definitions applies here as well.

EU member states may decide independently to extend the legal restrictions pertaining to the use of electronic messages in commercial communications to the business-to-business relationship (Article 13, Section 5, E-communications & Privacy Directive). This broadens their scope from individual data subjects (natural persons and small office/home office settings) to legal entities.

Use of Electronic Messages for Commercial Communication

As a general rule, the use of electronic messages for commercial or charitable purposes is permitted only with the prior consent of the recipient. Article 2h of the E-communications & Privacy Directive defines such a message as:

> any text, voice, sound or image message sent over a public communications network which can be stored in the network or in the recipient's terminal equipment until it is collected by the recipient.

In addition, this definition covers such technologies as SMS and MMS messaging and voice-mail. The sender must be able to prove that the recipient has given his prior consent (opt-in) to be sent such messages. Also, every electronic message sent for commercial or charitable purposes, must (Article 13, Subsection 4, E-communications & Privacy Directive):

- state the true identity of the person or organization on whose behalf the communication is being sent; and,
- contain a valid address which the recipient can contact in order to cancel future receipt of such messages/withdraw the opt-in.

Legal Definition of Consent (Opt-in)

For EDM using electronic contact data, the prior consent of the recipient must be obtained. This is defined, using the term "data subject's consent," in Article 2h of the Data Protection Directive, as:

any freely given specific and informed indication of his wishes by which the data subject signifies his agreement to personal data relating to him being processed.

Such consent does not have to be given in writing. A subject's behavior or actions may also imply consent—for example, checking a box on a website. But such behavior must be unambiguous enough that it is obvious that the data subject is giving his consent. And it must be clear what specific activities he is consenting to. The senders of electronic messages for EDM purposes are subject to a burden of proof: in the event of any doubt, they must be able to demonstrate that consent has indeed been given. The fact that a data subject has not exercised his right to object in previous messages for commercial electronic communication does not indicate prior consent, the legal definition of which implies a positive expression of agreement.

The "Soft" Opt-in

There is one legal exemption to the general rule that a data subject must opt-in to receiving electronic messages for commercial communication. That applies to a specific situation in the context of the sale of goods and services, including the pre-contractual phase. If a company has obtained a subject's electronic contact details as part of the selling process, it is permitted to use them to offer its own similar products and services. One important condition for this exemption to apply is that when the details were obtained, the subject must clearly and explicitly have been offered the opportunity to object (to do so easily and free of charge) *and* if the subject does not exercise that right to object, he must be offered it, under the same conditions, each time his electronic contact details are used. In other words, every electronic message must include an "unsubscribe" option. This exception to the general rule of opt-in is known as a "soft opt-in."

Like all exceptions to a general legal rule, it is interpreted narrowly. The terms "similar" and "own" are decisive for seeking compliance with this legal exception. For instance, the use of an email address for cross-selling without the recipient's prior consent is not allowed. Up-selling and deep-selling of one's own similar products and services may be allowed, depending upon the circumstances, but only if and insofar as each electronic message sent offers the right to object to further use of the email address for commercial communications. To be on the safe side, it is always sensible to ask for consent before using a person's electronic contact details for any electronic commercial communication.

Channel Management: A Legal Necessity

Article 13 of the E-communications & Privacy Directive relates to the recording of, blocking of, or consenting to each sort of electronic channel of communication. For this reason, it is increasingly important that channel management is to be used in event-driven campaigns. Two aspects are important here:

1. The withdrawal of consent, when the data subject consented to electronic commercial communication from the event-driven marketer in accordance with Article 13, Section 1, E-communications & Privacy Directive.
2. The right to object to data processing for commercial communication, regardless of the electronic channel, in accordance with the Data Protection Directive.

The rationale behind channel management is based in part upon the notion of an "open direct marketing" thought. If the data subject withdraws his consent, the sender (the Controller) is not obliged to end all data processing related to that subject, only, for instance, that of his email address. The complete blocking of data processing is an effect of the absolute nature of the right to object (Data Protection Directive). To prevent such a total block, the Controller should inform the data subject about the possibility of withdrawing consent to the use his email address. Adjusting the messages then becomes a legal necessity so that all available channels can continue to be used for commercial communications.

Outbound Telephony

Under Article 13, Section 3, E-communications & Privacy Directive, the use of electronic contact details such as telephone numbers, mobile or fixed-line, for outbound telephony is not subject to an obligatory prior consent (opt-in) regime. EU members may choose between opt-in or an objection-based (opt-out) system.

Channel Management Matrix

The matrix in Exhibit 8.3 summarizes the opt-in and opt-out possibilities available to data subjects in each channel of communication. If data subjects are able to withdraw their consent, this does not necessarily mean that all data processing in respect of them has to end. Allowing subjects to withdraw consent on a channel-by-channel basis can often prevent invocation of the absolute right to object. If data subjects have at any time exercised their right to object to the use of their email address for commercial communications, then sending them any further emails for that purpose is prohibited until such time as they once again give their consent for commercial communication by email.

Legal Information Requirements under the E-Commerce Directive

The E-Commerce Directive contains both general rules related to information and specific ones covering contracts agreed in electronic form within the context of commercial communications. It does not cover data protection issues directly, but it does apply to any service normally provided for remuneration, at a distance, by

Exhibit 8.3. Channel Management Matrix

Event-driven marketing by . . .	Targeting	Regime	Prior consent	Inform about right to object to the processing of personal data (Data Protection Directive, Article 14)	Inform about right to object and right to withdraw consent to use electronic contact details (E-communications & Privacy Directive, Article 13)
Automatic calling machines playing pre-recorded commercial message	Every recipient	Opt-in	Yes	Yes, when personal data is collected, unless subject has already been informed	No, since prior consent is required
Fax	Every recipient	Opt-in	Yes	Yes, when personal data is collected, unless subject has already been informed	No, since prior consent is required
Email, SMS, MMS, voicemail	Prospects	Opt-in	Yes	Yes, when personal data is collected, unless subject has already been informed	Yes
	Existing and former customers, with your own similar products and services	Soft opt-in	No, providing right to object is offered in message when data is collected	Yes, when personal data is collected, unless subject has already been informed	Yes
Telemarketing (outbound)	Every recipient	Opt-out or Opt-in	Depending on opt-in regime (see Outbound Telephony)	Yes, when personal data is collected, unless subject has already been informed	Yes
Direct mail	Every recipient	Opt-out	No	Yes, when personal data is collected, unless subject has already been informed	Not applicable

electronic means and at the individual request of a recipient of services (Article 2a, E-Commerce Directive with reference to Directive 98/34/EC).

The local "established service provider" is the entity to which the terms of the E-Commerce Directive apply. It is defined in Article 2c:

> A service provider who effectively pursues an economic activity using a fixed establishment for an indefinite period. The presence and use of the technical means and technologies required to provide the service do not in themselves constitute an establishment of the provider.

The service provider will usually be the same entity as the Controller, but this is not necessarily the case in EDM campaigns with third parties or partners involved.

The E-Commerce Directive contains a general obligation to inform. Article 5 ensures that the service provider shall render easily, directly, and permanently accessible to the recipients of the service and competent authorities, at least the following information:

- The name of the service provider.
- The geographical address at which it the service provider is established.
- Details, including an email address, which allow the service provider to be contacted rapidly and communicated with in a direct and effective manner.
- Where applicable, the trade or similar public register in which the service provider is entered and its registration number or equivalent means of identification.
- Where service provider's activities are subject to an authorization scheme, the particulars of the relevant supervisory authority.
- In the case of so-called "regulated professions", any professional body or similar institution with which the service provider is registered, their professional title and the Member State in which it was granted plus a reference to the applicable professional rules in the Member State of establishment.
- Where applicable, the service provider's VAT number and whether any prices quoted include tax and delivery costs.

Articles 6 and 7 of the E-Commerce Directive lay down rules with which electronic commercial communications have to comply:

- The commercial communication must be clearly identifiable as such.
- The natural or legal person on whose behalf the commercial communication is made must be clearly identifiable.
- Promotional offers, such as discounts, premiums and gifts, where permitted in the Member State where the service provider is established, must be clearly identifiable as such, and the conditions that are to be met to qualify for them should be easily accessible and be presented clearly and unambiguously.

- Promotional competitions or games, where permitted in the Member State where the service provider is established, must be clearly identifiable as such, and the conditions for participation must be easily accessible and be presented clearly and unambiguously.
- Unsolicited commercial communications by email must be clearly and unambiguously identifiable as such as soon as they are received.
- Those on behalf of whom the commercial communications are being sent must ensure that those who have exercised their right to unsubscribe from commercial communication by email are not approached to receive such commercial communication.

What significance for EDM activities can be given in relation to the other information requirements in the Data Protection Directive and the E-communications & Privacy Directive? Even where the Controller has informed data subjects about the processing of their data and asked for the consent for the use of email for commercial purposes, this does not give the Controller a green light to approach them for commercial purposes with, for instance, a game of chance. It must be considered whether or not the promotional activity in question is permitted in the country where the service provider is established. As already mentioned, the service provider is often the same entity as the Controller. But if that is not the case, and the Controller is based in another EU Member State than the service provider, it may occur that the EDM campaign is permitted where the Controller is established, but not where the service provider is located. Again we encounter a legal area of tension: the data can be processed in the database, but may not be used instantly for an EDM campaign because the laws relating to promotional activities have not been harmonized as yet within the EU.

Legal Information Requirements under the Distance Selling Directive

The Distance Selling Directive contains a more intensive obligation to inform: the consumer must be notified of his rights both prior to the conclusion of a distance contract and during its operational performance. The possible restrictions on the use of electronic channels (distance communications technologies) also apply to the conclusion of Distance Selling (Article 13, E-communications & Privacy Directive).

A distance contract is defined (Article 2, Distance Selling Directive) as:

> any contract concerning goods or services concluded between a supplier and a consumer under an organized distance sales or service-provision scheme run by the supplier, who, for the purpose of the contract, makes exclusive use of one or more means of distance communication up to and including the moment at which the contract is concluded.

This definition uses the same term *distance* as defined and referred to under "information society services" in the E-Commerce Directive: "(. . .) without the simultaneous physical presence of the parties." The parties to a distance contract are "the supplier" and "the consumer." Certain contract types, including those related to financial services providers, are not covered by the Directive.

In good time prior to the conclusion of any distance contract, the consumer shall be provided with the following information (Article 4, Section 1, Distance Selling Directive):

- The identity of the supplier and, in the case of contracts requiring payment in advance, the address.
- The main characteristics of the goods or services.
- The price of the goods or services, including all taxes.
- Delivery costs, where appropriate.
- The arrangements for payment, delivery or performance.
- The existence of a right of withdrawal, except in the cases referred to in Article 6, Section 3.[18]
- The cost of using the means of distance communication, where this is calculated at other than the basic rate.
- The period for which the offer or the price remains valid.
- Where appropriate, the minimum duration in the case of contracts for the supply of products or services to be performed permanently or recurrently.

A customer must receive written confirmation or confirmation in another durable medium available and accessible to him of the information referred to in Article 4, Section 1, Distance Selling Directive (see above), in good time during the performance of the contract, and at the latest at the time of delivery where goods not for delivery to third parties are concerned, unless the information has already been

---

[18] Article 6, Section 3, Distance Contract Directive states: "Unless the parties have agreed otherwise, the consumer may not exercise the right of withdrawal provided for in paragraph 1 in respect of contracts:
- for the provision of services if performance has begun, with the consumer's agreement, before the end of the seven working day period referred to in paragraph 1,
- for the supply of goods or services the price of which is dependent on fluctuations in the financial market which cannot be controlled by the supplier,
- for the supply of goods made to the consumer's specifications or clearly personalized or which, by reason of their nature, cannot be returned or are liable to deteriorate or expire rapidly,
- for the supply of audio or video recordings or computer software which were unsealed by the consumer,
- for the supply of newspapers, periodicals and magazines,
- for gaming and lottery services."

given to the consumer prior to conclusion of the contract in writing or on another durable medium available and accessible to him (Article 5, Section 1, Distance Selling Directive).

Article 5, Section 1, Distance Selling Directive, further states that during the performance of the contract, and at the latest at the time of delivery to the customer, the following information has to be provided in any event:

- Written information on the conditions and procedures for exercising the right of withdrawal, within the meaning of Article 6, including the cases referred to in Article 6, Section 3 (see footnote on page 187).
- The geographical address of the place of business of the supplier to which the consumer may address any complaints.
- Information on any after-sales services and guarantees which exist.
- The conclusion for cancelling the contract, where it is of unspecified duration or a duration exceeding one year.

Every distance contract must state that the customer is entitled to a statutory withdrawal or "cooling-off" period of at least seven days. If this is not done, a default withdrawal period of three months applies. In the case of goods, this period begins on the day of receipt by the consumer. In the case of services, it applies from the day of conclusion of the contract or from the day on which the obligation to inform is complied with, provided that the three-month default withdrawal period is not exceeded.

In the case of unsolicited supply of goods or services, the customer is exempt from any obligation in respect of them. The absence of a response from the customer does not constitute consent to supply (Article 9, Distance Selling Directive).

EDM-related Directive: the Unfair Commercial Practices Directive

The Unfair Commercial Practices Directive prohibits unfair commercial practices prior, during and after any commercial transaction involving a product. A product is defined (Article 2c, Unfair Commercial Practices Directive) as "any goods or service including immovable property, rights and obligations." The scope of the prohibition extends to aspects of commercial practices such as misleading practices and omissions that would be regarded as unfair by the average consumer and a list of commercial practices (misleading and aggressive) which are regarded as unfair under all circumstances. The Directive does not apply to legal regulations on taste and decency, which vary widely between EU Member States.

A commercial practice is defined as (Article 2d, Unfair Commercial Practices Directive):

any act, omission, course of conduct or representation, commercial communication including advertising and marketing, by a trader, directly connected with the promotion, sale or supply of a product to consumers.

Regard "consumers" as "customers," and the Unfair Commercial Practices Directive has direct relationship with EDM. Starting on September 12, 2007, the Directive's national implementation date, complying with the obligation to inform under the Directives related to data protection will no longer be a remedy but will have a sanctioning effect. Annex I of the Unfair Commercial Practices Directive includes a list of commercial practices regarded as aggressive and hence prohibited, amongst them the following:

- Making persistent and unwanted solicitations by telephone, fax, email or other remote media except in circumstances and to the extent justified under national law to enforce a contractual obligation. This is without prejudice to Article 10 of Directive 97/7/EC[19] and Directives 95/46/EC[20] and 2002/58/EC[21].
- Requiring a consumer who wishes to claim on an insurance policy to produce documents which could not reasonably be considered relevant as to whether the claim was valid, in order to dissuade a consumer from exercising his contractual rights.

It will soon be possible to cite a specific action or business activity—for example, defining calling three times or more as "persistent solicitation"—as grounds for imposing a temporary or permanent ban on commercial communications, even though the applicable obligation to inform has been complied with. The United States already has similar regulations under its Federal Trade Commission Act.

Development: Event-Forbidden Marketing

Every development in marketing brings its own rules with it—from doormat to data, from traditional to multimedia, each time, the regulations respond. For example, you have to be extremely careful with the use of special categories of personal data.[22] In practice, processing personal data of this kind for direct marketing purposes is in fact not possible other than with the explicit consent of the data subject. In the period of database marketing to EDM, the call for protecting certain

---

[19] Distance Selling Directive.
[20] Data Protection Directive.
[21] E-communications & Privacy Directive.
[22] Data concerning a person's philosophy of life or religion, race, political persuasion, health, sexual life, personal data concerning trade union membership, concerning a person's criminal behavior or unlawful or objectionable conduct connected with a ban imposed with regard to such conduct.

groups against data-based marketing has led to the first specific rules, in self-regulation, for children (younger than 14 years of age). It is to be expected that the use of events will generate a reaction. Indeed, the first examples have already appeared—a long way from Europe, but still illustrative for event-forbidden marketing. A specific regulation in Florida forbids lawyers to use direct mail to contact accident victims or their immediate relatives within 30 days "for the purpose of obtaining professional employment".[23] This ban on "ambulance chasing" is based upon a description of a specific event, with the effect that it imposes a temporary prohibition upon commercial communications. In this case, a prohibited communication due to an event is further reinforced and perhaps justified by the prevailing culture of litigation in the United States. In other words, there is a movement to be signalled from event-driven marketing to event-forbidden marketing.

Transborder Event-Driven Marketing: Good Taste and Decency

One issue that has not attracted much attention so far in the debate, but could influence EDM, is the role of good taste and decency, particularly for companies operating in a variety of countries and cultures. What in one place can be regarded as a useable event might be seen as totally inappropriate somewhere else. Is this new? Of course not: it has long been a factor in direct marketing. But when the marketer comes much closer to the "customer," as is the case in EDM, it gains a new dimension. Good taste and decency lie in very much the same domain as the development of event-forbidden marketing as just described. So be aware that the defining of events which may not be used for marketing purposes is going to impose much greater limitations than currently is the case. Let us hope that things do not go that far, although "good taste and decency" will remain a subjective criterion determined on an individual basis.

Conclusion

Depending upon the extent to which an "event" is related to individual (still living) persons or whether personal data is processed for the purposes of EDM, data protection regulation and other regulations described above are applicable. Sending electronic messages, and hence the use of electronic contact data, demands more detailed interpretation (recording of channel blocks) and further development of advertisers' obligation to inform the data subject. Since event-driven marketing is "closer" to the skin of the customer, factors like good taste and decency have a bigger part to play in it.

---

[23] Florida Rule 4–7.4, Direct Contact with Prospective Clients.

It is to be expected that EDM in the near future will not be governed by regulations associated with data protection alone, but also those concerning unfair commercial practices. If this type of regulation can make certain commercial practices impossible by prohibition, then the impact of regulation will be heading towards event-forbidden marketing. But the impact of considerations of good taste and decency upon the discipline, possibly enshrined in EU regulations, must not be underestimated, not by the legislator, and not by the marketer.

Forthcoming Event: Revisions and Discussions

Early 2010 the E-communications & Privacy Directive was revised. This revision, which must be implemented before May 2011 in the member states, introduces a more severe regulation on cookies. The "storing of information, or the gaining of access to information already stored, in the terminal equipment of a subscriber or user is only allowed on condition that the subscriber or user concerned has given his or her consent." So this is not only applicable to cookies, but to all the different techniques, such as flash-cookies etc. When asking the consent the data subject should be provided with clear and comprehensive information like the identity of the "controller" as meant in the Data Protection Directive and the purposes of the data processing.

There are some exceptions to this requirement, like when it is necessary to store or access information in the terminal equipment for the sole purpose of carrying out the transmission of a communication over an electronic communications network. Another exception applies when it is strictly necessary in order for the provider of an information society service to provide the service and there is an explicit request by the subscriber or user. Using the common terms on first and third party cookies, the biggest issue here is third party cookies. Because these are in general not compliant with the aforementioned exceptions.

Heavy discussions are expected among member states, since some have said that browser settings on cookies are sufficient for the implementation of this obligation. Other member states do not agree on this. Anyway, this can have a major impact on the industry.

The second issue in the European Union and the US is OBA, online behavioral advertising and regulation. This is very close to the çookie issue but even goes beyond. OBA, if it is processing personal data, must be in accordance with the rules and legislation in the field of data processing. But it is unclear whether it can be said that OBA is always done on the basis of personal data because there is a discussion as to whether an IP-address is personal data.

The third, closely related, issue is one not within the European Union, but in the Council of Europe. In a draft recommendation of the Council of Europe there are conditions introduced for profiling. Profiling is forbidden unless this is done in accordance with the rules in the draft recommendation, which means prior consent and a list of information that should be provided to the data subject. In Article 5.1 the information that should be given is mentioned:

Article 5.1 (version April 2010)

5.1 Where personal data are collected in the context of profiling, the controller should provide the data subjects with the following minimum information:

- a. the existence of profiling;
- b. the purposes for which the profiling is carried out;
- c. the effects of applying the profile to the data subject;
- d. the categories of personal data used;
- e. the identity of the controller and, if necessary, his or her representative;
- f. the existence of appropriate safeguards;
- g. all information that is necessary for guaranteeing the fairness of recourse to profiling such as:
  - —the categories of persons or bodies to whom or to which the personal data may be communicated, and the purposes of doing so;
  - —the possibility, where appropriate, for the data subjects to refuse or withdraw consent, and the consequences of withdrawal;
  - —the conditions of exercise of the right of access, objection or correction as well as the right to bring a complaint before the competent authorities;
  - —the persons or bodies from whom or which the personal data are or will be collected;
  - —the compulsory or optional nature of the reply to the questions used for personal data collection and the consequences of not replying for the data subjects;
  - —the duration of storage.

Note that a recommendation of the Council of Europe is not a European Union Directive. A Directive of the European Union must be implemented by the member states, a recommendation is not mandatory. But since the Euro-Commissioner Vivane Redding is evaluating the Data Protection Directive before the end of 2010 there is a big danger that the (draft) recommendation will be implemented directly in the revised Data Protection Directive.

Finally also various directives[24] are brought together and revised under the

---

[24] *Sale of consumer goods and guarantees (99/44/EC)*
Unfair contract terms (93/13/EC)
Distance selling (97/7/EC)
Doorstep selling (85/577/EC)

Exhibit 8.4. Media Regulation—EU

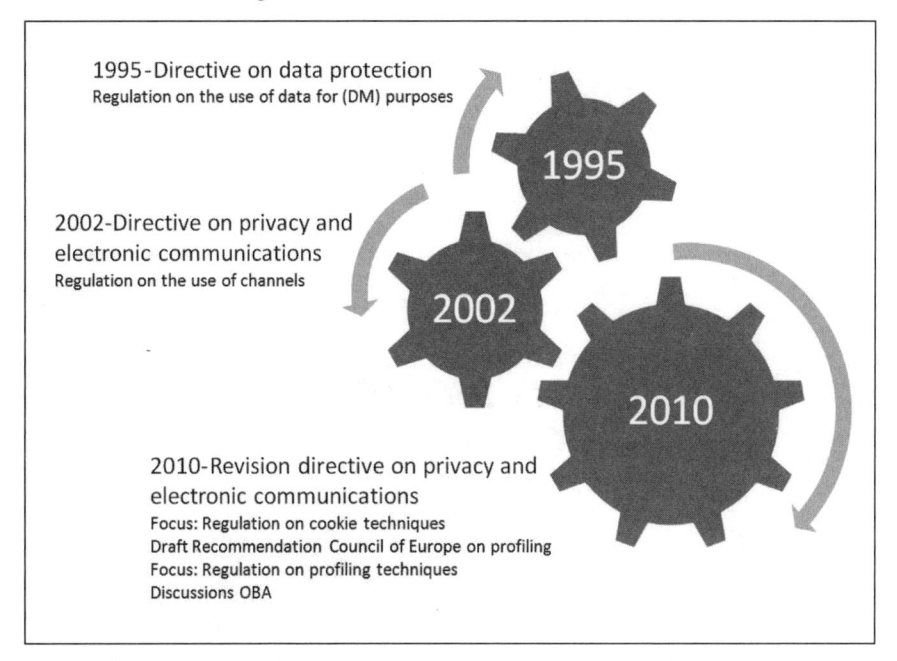

1995 - Directive on data protection
Regulation on the use of data for (DM) purposes

2002 - Directive on privacy and electronic communications
Regulation on the use of channels

2010 - Revision directive on privacy and electronic communications
Focus: Regulation on cookie techniques
Draft Recommendation Council of Europe on profiling
Focus: Regulation on profiling techniques
Discussions OBA

Consumer Aquis Directive (proposal for a Directive on Consumer Rights). It is remarkable that the E-Commerce Directive is not brought in the Consumer Aquis "project" of the European Union. This means that consumer rights are part of the the forthcoming Directive on Consumer Rights while for the online world there will be an additional e-commerce directive.

The History of Legislation for Direct Marketing

In 1995 the first directive on the protection of personal data was issued. In this Data Protection Directive it was allowed to process data for DM (and thus EDM) purposes.

In 2002 the Directive on privacy and electronic communications was issued that introduced opt-in and opt-out on the use of communication channels for DM.

In 2010 the Regulators are preparing regulation on techniques such as cookies and profiling.

This means that the Direct Marketing industry is severely regulated, starting with regulation on purposes for the processing of data, followed by regulation on the use of channels. Today regulators go even beyond this: techniques. And so—as can be seen in Exhibit 8.4—we have come full-circle, because the results of the used techniques are recorded in databases.

EDM and Legislation in the United States

Introduction

The practice of Event-Driven Marketing in the US market is somewhat more widespread than in Europe, just as the share of the advertising spend in the US attributable to "direct marketing" is greater than in Europe. According to the US Direct Marketing Association, it stands now at 53% of advertising spend. While there is no guarantee that all, or even a majority, of that investment is made with the principles set out in this work in mind, there is no doubt that a substantial portion of it is.

The entire marketing world has been forced by the growth of interactive marketing in a digital world to come to grips with two revolutions:

1. consumers now "pull" advertising messages, on demand.
2. making the right offer, at the right time, to the right person, in the medium of their choice, is imperative.

The "right" word means the "event," which makes it the correct choice. And that "event" is premised on an action by or arising around a consumer, which means it is expressed in marketing terms as "personally identifiable information," or PII, the American equivalent of European "personal data." Miss Smith has overdrawn her bank account twice in the last month; Miss Brown has graduated with honors from university and has purchased a new iPhone; Miss Smith and Miss Brown have become engaged and will be married in the Congregational Church on Main Street in July. All of these are events with marketing implications, and only one of them suggests a legal problem—the overdrafts.

Given this economic context for the discipline, it is not surprising that the law has also developed to take into account how businesses and government use PII. However, this development has been significantly different from the evolution in Europe.

US and European Law Briefly Compared

In the United States, laws protecting data and information employ much more specificity and detail than European legislation, since they relate to specific industries or subjects and are focused on protecting property and people from harm in specific contexts. They thus focus less on rather general principles and concepts, such as "processing of data" or "data controller," and more on controlling in a generally focused manner the gathering, storing, and sharing of particular kinds of information, in particular circumstances, and also on what sorts of warnings/ options must be given to individuals.

Most of the statutes in the area of privacy and data protection have been adopted either as a result of experienced market failures and personal injury, or the agreed perception that there was imminent threat of serious damage or injury if a statute were not adopted prohibiting certain uses of PII. In US law, there is no equivalent to the Data Protection Directive, but numerous targeted laws at both the Federal and State levels, which provide how certain kinds of information may be accessed or used.

For example, in the past it was possible for anyone to obtain for a nominal fee the information contained in an automobile driver's license or car registration from the Department of Motor Vehicles of each state. This information was also sold or rented by these agencies to marketing companies and others. It is highly accurate and thus was prized for segmentation and list enhancement. Unfortunately, a deranged man in California obtained the address of a young actress, Rebecca Schaeffer, from the Motor Vehicle Bureau, and stalked and murdered her. In 1997, a federal law was adopted requiring the States to adopt legislation regulating and limiting the manner and purpose for disclosure of this data. In short, it created a right to privacy for this information in order to thwart criminal misuse of the government-maintained personal information.[1]

Stated differently and with only a slight bit of exaggeration, European data protection law begins with the principle that data protection is a form of civil or human right, and enshrines a concept of "informational self-determination," to paraphrase German law, and then proceeds to work out what may permissibly be done with such data by other actors, be they government, average persons, or businesses. In short, data relating to identifiable persons may not be used/processed/

---

[1] The Driver Privacy Protection Act of 1994 (DPPA) also created an exception for the sale of this data for marketing purposes provided that State offered drivers the ability to opt-out of this sale. In some States, up to 50% of the population exercise this right. The DPPA is in many respects an example of a European Directive in that it requires the States to adopt conforming legislation. Unlike in Europe, however, States frequently challenge on Constitutional grounds the authority of Congress to force them to do so and this is true with respect to the DPPA. Thus, the availability of this information for marketing purposes varies from state to state.

manipulated unless the law permits it for a particular purpose. What is not permitted is prohibited.

On the other hand, in the United States, despite the best efforts of privacy advocates extending back at least to the beginning of the 20th century, US law in this area begins from the premise that information about citizens and consumers is basically not personal property. It is worthy of special protection only when its use or misuse could result in injury of a physical, financial, or psychological form. In short, personal information is free to flow unless someone is likely to be hurt; privacy law is more a matter of consumer protection, than of human rights.

There are of course some exceptions to this generalization that are not relevant to the issues posed for marketers, but they are worth noting.

First, the US has had privacy legislation at the federal level since the 1970s beginning with the Federal Privacy Act of 1970. This act has been amended numerous times and in effect sets controls and guidelines on access to and use and disclosure of information on citizens and lawful resident non-citizens contained in US government files. This raises no concerns for EDM.

Second, although not really considered "data protection" law, in effect that is what was accomplished at least vis-à-vis the government by the protection of individual "privacy" embodied in the Bill of Rights, the first 10 amendments to the Constitution. Two of these are in fact expressions of data protection as civil rights. The first protects an individual's personal privacy and papers within his residence unless a court orders that sanctity is invaded on reasonable grounds, and the second protects an individual's right not to be forced to incriminate himself before justice. But, an American would probably say that these privacy rights are less about "informational self-determination" and privacy as a human right, than they are about protecting the citizen against the State's power, a political right to freedom from repression or coercion. This is the US equivalent of Article 8 of the European Convention on Human Rights[2].

Third, while much of US legislation is informed by the fundamental principles of data protection expressed in the OECD Guidelines on the Protection of Privacy and Transborder Flows of Personal Data[3], many observers note that much of the

---

[2] 1. Everyone has the right to respect for his private and family life, his home and his correspondence.
2. There shall be no interference by a public authority with the exercise of this right except such as is in accordance with the law and is necessary in a democratic society in the interests of national security, public safety or the economic well-being of the country, for the prevention of disorder or crime, for the protection of health or morals, or for the protection of the rights and freedoms of others.

[3] Recommendation of the Council Concerning Guidelines Governing the Protection of Privacy and Transborder Flows of Personal Data (23rd September, 1980). The principles are Collection Limitation, Data Quality, Purpose Specification, Use Limitation, Security Safeguards, Individual Participation, and Accountability.

legislation would fall terribly short of implementing these principles to the satisfaction of European commentators.

Industry and Media-Specific Legislation

There is, thus, no single set of legislated standards regarding permissible use of personal data in the United States to guide one in making choices. However, because there is a long tradition of database compilation and direct marketing communication, there is also a history of data protection within industries/disciplines where misuse of data could cause serious damage. In addition, there has been specific media regulation for both data protection purposes and consumer protection purposes. These impact marketing directly and marketers are expected to know the limits.

Consumer Credit Information

Turning first to the subject areas which have received close attention, it may interest European readers that two important laws treat financial information as something close to "sensitive information". The first is the Fair Credit Reporting Act (FCRA)[4]. This regulates the collection, dissemination, and use of consumer credit information. Along with the Fair Debt Collection Practices Act (FDCPA) and the Gramm-Leach-Bliley Act, it forms the base of consumer credit rights in the United States. It was originally passed in 1970 and is enforced by the US Federal Trade Commission. Consumers have rights of access and correction of the files maintained by consumer reporting agencies and must be notified if they are denied credit or insurance on the basis of such a report. Access to the data collected by these agencies is limited to entities with a legitimate business reason. There are three main credit bureaus in the United States who receive credit information from banks, insurance companies, credit card companies, retail chains and other sources: Experian, Equifax, and TransUnion. Consumers may receive one copy of their credit report each year for free.

Information Notices by Financial Institutions

The Gramm-Leach-Bliley Act (GLB)[5] introduced a program to systematically govern the collection, disclosure, and protection of consumers' and customers' non-public personal information acquired by financial institutions. Part of GLB established three privacy-related rules: Financial Privacy, Safeguards, and Pretexting Protection. Only the first is relevant here, since it would limit third parties' potential use of customer information held by financial institutions.

---

[4] 15 U.S.C. § 1681 et seq.
[5] Pub.L. 106-102

The Financial Privacy Rule requires financial institutions to provide each new customer with a privacy notice when the relationship is established and annually thereafter. The privacy notice must explain what information is collected, where it is shared, how it is used, and how it is protected. The notice must note that the consumer has a right to opt-out of the information being shared with unaffiliated parties. Importantly, customers can not opt-out of sharing of information with defined service providers and companies that provide marketing services to the institution. Service providers are companies hired to perform a specific service, such as printing checks, and joint marketers are companies that have an agreement with the financial company to offer other financial products or services. However, customers can opt-out of sharing with third-party nonaffiliates, i.e., companies renting the company's mailing list.

One piece of information cannot be transferred, however. Customers' account numbers may not be disclosed to nonaffiliated companies when it comes to telemarketing, direct mail marketing or other marketing through email, even if the individuals have not opted out of sharing the information for marketing purposes.

Thus, if Miss Brown's bank was to begin a program to market new services to customers who had overdrawn their accounts twice, they would have to carefully review their notice, determine whether she has exercised an opt-out, and if they will do this themselves or provide data to a nonaffiliate.

Protected Health Information

Also an "industry specific" statute is the Health Insurance Portability and Accountability Act (HIPAA)[6], a very complex statute addressing medical insurance portability, identification of providers, plans and employers, administrative issues, and privacy and security of personal health information. As concerns privacy, "covered entities" are restricted as to how and to whom Protected Health Information (PHI) may be disclosed. They have notification and security obligations regarding this information. PHI is any information about health status, provision of health care, or payment for health care that can be linked to an individual, in short, any part of a medical record or payment history maintained by a covered entity.

Individuals have access and correction rights. There are detailed rules on to whom and for what purpose PHI may be disclosed, in general only to facilitate treatment, payment or health care operations, or with the consent of the patient. Covered entities must notify the uses to be made of PHI.

The impact on marketing seems to have been negligible, since confidentiality has been a hallmark of the medical profession for thousands of years. However, hospitals have changed many practices. For example, they no longer disclose to local newspapers news of births, which was useful data to some merchants. Moreover, medical research projects have found it extremely difficult to recruit volun-

---

[6] Pub. L. 104–191

Exhibit 9.1 Media Regulation—US

Channel	Target	Opt-in/out	Comment
Telephone	Customers and inquirers	Opt-out	Government Do-Not-Call list opt-out not applicable, but in-house Do-Not-Call list required
Telephone	Prospects	Opt-out	Do-Not-Call list applies
Mobile phone, SMS, Fax	Customers and prospects	Opt-in	
Direct Mail	Customers and prospects	Opt-out	Self-regulation only
Email	All	Opt-out. Notice required in message unless "relational or transactional"	In-house suppress required

teers for drug and procedure tests because they no longer have access to records of patients who might participate and required warnings surrounding permission to transfer data frighten patients.

Media Channels

As concerns media channels, the two most important governing telemarketing and email marketing area shown in Exhibit 9.1.

Telephone, Mobile, SMS, Fax

The federal Telephone Consumer Protection Act of 1991 (TCPA)[7] is the primary law governing telemarketing. TCPA restricts the use of automatic dialing systems, artificial or prerecorded voice messages, SMS text messages received by cell phones, and the use of fax machines to send unsolicited advertisements. It also specifies several technical requirements for fax machines, autodialers, and voice messaging systems—principally with provisions requiring identification and contact information of the entity using the device to be contained in the message. The Federal Trade Commission (FTC) and Federal Communications Commission (FCC) each have enforcement and rule-making authority under the TCPA.

Of relevance here, unless the recipient has given prior express consent, the TCPA and FCC rules thereunder require:

- The marketer must maintain a "Do Not Call" (DNC) list for in-house suppress, which must be honored for 5 years.
- Marketers must provide their name, the name of the person or entity on whose behalf the call is being made, and a telephone number or address at which that person or entity may be contacted.

---

[7] 47 U.S.C. 227

- Marketing calls cannot be made to residences with artificial voices or recordings.
- Calls cannot be made to mobile phones or to any service in which the recipient is charged for the call.
- Prerecorded or autodialed calls cannot engage two or more lines of a multi-line business or to any emergency number.
- Marketing faxes may not be sent.

With the growing adoption of auto-dialing equipment starting in the 1990s, it became apparent that a major weakness in this law was that that the consumer had to request each telemarketer who called to be put onto that telemarketer's list. Reacting to very intense and sustained public pressure, Federal legislation resulted in the creation of the National Do-Not-Call list by the FTC in 2003. Only residential phone numbers may be listed, and there are a number of exceptions to the calling prohibition, notably for existing business relationships. It bears noting that the TCPA also specifically mentions that it applies to calls and faxes from outside the United States.

Something like 75% of the American public has registered their phone numbers. Consequently, marketers are increasingly obliged to obtain express consent for calls. And, of course, they must clean their calling lists against the DNC list to remove prospects from it. However, companies can call consumers with whom they have an existing business relationship (EBR), defined as 18 months after a purchase or delivery, and 3 months after an inquiry.

The situation is complicated further by the existence in many States of their own statutory DNC lists, which often have different exceptions as to coverage. For example, in some States, newspaper subscription sellers need not use the DNC list.

Also of relevance to EDM, at least as it might be practiced by a telephone services provider, is the Telephone Records and Privacy Protection Act of 2006 which protects Customer Proprietary Network Information (CPNI) generated with a landline, mobile, or VOIP carrier. This data may not be used by a company to market products to its own customers unless the company has given the customers the ability to "opt-out" of this use. In addition, the company may not disclose the data to any unrelated third party without the customer's "opt-in" to the practice. There are exceptions for law enforcement.

Email

The other channel regulation, the CAN-SPAM Act of 2003[8] established that the opt-out principle would prevail for commercial email messages. Commercial offers, but not "transaction or relationship messages" must comply with certain requirements.

---

[8] 15 U.S.C. 7701,et seq. Controlling the *Assault of Non-Solicited Pornography And Marketing Act of 2003.*

"Commercial" has come to be understood to be defined by a combination of the content in the subject line and "above the fold content" in the body of the message. If this content contains a solicitation and it can be determined that the majority of the content is selling something—it is a commercial offer. If the subject line and body content are majority invoicing information, a sales receipt, account information, etc. the offer is considered transactional.

There are no restrictions against a company emailing its existing customers or anyone who has inquired about its products or services, since these are classified as "relationship" messages. Nor are their restrictions against renting or selling one's email database. Nevertheless, the practice of many email service providers and of most companies is to place an opt-out message in all but transactional messages and not to rent their lists.

If a user opts out, a sender has ten days to cease sending and can only use that email address for compliance purposes. An email address may not be sold or rented after an opt-out request and the unsubscribe mechanism must work for at least 30 days after transmission. The sender must include a physical address or post office box of the publisher or advertiser.

Finally, it bears noting that sexually-oriented spam must have "SEXUALLY EXPLICIT" in the subject line.

The marketing community itself has been stricter in this area than government, and the general practice among companies is to elicit an opt-in for email messages, and in some cases, a double opt-in, and to commit not to rent or sell the address. The following notice at the end of a loyalty club emailing is representative of this practice, and its "no sharing" commitment is also increasingly common:

This email was sent because you joined the Boston Market VIP Club in one of our locations, online or at one of our events. Your email address will not be shared with anyone. You can take your name out of the Boston Market VIP Club at any time by clicking the unsubscribe link on this email and you will be removed from our list immediately. Boston Market Corporation, 14103 Denver West Pkwy, Golden, CO 80401.

Direct Mail

There is not yet any legal restriction on marketing in the mail channel, although there is a very active movement calling for the establishment of a national "do not mail list" similar to the federal DNC list. For many years, the Direct Marketing Association (DMA) has maintained both do-not-call and do-not-mail lists which consumers were free to subscribe to. The DMA requires its members to both maintain in-house suppress lists and to use the DMA's lists, although it is phasing out its

DNC list and has recently changed its do-not-mail system to eliminate the list creation and put consumers in direct contact with companies.[9]

It should be noted for non-US readers that in the United States only the postman may put materials in a mailbox or mailslot, and thus all direct mail has paid postage of some sort. Thus, there is no unaddressed mail in householders' mailboxes of the sort experienced elsewhere. This is not to say that every piece of the some 600 or so direct mail pieces received annually by the average home is relevant or targeted, but it is at least addressed.

Enforcement and Conclusion

As we have seen, the US has no overarching Directive regarding privacy as a civil right. There are two consequences of this "nonelevation" of privacy concerns to the level of civil right. First, if the use of PII is to be controlled in generally limited circumstances, these circumstances must be carefully defined and a structure created to enforce the protections created. Second, since law is an imperfect implement of regulation of societal norms, which mutate and evolve much faster than the law, there must be other "regulatory" forms that can function more swiftly, and in the lacunae left by the legislative processes.

The federal and state governments have responded to citizen concerns with legislation that places enforcement primarily in the hands of powerful Federal regulatory agencies such as the Federal Communications Commission and the Federal Trade Commission, and the States Attorneys General. Consequences of violation of these protections range from "cease and desist" orders to civil penalties and possible criminal fines and imprisonment. In a few instances, citizens have been given the ability to sue for statutory (minimum) damages, as in the case of commercial fax messages which were unauthorized.

Businesses and individuals have responded in sensible economic fashion by investing in compliance and self-education. For example, there now exists a profession and a corporate position of Privacy Officer, and an educational/certification association—International Association of Privacy Professionals[10]—with some 5,200 members from academia, business, and government. These participants have helped to raise issues of privacy and data protection in their areas. As a consequence businesses, especially in the face of the voices heard in Internet social media, are becoming more self-regulating and cautious in their use of personal information.

Nevertheless, this new caution, especially with respect to the use of the telephone and Internet data, has not prevented the continued growth of Event-Driven Marketing in the US, but in fact may have resulted in marketers becoming more disciplined in spotting the "right" time, offer, product, person, and data.

---

[9] www.dmachoice.org/
[10] https://www.privacyassociation.org/

Appendix 1. Tips and Checklists

In this appendix we provide tips and checklists that we hope will help you when setting up your own EDM program.

Eleven Lessons Learned

The case studies in this book are of course summaries of a number of programs implemented by various businesses. They are the product of many years of development, ROI calculation and testing. There is much more to them than meets the eye, particularly when it comes to their whole organization and the use of database technology behind the scenes. But they still teach us some clear lessons. What are the critical factors when setting up an event-driven marketing program?

1. **Make sure your sources are good.** A good EDM program begins with data gathered accurately and promptly from a reliable source. With timing crucial to EDM, data soon becomes worthless if it arrives too late. There is little point in offering products if the consumer is no longer going to use them. Reliability is just as important, since you want as little waste and irrelevant communication as possible in your program. One manufacturer of premium pet foods, for example, discovered that a few breeders were taking advantage of its generosity by sending in names plucked at random from the telephone directory, pretending that they had bought pets in order to claim extra free food. The closer the source is to the customer, the more reliable the data usually is. Ideally, then, your information will come directly from customers themselves.

2. **Think like the customer.** Put yourself in the customer's shoes. Adopt a user rather than a product perspective. Product and brand managers are all too often so blinded by their own perceptions that they fail to realise that customers are using the product in a completely different way. This 'Marketing Myopia' can lead to discrepancies between the actual and theoretical timing of events, as we saw in the premium pet foods case study.

3. **Make the right calculations.** First check that the program works in theory. Especially given the fact that margins in some sectors can be very tight, calculating a program's profitability is an absolute necessity. Our pet food manufacturer worked out that a retention program aimed at cat owners would barely increase its profits because cats eat less and so the additional margins would only just exceed the program costs. Before presenting your plans to management or putting them into practice, use the formulae in Chapter 7 to calculate whether the program can be profitable in theory.

After implementation, check on a regular basis whether the assumptions made in those calculations do still apply in the "real world".

4. **Test on a small (but statistically large enough) group.** The complexity of EDM programs, together with the high degree of differentiation they require, means that they are not the cheapest form of marketing. Think of all that expensive coordination, customisation of (e)mailings and database management. On the other hand, their perfect timing does make them the most effective form in many cases. Once you have made the necessary initial profitability calculations, it is a very good idea to test your assumptions regarding response rates, retention and share of wallet on a trial group. Compare the results with those from a comparable control group that has not been included in the EDM program. If the test shows that the program can be profitable, it can be rolled out to all potential customers.

5. **Keep asking questions.** Use every contact with the customer to check your data and enrich your database. Always give the consumer the chance to contact you so that he can update his own details. Not only does this keep your database up to date, it also minimises the danger of incorrect information causing irritation or upset.

6. **Be relevant.** The more relevant the communication, the more effective it will be. As the case studies show, achieving relevance often requires a good deal of brainwork on the database side as much as anywhere. Make sure that everything is properly structured and has been thoroughly tested.

7. **Keep the database clean and up to date.** Enter changes to the database as quickly as possible, and always before making the next mail selection. Screen the content of every field regularly, for both quality and logic. Look for discrepancies. Do not blindly trust the accuracy of your data-entry department. As database marketing guru Arthur Middleton Hughes once wrote, *'You can't do good database marketing unless you are constantly monitoring your delivery methods and your output. Your customers see your output. You can ruin your reputation with thousands—or millions—of customers overnight if you are not constantly vigilant.'*

8. **Check, check, and double-check.** It is often highly advisable to check the information in a database thoroughly before rolling out a program. Nothing is more devastating than receiving an upbeat letter for a cat or dog that died a couple of months earlier. And as for the expectant mothers described in Case Study 4, just think what the impact would be if you failed to check for subsequent miscarriages before including them in your EDM program.

9. **Remember your lead times.** Bear in mind that in case of regular direct mail there is delay between a message being sent and its receipt. This is particularly important when it is timed to coincide with a particular event. Is

the message on time and still relevant? How long before or after the event should it be sent? This is one of the key factors determining how frequently you should, say, generate a new run of letters. Once a day? Once a week? Once a month? This is a also particularly important consideration in the case of international direct-mail programs, where you are at the mercy of what can be considerable postal delays.

10. **EDM is a permanent process, not a one-off promotion.** As we've seen in Chapter 5, the triggers in your database, which in turn are derived from events, determine *when* something is done and *what* it is. This demands an approach entirely different from that used when sending a mailshot announcing a new product to everyone in your database. We recently heard a marketing manager say, "OK, we'll do the product launch in March and the EDM program in June and July." She had totally missed the point!

11. **Be different.** Like most products and marketing activities, the communications in your EDM programs are often relatively easy for your competitors to copy. So make sure that you are the first in your market to introduce EDM, and make it distinctive and special enough that people stick with your program even after competing versions appear.

Preparing an EDM Program

The first thing you need to do when starting an EDM program is a lot of thinking. Event-driven marketing is not about **individual actions**, it is about **ongoing programs**. Events identified on, say, a monthly, weekly or daily basis trigger communications. You cannot just say, "Let's do something this quarter for everybody who has had a baby in the past three months." Once you have started, you have to see it through. Otherwise you are better off spending your money on other things. If you want to be customer-oriented, innovative and original, then EDM is a good option for you. Here are some things to think about.

Vision

- My business is facing growing competition.
- In a highly competitive market, the customer is increasingly important to me. They are not a fixed target, but constantly changing individuals.
- In general, customers are poorly "managed". As a customer of other businesses, who gives me the best service? How?
- Event-driven marketing is a good way of serving customers in accordance with my business requirements.

Strategy

- I can improve my customer relationships in order to strengthen my competitive position if I am to make the most of an EDM program.
- The relationship I have or which I am looking for with an individual customer is a question of:
  —Past customer value and relations (loyalty).
  —Future customer value (potential and contribution).
  —Real-time customer knowledge (see "Marketing" below).
- A good understanding, theoretical and practical, of customer profitability methods and models is essential if I am to develop a sound strategic framework for the management of customers and my relationship with them. As part of this, I need to identify points requiring improving or change if I am to meet my own business requirements.

Marketing

- I must take a good look around my customer database in order to understand my customer in a dynamic way.
- I must use segmentation and behavioural models in order to identify my target groups and individual customers.
- I should compile a list of "events" related to customer clusters and to the use of media and channels. I need to develop a strategy for testing, evaluating and analysing a range of offers, channels and communications (media, resources, strategy).
- Can the effectiveness of an EDM program be described in concrete terms? What are the key issues involved here?
- What real, achievable opportunities does EDM open up?
- How can these opportunities be exploited and gain the organisation's commitment?
- Can I analyse trends, finances, market shares, profitability, channels, media choices and the relationship between them?
  —For example, finding cost-effective channels for "low-profit" customers.
  —Establishing predictive behavioural models.
  —Establishing cross-selling models.
- Can profitability be used as the basis for segmentation, to identify such determinants as the following:
  —Lifestyle or life-stage segmentation, behavioural measurements and behaviour forecasts so as to develop customer-specific propositions.
  —The formulation of appropriate events so as to develop propositions for individuals within the target group as a whole.

Sit down at your desk and ask yourself the following questions:

- What is my vision of direct and interactive customer contact?
- What do I know about this subject? Will everybody in my organisation understand it, or want to? What experience do we have with it?
- Do I have the power to be interactive in this way? Do I have the technology, the organisation, the right conditions and the budget? Can I carry my organisation with me?
- Can I "map" my customers in terms of their needs, customer value, share of wallet and potential?
- Are my procedures clear and efficient? Can I measure and steer marketing processes?
- Can I do it all myself? Or do I need to outsource?
- Do I have enough information about the competition?
- Do I want to do it? Does the customer need it?

EDM in Practice

Here are some practical tips for implementing an EDM process.

Organization

Initiation. It is not advisable to start with too many EDM programs at once. Allow your organisation and your suppliers time to get used to the process and complexity of event-driven marketing. No more than three programs should give you a good start.

Creation. Research the production of mail packs and the potential—as well as the limitations—of digital printing, printing on demand (POD) and select feeding. They could save you money and increase the flexibility of your stock control.

Processes. Make sure that the processes involved in every EDM program are described clearly, including any exceptions that may arise. Before the program goes "live", it is advisable to conduct a full test.

Performance. To safeguard communications and response times, service-level agreements (SLAs) are essential. And not just with external suppliers, but also with those departments within your organisation that form part of the EDM chain. An SLA covers such matters as delivery dates, turnaround times, production capacity and quality control.

IT Systems

Communications and data flows. Think carefully about how you bring together all your communications and data flows. Channelling them makes it easy to monitor processes centrally.

Triggers. You want to trigger communications automatically, using predefined decision rules. To keep the management and organisation of your EDM processes under control, draw a distinction between two types of business rules:

- Campaign rules.

    Example

    —If response = "yes" and . . .
    - Customer value is greater than X, then . . .
        - Send pack A.
    - Customer value is less than X, then . . .
        - Send pack B.

- Enterprise rules.

    Example

    —Never send more than X (direct-marketing) communications within Y weeks.

Data-interchange protocols. Define standard import and export formats and record layouts. If at all possible, make your suppliers adopt these. That makes it easier for you to switch supplier or add new ones as capacity demands.

Reports. Before your EDM program goes "live", decide what reports need to be generated and in what form: real-time, daily, weekly and so on. Do not confine these just to response and conversion data. Also consider reporting on budgets, stocks and notification thresholds (who should be notified, and when, in the event of an impending stock shortage).

—By Dick Vanderzaken and Ronald Marcus, 2Organize Holland

Appendix 2. ROI Case Studies

To work through the example cases, first download the Excel workbook online at www.eventdrivenmarketing.net. Open the file and look across the tabs at the bottom of the workbook to find the concerned exercise. When you click on it, you will find a spreadsheet similar to what you see in the book.

The "answers" to the case questions can be downloaded at www.eventdrivenmarketing.net separately, so you can check your work and make sure you are using the formula properly.

Break Even Exercise

John Goodman is planning to do a birthday promotion to customers of a budget direct retail jeweler. John has reviewed past promotions that were similar, and within the customer list he expects a response rate of 3.0% (in this case response rate is considered to be an actual sale). The featured gift item sells for $100, which is the expected average order. John plans to send out a fairly elaborate mail piece, which will cost $1.75 with postage. The company will send each item in a gift wrapped box including a birthday card.

John is concerned that given the cost of the mail piece, they might not be making a profit. He does not want to market to customers below break-even.

Start by entering the numbers below in the Break-Even tab of the spreadsheet to find the answers to the four questions below:

Average Order:	$100
Cancels, Bad Debt:	1%
COGS* %:	50%
Fulfillment Cost:	$7.00 (data entry, processing, gift wrap, card)
Cost per Reach:	$1.75

*Cost of Goods Sold

Question 1: Would you say they are likely to break-even?

Question 2: What is the break-even $ per name?

Question 3: If John offered an item with a COGS of 75% instead and it increased the average gift (average order) to $175, would break-even response% go up or down? Would break-even $/name, go up or down? Assume Cancels, fulfillment, and Cost per Reach stay the same.

Question 4: If you wanted the lowest break-even response rate, would you go with the $100 item with 50% COGS, or the $175 item with 75% COGS?

Profitability by Campaign Exercise

A furniture retailer runs a semi-annual sale directed at new, first time homebuyers. The marketing manager generates as much floor traffic as possible, but doesn't apply profitability measures to the results. The business manager wants to bring some business discipline to the marketing numbers, and wants to "balance out" the skills of the marketing and sales team with greater financial discipline.

Marketing has a budget of $50,000 to advertise for the upcoming sale. The ads themselves are well-designed ads and the marketing manager negotiates good deals with the local newspapers and radio stations. They spend $10,000 of the $50,000 creating new advertisements. That covers design, copyrighting, photography, and so on. This leaves $40,000 for placing the ads in the paper and on the radio.

Because first time homebuyers are likely furniture buyers anyway, the business manager would like to get a relatively high 30% Contribution to profit and Overhead from the sale.

You have come up with the following estimates based on results from past sales:

Gross Sales:	$500,000
Returns, Cancels, etc.:	5.00%
COGS%:	50%
Average Order:	$750
Fulfillment Cost/order:	$75 (delivery)

Question 5: With these numbers will they meet or exceed the business manager's goal?

Question 6: The sales manager suggests we should place more ads. $40,000 only covers one newspaper ad and a few radio stations, and with twice placement budget, they think they can get twice the sales. If printing and placement was doubled to $80,000 and sales also doubled to $1 million, would they meet or exceed the 30% goal? (No other numbers change.)

Question 7: Based on Question 6, do they make exactly twice the profit?

Question 8: The Company's chief accountant suggests they are spending too much creating new ads. He wants them to re-use some photos and make smaller changes. He wants to see if we can lower our design of advertising costs to $5,000.

Going back to the numbers in Question 5 (sales $500,000, placement $40,000), if we could lower design of advertising to $5,000 without losing sales, would they meet or exceed the 30% goal?

Sample Profitability of Multistep Campaigns Exercise

You are part owner of a restaurant that offers a catered facility for wedding receptions. It is a very large facility, with an average reception selling for $20,000.

A major marketing expense has been participating in bridal fairs. Few sales are made at each bridal fair, and it often takes several contacts with prospective brides and their families before they buy. This is causing a problem for the marketing department, because the Chief Operating Officer has realized that they don't make enough sales after the first contact to the families they met at bridal fairs to justify the cost. The COO thinks going to bridal fairs is a waste of money and should be dropped.

The sales manager argues that most brides and their families require a series of contacts before they will buy. The bride has to have her questions answered so she will specify our facility. We have to get the approval of the family, who is often paying for the reception. We have to work out terms and prices with each buyer. So we rarely make a sale at a bridal fair, and it often takes months of re-contacts. Only on rare occasion do they buy right away, or without going through the entire decision process.

Currently, all prospects gathered at trade shows get the following contacts:

Initial: Call to qualify their needs, gather information, and determine the best things to offer

2nd Contact: Menu, brochure, and small food samples

3rd Contact: Follow-up call to talk with bride and family

4th Contact: Specific offer geared to their needs

5th Contact: Negotiate with buyer

For the sake of simplicity we will assume that an order requires all five contacts and no purchases are made before the 5th contact. Along the way customers will however drop out and decide not to be interested in the company's services. Note: the drop-out rate is the percentage of customers contacted in a specific phase that do not wish another contact. The cost per contact and drop-out rate per contact can be found in the table below. Customers remaining after the 5th contact will make a purchase.

	Cost of Contact	Drop-Out Rate
Initial Contact:	$10.00	0%
2nd Contact:	$15.00	20%
3rd Contact:	$7.50	15%
4th Contact:	$5.00	20%
5th Contact:	$25.00	20%

You are the CFO and want to determine whether or not the sales manager has a valid argument. After gathering and analyzing the data, you have come up with the following numbers:

Bridal Fair (Advertising) Cost:	$50,000
Prospects per Bridal Fair:	50
Cost to Enter Data:	$5.00 per name
Average Sale:	$20,000
COGS:	75%
Returns, Cancels, Bad Debt, etc:	2%
Fulfillment Cost	$250.00

You will side with the sales manager if they have at least broken even on bridal fairs by the 5th contact. But, if bridal fairs still don't cover their costs by then, you will side with the COO.

Question 9: Do you agree that bridal fairs are covering their costs by the 5th contact?

Question 10: What would your answer be if we gathered only 25 names per trade show?

Question 11: Would your answer to question 10 be different if entry cost of names was $1.00 and not $5.00?

Sample Lifetime Value Exercise

This exercise uses a method of calculating Lifetime Value that differs from the approach in the example in Chapter 6. One item requiring explanation in the Lifetime Value formula used in this calculation is Response Rate per Contact. Where it says "per year", Year One is the first year they are a customer, Year Two is the second year, and Year Three is the third year. It is NOT their "recency" or year or most recent activity. The response generally goes down over time, because some customers go away each year (even though your best customers stay.)

The Response Rate per Contact is set up that way so marketers can vary the number of contacts per year, which is useful when customers are all contacted the same number of times per year, or when customers could be contacted more frequently.

To determine or estimate response rate per contact, you will need to determine response rates for all the customers first acquired in the most recent year, 1–2 years ago, and 2–3 years ago. Since the day a customer first made a purchase is usually tagged in their customer record, it may be difficult to do this—but not impossible!

The owner of a toddler and young children's clothing cataloger is concerned that the company is spending too much to acquire new customers. Customers tend to outgrow their offerings by the time they enter grade school, so if they acquire parents of a newborn or 1 year old, they only have a few years to sell them products.

The manager of the finance department looked at the numbers for customer behavior over time. With access to sales records, the costs of marketing campaigns, and the frequency of marketing campaigns, they have come up with the following numbers to put into a lifetime value calculation:

Cost to Reach a prospect:	$1.00
Average Prospect Response Rate:	0.90% (Avg. response to prospecting efforts)

Based on these figures, the acquisition costs for a new customer can be calculated.

Average Initial Order:	$80.00
Average COGS %:	47%
Initial Fulfillment Cost:	$7.00

With these figures the profit on the initial sale and the initial investment per customer can be calculated.

Cost to Reach A Customer: $0.95
Number of Customer Contacts per year: 12

With these figures the annual marketing costs can be calculated.
Response Rate per Contact from:

1st Year Customers:	18% (per each contact, 1st year customers)
2nd Year Customers:	15% (per each contact, 2nd year customers)
3rd Year Customers:	10% (per each contact, 3rd year customers)

Since they have a limited time horizon as a customer, only a 3-year window will be considered.

Average Repeat Order:	$85.00
Fulfillment Cost:	$5.60
Discount Rate:	20% (represents required return, should exceed return on equity, plus risk factor)

Question 12: How much more do they spend on advertising to gain a new customer compared to what we make on the first sale, on average? In other words, what is their initial investment per customer?

Question 13: Do they make back the loss over time, given a time value of money of 20%?

Question 14: Do they make back the loss in less than one year or more than one year, not counting time value of money? In other words, does *Profit Per Customer in Year One* exceed Initial Investment Per Customer or not?

Payback Period Exercise

The marketing manager of a financial services provider is planning a campaign to generate leads for their intermediaries. Business-to-business customers will receive a simple mailing (costs $1 per piece) that invites them to visit a web site and calculate their monthly fee when financing their next investment by leasing. The online calculator features a form that customers can fill out to be visited by an account manager of their local intermediary. Non-response to the mailing is called by a telemarketing call center (costs $8 per call). The whole campaign is managed by the company's database management agency at a project management fee of $15,000.

The CFO has given the marketing department the goal of recouping any acquisition investment within 10 months. He has also calculated that the annual profit gained from a lease contract of the concerned target group is $1000 (after deducting the commission for the intermediary). A selection from the database proves that 10,000 customers fall within the criteria of the target group.

Participating intermediaries will pay a contribution of $5 per customer. These contributions are deducted from the campaign costs when calculating the payback period. Since the sales staff of the intermediaries makes the visits, these costs are not included in the payback period calculation.

From experience the marketing manager expects to get a 2% response from the mailing and another 8% from the telemarketing follow-up.

Question 15: Based on these assumptions, will the marketing manager be able to run the campaign according to the CFO's payback period goal?

Question 16: The marketing manager doubts if all intermediaries will participate when they need to pay a contribution of $5 per customer. He suggests lowering the contribution to $2 per customer. Will the payback period goal still be reached under these circumstances?

Question 17: Instead of decreasing the contribution per customer the company decides to go ahead as planned. Unfortunately the marketing manager was right. A substantial number of intermediaries do not participate in the campaign and only 4,000 customers are reached. Does the campaign still meet the payback period goal?

Appendix 3. List of Exhibits

Exhibit 1.1. Differences between direct marketing and event-driven marketing
Exhibit 1.2. DM and EDM Processes
Exhibit 1.3. Positioning of EDM-related marketing tools and concepts
Exhibit 1.4. The returns from EDM: better results at lower contact costs per customer
Exhibit 1.5. From production to process orientation: where do you stand?
Exhibit 1.6. The top ten EDM considerations
Exhibit CS1.1. Online registration form
Exhibit CS1.2. Customer request form
Exhibit 2.1. Market segmentation, definition and positioning
Exhibit 2.2. Traditional versus Event-Driven Marketing
Exhibit 2.3. Sales Funnel
Exhibit 2.4. Analysis of patrons of a symphony orchestra
Exhibit 2.5. Loyalty Rate
Exhibit 2.6. Average Annual Sales
Exhibit 3.1. Contact planning steers individual actions
Exhibit 3.2. From event to action
Exhibit 3.3. Scorecards and triggers play an important role in contact planning
Exhibit 3.4. Selection of an action based upon the contact plan
Exhibit 3.5. Roles in the marketing process
Exhibit 3.6. Events, Indicators, Actions and Media
Exhibit 3.7. The EDM Quadrant
Exhibit 3.8. Application levels of EDM
Exhibit 3.9. Examples of different applications of the EDM Quadrant

Exhibit 4.1. Variable process chains
Exhibit 4.2. The event-driven marketing cycle as a variant of the direct marketing cycle
Exhibit 4.3. Response Example A
Exhibit 4.4. Response Example B
Exhibit 4.5. Difficult-to-manage campaign execution
Exhibit 4.6. Marketing Campaigns versus EDM Programs
Exhibit 4.7. The Complexity of EDM
Exhibit 4.8. From DM to EDM: Increasing Complexity
Exhibit CS3.1. Effect of Travelers' Retention Program
Exhibit CS3.2. Risk/Revenue Matrix
Exhibit CS3.3. Communications Testing Matrix
Exhibit CS3.4. The effect of the retention program on churn

Exhibit CS3.5. The effect of the retention program on revenue
Exhibit CS3.6. The effect on phone usage of the retention program
Exhibit CS3.7. The effect of the new retention program on costs per customer in 3 years
Exhibit 5.1. Loyalty versus Retention
Exhibit 5.2. The Causes of Low Retention
Exhibit 6.1. The Customer Value Cube
Exhibit 6.2. The Importance of Retention
Exhibit 6.3. A Sample Break-Even Calculation
Exhibit 6.4. Profitability by Campaign Calculation
Exhibit 6.5. An example Profitability by Campaign Calculation
Exhibit 6.6. Profitability by Multistep Campaign Calculation
Exhibit 6.7. Customer Value Structure
Exhibit 6.8. Calculating Retention Rate
Exhibit 6.9. Calculating Lifetime Value without the marketing program
Exhibit 6.10. Calculating Lifetime Value with the marketing program
Exhibit 6.11. Calculating Payback Period
Exhibit CS4.1. Spending on Baby Care Products in The Netherlands
Exhibit CS4.2. The Happy Box and Baby Box by WSM
Exhibit CS4.3. WSM communication program
Exhibit CS4.4. The Felicitas media pack
Exhibit CS4.5. Zwitsal's Communication Program
Exhibit CS4.6. Zwitsal shifts EDM to the Internet
Exhibit CS4.7. The Nutricia Growth Guide
Exhibit CS4.8. Nutricia's Growth Guide Communication Program
Exhibit CS4.9. Nutricia MMoves EDM from Print to the Internet
Exhibit CS5.1. The Smile Theory
Exhibit CS5.2. The Pet Lifecycle
Exhibit CS5.3. Examples of "Puppy Packs"
Exhibit CS5.4. Dog Lifecycles by Breed Size
Exhibit CS5.5. Consumer Transition to Adult Pet Food
Exhibit CS5.6. Retention Program Timetable
Exhibit CS5.7. Events, Triggers and Actions
Exhibit CS5.8. Lifetime Value Without Retention Program
Exhibit CS5.9. Lifetime Value with Retention Program
Exhibit CS6.1. Weight per Predictable Variable
Exhibit CS6.2. Example of Weight per Value of Variable
Exhibit CS6.3. Risk/Revenue Matrix
Exhibit CS6.4. Retention Probability Segments
Exhibit CS6.5. Customers assigned to the Risk/Revenue Matrix
Exhibit CS6.6. Data per priority segment
Exhibit CS6.7. Goals and additional gross margin per priority segment

Exhibit CS6.8. Program Costs and Payback period
Exhibit CS6.9. Leaflet for priority group A
Exhibit CS6.10. Leaflet for priority group B
Exhibit CS6.11. Leaflet for priority group C
Exhibit 8.1. The Legal Big Picture
Exhibit 8.2. Applicability of European Legislation
Exhibit 8.3. Channel Management Matrix
Exhibit 8.4. Media Regulation—EU
Exhibit 9.1. Media Regulation—US

Sources

(where other than the authors)

E.J. van Bel / Paul Postma—Handboek Direct Marketing 1999, 1.1
Ruud Verduin, 1.2, 4.1, 4.2, 4.3, 4.4, 4.9
Verduin Marketing Consultants, 1.4, 1.6, 1.7, 4.5, 4.6, 4.7, 5.8
Gartner, 1.5
E.J. van Bel, 4.8, 4.10
2Organize, 5.5, 5.6, 5.7
McGraw-Hill, 6.2
TNS NIPO, CS4.1
Willem Smit, CS5.2
Based on model by Exchange Applications, 7.1
Based on Reicheld & Sasser, 7.7

Index

Absolute reference 37
Absolute right to object 177–78
Acquisition 96, 97
Acquisition costs 110
Actions 39
Added-value use 149
Addresspointe 68, 69, 71
Analytical objectives 157–59
Anticipative field, of the EDM quadrant 42–43
Aprimo 68, 69, 70
Average order 100, 103
Average spend per customer 110, 111

B

The Baby Box 126
Baby care market, and EDM 123–33
   the Baby Box 126
   database maintenance 133
   EDM quadrant 132–33
   Felicitas congratulatory service 126–28
   the Happy Box 125–26
   Nutricia growth guide 129–31
   retailers 132
   Zwitsal 128–29
Baby Dump 133
Baby Pack 127, 128
Bad debts 100
Baier, Martin 2
Behavioral segmentation 2, 25
BellSouth 45
Benefit segmentation 25
Bezemer, Jan C. 49
Birthday clubs 14–16
Bloomingdale's 25
Bond, Alison 73, 74, 75, 76
Boston Market 201
Brand(s)
   demise of 91
   and investment in relationships 86–87
   as mark of assurance 86
Branding, and loyalty 91
Break-even 99, 101–02
Breeders, as market influencers 136–38, 139

B2B contact types 10–11
Business, applying EDM to 10–13
Business processes
   allowing customers to steer 47, 50
   structuring for EDM 47–48, 65
Buyers 10–11, 33

C

Campaign, calculating profitability of 102–06
Campaign management 56–61, 65
Campaigns 38–39
Cancellations 100
CAN-SPAM Act of 2003 200
Chain integration 65
Churn 87–88
Coca-Cola 149, 150
Complementary products 31
Consumer Aquis 193
Consumer confidence 173, 174
Consumers, and privacy data 132
Contact planning 35
Controller 179
Conventional statistical techniques 155
Cookies 191
Cost of goods sold (COGS) 100
Cost per name 101
Cost per reach 101
Council of Europe 191, 192
CRM Association 8
Cross-selling 30–31
Cross-tabulation analysis 153
Customer churn, and revenue depletion 1
The Customer Connection 14, 15, 16, 17, 18, 20, 21
Customer Development Corporation (CDC) 73, 74
Customer dissatisfaction program 77
Customer lifecycle 23
Customer lifetime value *See* Lifetime value
Customer list, value of 1
Customer loyalty 23, 73
   myth of 84–86, 88–90
Customer loyalty program 85, 89

Customer needs
  anticipating 52–55
  internal planning and 34–35
Customer relationship management (CRM) 89
  debate over 93–94
  overlap with EDM 8–9, 11
Customer retention, importance of 1, 23
Customer(s)
  and access to information 1
  allowing to steer business process and difficulty in segmenting 53, 54
  as heart of EDM 3, 4
  creating relationships with 3
  defined 23
  identifying changing needs of 4
  keeping satisfied 90–91
  marketing power of 1
  overtargeting 4
  pampering 93, 94
  putting first 47–48
  seeing from the perspective of 26, 27
  and self-image 28–30
  and view of FBC 51–52
Customer satisfaction, measuring 20
Customer share 22, 84
Customer value 23
Customer value cube 95, 96, 112

D

Data
  access to in EDM 11
  as EDM driver 56
  versus information 149–51
Data analysis 152–54
Database
  importance of in EDM 4
  in triggering EDM activities 8, 9
Database analysis techniques 154–56
Database marketing, challenges in 146–49
Data mining 151–52
Data Protection Directive 176–77, 195
Data warehouses 146
Davidoff 91
Decency 190, 191
Decision-makers 11
Decision support system 145–46
Decision trees 156
Dell 53

Demographic segmentation 24
Design of advertising 101, 103
Development 96–97
Direct marketing
  and interactive electronic media 3
  roots of 2
  versus event-driven marketing 2
  versus traditional marketing 2
Direct marketing, distinctions from event-driven marketing 4–7
  campaign approach 6–7
  lead generation 4, 6
  response rate 6
Direct Marketing Association (DMA) 194, 201
Direct marketing legislation, in the EU 193
Discount rate 110
Distance Selling Directive 186–88
Do-Not-Call list 200
Doubleclick 69
Dutch Data Protection Authority 132

E

E-Commerce Directive 183, 185–86
E-communications & Privacy Directive 181, 191
EDM considerations 13
EDM exercises 209–15
EDM program, preparing 205–07
EDM program development, case study 160–71
  creative concept development 166–69
  financial lease contracts 160, 161
  operational lease 160
  predictive modeling 162–64
  program implementation 169–70
  retention analysis 161–62
  risk/revenue matrix 164–66
  selling program 169
  singular events 170
  success elements 170–71
EDM programs, versus direct marketing campaigns 63
EDM prospecting 7–8
EDM quadrant 40–43
  anticipative 42–43
  and baby care programs 132–33
  interactive 42
  recurring events 41

singular events 40
EDM tips 207–08
Einstein, Albert 95
Electronic messages 181–82
E-mail, regulations governing 200–01
E-mail marketing, use in FMCG 120
Emotional information 149, 150
Emotional involvement curve 135
Epiphany 69, 70
ERP systems 49, 50
Etos 126
EU directives 174–75, 192
European Convention on Human Rights 196
European law, compared to US 195
European Union (EU) legislation, and EDM 172–93 *See also US legislation*
  absolute right to object 177–78
  awareness 175
  channel management 182–83
  channel management matrix 183
  controller 179
  cookies 191
  Data Protection Directive 176–77, 195
  direct marketing legislation 193
  Distance Selling Directive 186–88
  E-Commerce Directive 183, 185–86
  E-communications & Privacy Directive 181, 191
  electronic messages 181–82
  EU directives 174–75, 192
  event-forbidden marketing 189–90, 191
  free flow of services 175–76
  good taste 190, 191
  local regulations 172–73
  online behavioral advertising (OBA) 191
  personal data outside of EU 180
  transborder flow of personal data 178–79
  transparency 173–74
  Unfair Commercial Practices Directive 188–89
Event-driven marketing (EDM)
  as adjunct to direct marketing 6
  aligning with communications and database marketing 4
  benefits of, xi, xii
  compared to direct marketing 3
  complexity of 63–64
  and data access 11
  definition of 3–4
  and development 97
  difficulty in implementing xi
  executing 62–65
  explaining to non-marketers 33
  lack of information on, xi
  lessons learned 203–04
  organizations best suited to 11
  overlap with CRM 8–9
  program preparation 205–07
  and retention 97
  roots of 2–4
  and segmentation 10
  success criteria for 121
  as successor to segmented marketing 25
  tips 207–08
  uses in mobile telephony 44–46
  versus traditional marketing 27
Event-driven marketing (EDM), distinctions from direct marketing 4–7
  campaign approach 6–7
  lead generation 4, 6
  response rate 6
Event-driven marketing (EDM), sales funnel and 30–32, 33
  buyers 33
  regulars 22
  tryers 33
Event-driven marketing cycle 56–61
  campaign implementation 59
  campaign selection 58–59
  follow up 61
  observation 59–60
  registration in the database 56–57
  response 60–61
  target group selection 57–58
Event-forbidden marketing 189–90, 191
Events 175, 176
  as marketing triggers 2, 36
Explicit indicators 37, 132
External data 57
External sources 57

F

Face validity 153, 154
Fair Credit Reporting Act 197
Fair Debt Collection Practices 197
Fast-moving consumer goods (FMCG), and EDM 119–23

consumer interest 119–20
criteria for EDM 120–21
Internet/e-mail marketing 120
point-of-market entry 121–23
  manufacturer 122, 123
  retailer 121, 122, 123
FBC formula 50–55
  and customer needs 52–55
  customer's view of 51–52
Federal Communications Commission 199
Federal Privacy Act of 1970 196
Federal Trade Commission 199, 200
Felicitas congratulatory service 126–28
Felicitas hostesses 127
Financial institutions, information notices by 197
Financial Privacy Rule 198
Folksam 66 *See also Moving Bird program*
Folksam liv 66
Folksam sak 66
Four rights 12
Free flow of services 175–76
Fulfillment cost 100

G

Galileo 59
General Services Administration (GSA) 147
Geodemography 24
Geographical segmentation 2, 24
Gillette 121
Goldfeder, Judd 14
Good taste 190, 191
Gramm-Leach Bliley Act (GLBA) 197
Gross sales 100

H

The Happy Box 7, 125–26
Harley-Davidson 91, 150
Health information 198
Health Insurance Portability and Accountability Act (HIPPA) 198
Heijn, Albert 132
Hills 136
Hoetmer, M. 85
Holy Cow! Direct Communications 166
Hospitality Technology 21
Hughes, Arthur Middleton xiii–xiv, 110, 111, 132

Hunt, Kendall 54

I

Implicit indicators 37, 132
Independent Insurance Agency Association 75
Indicators 36–37
Influencer marketing 135, 136, 137
Information, versus data 149–50
Information systems 144
Interactive field, of the EDM quadrant 42
Internal market 174
Internal planning, customer needs and 34–35
International Association of Privacy Professionals 202
Internet, use in FMCG 120
IT, merging with marketing 49–50, 65

J

Jaguar 29, 30

K

Kmart 123, 125, 132
KnowledgeBase Marketing, Inc. 76–82
  client retention program 76–77
  customer contact strategy 78–79
  results 79–80
  revenue increase 80–82
  risk/revenue matrix 77–78
Kotler, Philip 2

L

Land Rover 91
Lifecycle segmentation 24
Lifecycle stage, importance in EDM 3
Life-phase events 36
Life-stage triggers *See Event triggers*
Lifetime marketing 41
Lifetime value 94, 95, 99, 109–15
  versus payback period 117
Lift 105, 106, 117
Loyalty
  compared to retention 88–90
  myth of 84–86, 88–90
Loyalty cards 121, 122
Loyalty/frequency programs 16–23

LTV calculations 114, 115
LTV model 110, 112, 113

M

Magnehed, Staffan 67, 68, 69, 70, 71
Mailing list, mining 2
Makro 25
Management information system 145
Manufacturer, and access to consumer data 122
Marketing
 focus of 83–84
 goal of 83
 merging with IT 49–50, 65
Marketing campaigns, versus EDM programs 63
Market penetration 84
Marketing process, roles in 39–40
Marketing programs, calculating returns on 94
Market segmentation 2
 criteria for 24
 definitions of 24
 EDM as replacement for 26
 leads and 26
 outdatedness of 25, 26
Market share 22, 23, 84
Mass customization 3
Mass media, in baby care market 123
Media channels, and US legislation 199–202
Migration analysis 158–59
Mobile telephony industry 44–46
Moving Birds program 66–72
 brand benefits 71
 CRM initiative 66–67
 customer retention 71
 EDM solutions 68–69
 future programs 71
 learnings 70
 loyalty study 67
 moving bird 68
 Moving Birds campaign 69
 program implementation 69–70
 results 70
Multichannel campaigns 62
Multistep campaigns, calculating profitability of 106–09
Multivariate analysis 153

N

Net margin per order 100
Net present value 110
Net sales 100
Nutricia 125, 129–31

O

Olvarit 131
One-to-one marketing 3
Online behavioral advertising (OBA) 191
Opel Astra 150
Opportunity segmentation 25
Opt-in, EU legal definition of 181–82

P

Patton, 1, 8
Payback period 99, 115–18
 versus lifetime value 117
Pedigree Advance 136
Peppers, Don 3
Periodic reference 37
Periodic reference events 41
Personal data, outside of EU 180
Personally identifiable information (PII) 194
Pet lifecycle 136
Pine, Joe 3
Poiesz Triad 60
Point-of-market entry 121–23
Points programs 16–20
Postma, Paul 56
Predictability, and the EDM quadrant 43–44
Predictive modeling 155
Pregnancy Pack 127
Premium pet food market, and EDM 134–43
 breeders 136–38, 139
 emotional involvement curve 135
 events/triggers/actions 140–41
 influencer marketing 135, 136, 137
 lifetime value calculations 141–43
 retention program 138–40
Prénatal 125, 126
Printing/placement 101
Privacy data, and consumers 132
Processor 179
Processes

and complexity 54–55
and need for flexibility 55–56
Procter & Gamble 119, 120
Product analysis 158
Product-phase events 36
Products
   company's view of 83
   customer's view of 83
   and self-image 28–30
Profiling 155, 191–92
Profitability, by campaign 102–06
Profitability, by multistep campaign 106–09
Profit and loss by campaign 99
Profit and loss for multistep campaign 99
Protection of Privacy and Transborder Flow of Personal Data 196
Psychographical segmentation 25

R

Rabobank 42
Rational information 149, 150
Recurring event 40
Redding, Vivane 192
Relationship buyers 97
Relationship-phase events 36
Relative reference 37
Relative reference event 41
Response percentage 101
Responses, processing 60–61
Restaurants, and birthday clubs 14
Retailers
   and baby care EDM 132
   and access to consumer data 121, 122
Retention 97
   compared to loyalty 87–88, 89–91
Retention program(s)
   for premium pet food market 138–40
   as replacement for loyalty programs 89
Retention rate 110, 111
Retention strategy, organizing 92
Return on investment (ROI) 98, 109
Revenue analysis 158
Right 4 10
Right moment, identifying 11, 35–39
   actions 39
   campaigns 38–39
   events 36
   indicators 36–37
   scores 37–38

triggers 38
Risk discount factor 101
Rogers, Martha 3
Rolls-Royce 29, 30, 91

S

Sales funnel 30–32, 33
Sanoma 126
SAP 51
Sara Lee 128
Schaeffer, Rebecca 195
Scorecard 35, 38
Scores 37–38
Scoring 155
Sears, Richard Warren 2
Segmentation techniques 24–25
Self-image, and consumers 28–30
Seller-customer relationship 2
Shaping 86
Share of wallet 84
Sherlock Holmes 144
Siebel 51
Single-factor analysis 152
Singular event 40
Smile theory 135
Smit, Willem 135
Soft opt-in 182
Specifiers 11
Staff costs 103, 104, 105
Statistical validity 154
Strategy, and priorities 95–96
Supply and demand, harmonizing 147–48
Sutton, Willie 1
Switching costs, and loyalty 86–87

T

Taste 190, 191
Taylor, Frederic 49
Technology, use of in EDM 12
Telecombrief 87
Telephone Consumer Protection Act of 1991 199
Telephone Records and Privacy Protection Act of 2006 200
Temporal indicators 37, 41
Three rights principles 11
Time, and the EDM quadrant 43–44
Time value of money 101

Traditional marketing
   versus direct marketing 2
   versus event-driven marketing 27
Transaction buyers 97
Transaction processing system 144–45
Transparency, and EDM 173–74
Travelers Property Casualty Company 73–76
Triggers 38
Turnover analysis 158

U

Unfair Commercial Practices Directive 188–89
US legislation, and EDM 194–202 *See also European Union (EU) legislation*
   compared to European laws 195–97
   consumer credit information 197
   enforcement 202
   health information 198
   industry legislation 197
   information notices (financial institutions) 197
   media channels 199–202
Users 10–11

V

Variable costs 110, 111
Visualization techniques 155
Vodafone UK 44

W

Waiting list 58, 59
Wal-Mart 110
Ward, Aaron Montgomery 2
Web, and customer empowerment 48, 49
Wegener Direct Marketing 125
Wehkamp 34
Wij Special Media (WSM) 7, 125, 126, 127
Willenborg, Gijsbert 89, 90
www.eventdrivenmarketing.net 171

Z

Zip codes, using to segment markets 2
Zwitsal 125

About the Authors

Egbert Jan van Bel

Egbert Jan (1958) studied Marketing in The Netherlands (NIMA). He worked as marketer for the dBase product in the eighties, introducing the software to market leadership in Europe. He started his own company in 1989, helping business with customer-centric marketing. Egbert Jan has written six books in the field of marketing, CRM, and communications. He is keynote teacher since mid-90s at Beeckestijn Business School, member of the jury at the international Internet awards "Webby," and Faculty Member of Speakers Academy.

email: egbertjan@vanbel.nl

Ed Sander

After studying Marketing in Eindhoven, The Netherlands, Ed (1970) soon began to specialize in database marketing, online marketing, and CRM. This he has done in positions with multinationals in a wide variety of industries, including pet food, office supplies, tissue manufacturing, pharmaceuticals, and financial services. As a consultant, Ed also worked on projects for a CRM service provider, an email marketing agency and a database management agency. His past projects range from setting up marketing databases and implementing CRM applications, developing database marketing, and direct marketing programs and designing online marketing campaigns. Ed has published in various trade journals and provides guest lectures at seminars and marketing colleges.

email: ed@failsafe.nl

Alan Weber

Alan Weber is president of Data to Strategy Group, a firm specializing in using a company's existing customer data to drive their marketing strategy. With more than 15 years of experience in data-driven marketing, Alan has broad experience in applying data-driven tools to practical marketing challenges. He has helped both large and small companies, both B-to-B and B-to-C, both for-profit and not-for-profit. Before founding Data to Strategy Group, he was President of Marketing Analytics Group and Vice President, Database Marketing for J. Schmid & Associates.

Alan is author of *Data-Driven Business Models* (Racom)and co-author of *Desktop Database Marketing* (NTC) which is used as a textbook in many college-level database-marketing courses. Alan's articles have been published in various magazines, and he teaches marketing at University of Missouri/ Kansas City and the University of Kansas. He has trained direct marketers across North America, Mexico, and South America.

email: alan@d2sg.net

Racom Communications Order Form

QUANTITY	TITLE	PRICE	AMOUNT
_____	*Internet Marketing,* **Herschell Gordon Lewis**	$??.??	_____
_____	*Reliability Rules,* **Don Schultz/Reg Price**	$34.95	_____
_____	*The Marketing Performance Measurement Toolkit,* **David M. Raab**	$39.95	_____
_____	*Successful E-Mail Marketing Strategies,* **Arthur M. Hughes/Arthur Sweetser**	$49.95	_____
_____	*Managing Your Business Data,* **Theresa Kushner/Maria Villar**	$32.95	_____
_____	*Media Strategy and Planning Workbook,* **DL Dickinson**	$24.95	_____
_____	*Marketing Metrics in Action,* **Laura Patterson**	$24.95	_____
_____	*The IMC Handbook,* **J. Stephen Kelly/Susan K. Jones**	$49.95	_____
_____	*Print Matters,* **Randall Hines/Robert Lauterborn**	$27.95	_____
_____	*The Business of Database Marketing,* **Richard N. Tooker**	$49.95	_____
_____	*Customer Churn, Retention, and Profitability,* **Arthur Middleton Hughes**	$44.95	_____
_____	*Data-Driven Business Models,* **Alan Weber**	$49.95	_____
_____	*Creative Strategy in Direct & Interactive Marketing,* **Susan K. Jones**	$49.95	_____
_____	*Branding Iron,* **Charlie Hughes and William Jeanes**	$27.95	_____
_____	*Managing Sales Leads,* **James Obermayer**	$39.95	_____
_____	*Creating the Marketing Experience,* **Joe Marconi**	$49.95	_____
_____	*Coming to Concurrence,* **J. Walker Smith/Ann Clurman/Craig Wood**	$34.95	_____
_____	*Brand Babble: Sense and Nonsense about Branding,* **Don E. Schultz/Heidi F. Schultz**	$24.95	_____
_____	*The New Marketing Conversation,* **Donna Baier Stein/Alexandra MacAaron**	$34.95	_____
_____	*Trade Show and Event Marketing,* **Ruth Stevens**	$59.95	_____
_____	*Sales & Marketing 365,* **James Obermayer**	$17.95	_____
_____	*Accountable Marketing,* **Peter J. Rosenwald**	$59.95	_____
_____	*Contemporary Database Marketing,* **Martin Baier/Kurtis Ruf/G. Chakraborty**	$89.95	_____
_____	*Catalog Strategist's Toolkit,* **Katie Muldoon**	$59.95	_____
_____	*Marketing Convergence,* **Susan K. Jones/Ted Spiegel**	$34.95	_____
_____	*High-Performance Interactive Marketing,* **Christopher Ryan**	$39.95	_____
_____	*Public Relations: The Complete Guide,* **Joe Marconi**	$49.95	_____
_____	*The Marketer's Guide to Public Relations,* **Thomas L. Harris/Patricia T. Whalen**	$39.95	_____
_____	*The White Paper Marketing Handbook,* **Robert W. Bly**	$39.95	_____
_____	*Business-to-Business Marketing Research,* **Martin Block/Tamara Block**	$69.95	_____
_____	*Hot Appeals or Burnt Offerings,* **Herschell Gordon Lewis**	$24.95	_____
_____	*On the Art of Writing Copy,* **Herschell Gordon Lewis**	$34.95	_____
_____	*Open Me Now,* **Herschell Gordon Lewis**	$21.95	_____
_____	*Marketing Mayhem,* **Herschell Gordon Lewis**	$39.95	_____
_____	*Asinine Advertising,* **Herschell Gordon Lewis**	$22.95	_____
_____	*The Ultimate Guide To Purchasing Website, Video, Print & Other Creative Services,* **Bobbi Balderman**	$18.95	_____

Name/Title _____
Company _____
Street Address _____
City/State/Zip _____
Email _____ Phone _____

Credit Card: ☐ VISA ☐ MasterCard
              ☐ American Express ☐ Discover

☐ Check or money order enclosed (payable to Racom Communications in US dollars drawn on a US bank)

Number _____ Exp. Date _____
Signature _____

Subtotal _____
Subtotal from other side _____
8.65% Tax _____
Shipping & Handling _____
$7.00 for first book; $1.00 for each additional book.
TOTAL _____

Racom Communications, 150 N. Michigan Ave, Suite 2800, Chicago, IL 60601
312-494-0100, 800-247-6553, www.Racombooks.com